THE
HEALTHY
WOMAN
1995

THE
HEALTHY
WOMAN
1995

from **PREVENTION** Magazine Health Books and
the Rodale Center for Women's Health

edited by Alice Feinstein

Rodale Press, Emmaus, Pennsylvania

This book is being published simultaneously by Rodale Press as *Women's Health Advisor.*

Copyright © 1995 by Rodale Press, Inc.

Illustrations copyright © 1995 by Michael Gellatly and Paula Munck

ISBN 0–87596–231–9 hardcover
ISSN 1070–4361

Distributed in the book trade by St. Martin's Press

2   4   6   8   10   9   7   5   3   1   hardcover

——————— OUR MISSION ———————

We publish books that empower people's lives.

——————— RODALE BOOKS ———————

THE HEALTHY WOMAN 1995 Editorial and Design Staff

Editor: Alice Feinstein
Permissions Coordinator: Anita Small
Cover Designer: Debra Sfetsios
Cover Photographer: David De Lossy/The Image Bank
Art Director: Faith Hague
Book Designer: Karen C. Heard
Illustrator: Paula Munck
Technical Illustrator: Michael Gellatly
Studio Manager: Joe Golden
Page Composition: Kristen Page Morgan
Copy Editor: Stacey Ann Cortese
Office Staff: Roberta Mulliner, Mary Lou Stephen

PREVENTION MAGAZINE HEALTH BOOKS

Editor-in-Chief, Rodale Books: Bill Gottlieb
Executive Editor: Debora A. Tkac
Art Director: Jane Colby Knutila
Research Manager: Ann Gossy Yermish
Copy Manager: Lisa D. Andruscavage

CONTENTS

PART FIVE
THIN FOREVER

PART SIX
THE NUTRITION/HEALTH CONNECTION

INTRODUCTION

THE ANSWERS JUST KEEP ON COMING

You don't have to go far to see how hungry women are for information about their health. Next time you're standing in line at the supermarket, check out the magazine rack.

Women's magazines used to be all recipes and beauty, fashion tips and celebrity gossip. Now we're seeing breast cancer and orgasms, how to talk to your gynecologist, do chemical peels really make your skin baby-bottom smooth, how to lose those last ten pounds and which medical tests should you have this year. . . . Every issue, it seems, has a couple of articles on health, and the list of topics goes on and on. It's a good change.

Women's health was neglected for years, but once the subject got hot—just a few years back—it kept on sizzling. The Rodale Center for Women's Health keeps an eye on developments in women's health, and we've gathered some of the best writing on the topic this past year. We start with a survey that *Prevention* magazine did. They contacted 16,000 readers about dozens of current health issues of concern to women, then had the results analyzed by the American Medical Women's Association.

Women are not only demanding answers to *their* health problems, they're starting to get some answers. It's about time.

Alice Feinstein
Editor

PART ONE

TAKING CONTROL
OF YOUR HEALTH

PREVENTION'S WOMEN'S HEALTH CONFIDENTIAL

HOW EMPOWERED WOMEN TAKE CONTROL OF THEIR HEALTH: THE RESULTS OF AN EXCLUSIVE SURVEY CONDUCTED IN COOPERATION WITH THE AMERICAN MEDICAL WOMEN'S ASSOCIATION.

There are still some skeptics out there who say that it's not realistic to ask American women to eat a low-fat diet, to exercise frequently or to get regular mammograms and other screening tests. But women who are really concerned about their health are doing all these things. Many women are actually steering their course to a healthier future—and doing it with surprising success.

That message came through loud and clear in 1992 when editors at *Prevention* magazine analyzed the response to their Healthy Women Survey. An astounding 16,500 readers of the top health magazine in the nation took the time to fill out the eight-page questionnaire. And when a panel of physicians from the American Medical Women's Association (AMWA) looked over the responses, they were impressed.

WOMEN: TAKE CHARGE

"This group takes more action to stay well than any other group of women I've ever seen in a survey," says AMWA cardiologist Debra Judelson, M.D. "The rates of compliance with recommended health behaviors are exceptional." Janet Rose Osuch, M.D., AMWA breast cancer specialist and associate professor of surgery at Michigan State University in East Lansing, agrees. "These results show the media really can influence women's lifestyles for the better."

HERE'S WHAT THE SURVEY FOUND

Healthy women are proactive women! Ninety-two percent of the survey takers rated their health as excellent, very good or good. And the vast majority engage in regular aerobic exercise, try to eat low-fat, high-fiber foods and get needed medical screenings.

The older the women are, the more they exercise! There's a general perception that people become more sedentary as they get older. Surprisingly, the opposite was true among the survey takers: As age increases, activity levels rise. While 64 percent of the youngest survey takers, ages 18 to 34, exercise at least three times a week, the rate soars with age. Some 80 percent of women over 65 exercise at least three times a week, and 40 percent of the survey takers over 65 exercise nearly every day!

Pay attention to calcium. While low-fat, high-fiber eating has become an integral part of the survey takers' nutritional habits, they still aren't getting enough calcium. AMWA physicians said that even the well-informed *Prevention* audience doesn't seem to be consuming enough calcium to build and maintain healthy bones. If that's true of *Prevention* readers, imagine the deficit among women who aren't as well informed. Most worrisome of all: The women who benefit from calcium the most—women under age 35—are consuming the least.

"The years before age 35 are the most important to building bone," notes AMWA osteoporosis expert Sydney Bonnick, M.D., who is head of osteoporosis services at the Cooper Clinic Aerobics Center in Dallas. "That's when women can build up stores of bone to carry them through older age."

Find more pleasure in your lifestyle. There is no question that the survey takers are on the right track with their lifestyles, but are they having fun yet? Only about 40 percent of the women said that enjoyment of exercise got them moving, and only a third cited enjoyment of healthy foods as a motivation for eating right. They enjoy the way exercise and eating right makes them feel, but they're not fond of the process.

That's too bad, says AMWA obesity expert Susan Yanovski, M.D., of the National Institute of Diabetes and Digestive and

Kidney Diseases. "It's important to find a kind of exercise that you really like, because then you're most likely to fit it into your daily activities and stick with it." The survey supported that conclusion: Women who enjoy exercise are more likely to exercise at least three times a week.

Walking is No. 1. Nearly three-quarters of the women said they stride outdoors for exercise. Even for women ages 18 to 34, walking was almost twice as popular as aerobic dance.

Aerobics is the motivator. Three-quarters of the survey takers exercise aerobically at least three times a week. And 35 percent exercise nearly every day. Authorities say 20 minutes of aerobic exercise three times a week is the minimum for cardiac conditioning, so these women are doing well.

Time pressures are most likely to edge out exercise for women in their twenties to mid-fifties. Those women were nearly twice as likely to say they're too busy to exercise as women over age 55.

Even women who describe their health as fair or poor are exercising. Half of the women in this group are exercising three times a week or more. "I'm very impressed that even those women are out there plugging away to feel better," says Dr. Judelson.

Low-fat and high-fiber are in. AMWA physicians were pleased that 84 percent of the survey takers say they try to eat low- or nonfat foods, making it their number-one diet priority. Along with weight control, less fat means a reduced risk of heart disease, the leading killer of American women, and possibly even reduced rates of cancer.

It also came as good news that eating high-fiber foods was the second most popular priority. "The fact that nearly 70 percent of respondents say they're eating a high-fiber diet is very good," says AMWA internist Mary Guinan, M.D. "High-fiber diets can prevent colon cancer, which is a common type of cancer for American women." It may also help prevent other cancers as well as heart disease and other ailments.

MOST WOMEN NEED MORE CALCIUM

Overall, women's intake of calcium seems alarmingly low, especially for the youngest women, who would benefit most from higher calcium levels. The evidence: Eating more calcium-rich foods was the lowest priority for the survey takers.

In addition, milk isn't popular. An incredible 96 percent of survey takers said that they abstain from whole milk entirely. That's good because it reduces fat, but they're not drinking much skim or low-fat milk to make up for the lack of calcium. Forty percent of the survey takers drink none. Another 40 percent drink just one glass, and very few drink more.

"This may be a lot of milk compared with the general population, but it's still not enough," says Dr. Bonnick.

Calcium supplementation among the survey takers is low, especially for younger women. Only 19 percent of women ages 18 to 34 report taking calcium supplements. The rate increases with age: Up to 57 percent of women who are 65 and older are taking calcium pills.

Calcium supplementation is mandatory for women who don't regularly drink milk or eat dairy products, says Dr. Bonnick. She explains that it's very difficult to get 1,000 milligrams of calcium daily (the level most women need) relying on foods alone and virtually impossible (without supplements) to reach 1,500 milligrams daily (the level suggested for postmenopausal women who aren't on estrogen).

"Someday, I'd like to see a survey where 100 percent of women, young and old, are meeting their Recommended Dietary Allowance (RDA) for taking calcium," says Dr. Bonnick. "At least the results show that older-age groups are getting the message a little better than younger women. Young women really need to take extra calcium to prevent a long-term future of bone fractures."

CONCERNS ABOUT WEIGHT CONTINUE

The young women in the survey are more motivated by weight concerns than the older women, even though the young women are less likely to be overweight. For the survey takers, weight control is the number-one reason to exercise and eat right. Feeling better and more energetic and preventing health problems are next in importance.

Nearly 90 percent of young women ages 18 to 34 consider

weight control a major reason to exercise, but the rate drops steadily with increasing age, down to 61 percent of women over age 65. Past age 55, however, preventing and controlling health problems ranked before weight loss as a reason to exercise, motivating about 68 percent of the women.

Next, *Prevention* tabulated the weights, heights and body-frame sizes reported by the survey takers with standards set by the Metropolitan Life Insurance Tables of healthy weights for women. Here's the irony: Younger women were the least likely to be overweight. And, the least overweight women are the most concerned about their weight. Dr. Yanovski didn't need all the figures to tell her that. "If you sit with a group of young women, they discuss how fat they are, even when they're not."

Former AMWA president Leah J. Dickstein, M.D., a professor of psychiatry at the University of Louisville in Kentucky, was disturbed by these findings. "It's dangerous and very sad that women who are at a healthy weight, or even underweight, are trying to lose weight. We know that girls these days are starting to diet in fourth grade. That's coming from the media—images on television, in teen magazines and in department store windows. As parents and educators, people must protest these unhealthy images.

"Women have to learn that the number on the scale is not what's important," continues Dr. Dickstein. "What's important is percentage of body fat, the proportion of their hips to their waists (since studies show that women with waists that are larger than their hips run more health risks), how their bodies are working and how they feel."

When it comes to a woman's relationship with food, here's what the survey found.

Sweets and snacks are diet busters. When women were asked what bad habit they'd most like to break, the largest number (37 percent) chose eating too many sweets. Other studies agree, says Dr. Yanovski. "Research shows that women especially love sweets, while men go for high-fat, high-protein, like meat."

Snacking came second, with a quarter of the women calling it a problem. Other habits survey takers want to break include drinking too much caffeine (17 percent), watching too much television (17 percent), food bingeing and/or purging (12 percent), smoking (7 percent), taking prescription drugs (6 percent) and drinking alcohol (5 percent).

Thin women exercise longer. The survey found that over-weight people tend to have shorter exercise sessions—20 to 30 minutes per session—than women whose weight is within their ideal range, who are more likely to exercise for 45 minutes or more per session. This may support a theory propounded by some exercise physiologists: For maximum weight loss, they say, you're better off exercising longer at a slower pace than for short periods at a fast-and-furious rate.

Bingeing a younger issue. Twenty-five percent of women ages 18 to 34 said they want to stop bingeing and/or purging, compared with only 13 percent of the women ages 35 to 54, and less than 10 percent of the women over 55 report it as a problem.

Does this mean a quarter of the youngest survey takers are bulimic or have a full-blown binge-eating disorder? Probably not, says Dr. Yanovski. "A binge is in the eye of the beholder—someone might call it a binge if they eat a couple slices of pizza." But it does reinforce the point that young women may be excessively concerned about weight control. Women who are concerned that they may be bingeing too much or who are purging at all should seek counseling.

MEDICAL SCREENING GETS A YES

The vast majority of the survey takers have blood pressure checks and cholesterol level checks annually or even more frequently. Given that heart disease is the number-one cause of death among American women, that was heartening news indeed.

Most women are taking action to catch breast cancer early, but the highest-risk women (those over age 65) may be letting down their guard. An impressive 87 percent of the survey takers report that they're getting breast examinations by a health professional annually, which is the rate that AMWA recommends, particularly for women over 40. "This is phenomenally good," says Dr. Osuch.

As for mammograms, survey takers are also doing well. Sixty-eight percent of the women ages 35 to 44 have had at least one. For the women ages 45 to 54, an impressive 87 percent get mammograms at least every two years, while 62 percent of that age group get them annually. Seventy-four percent of the women ages 55 to 64 get mammograms at least annually.

The figures put most of these women who are 64 and under solidly within AMWA's recommendations that women get their first mammogram by age 40, repeat them at one- to two-year intervals, then have them annually after age 50. "I only wish these figures held for all American women," comments Dr. Osuch.

The bad news is, however, that there is an unexplained dropoff in annual mammogram rates for women over age 65, down nearly ten points to only 65 percent having it done annually. Why? Is it because older women are less likely to be able to afford mammograms? Whatever the reason, we're concerned: Breast cancer risk increases with age, and senior women need to be the most vigilant about testing.

Breast self-examination rates could be much better for all adult women, but especially for older women. Only 47 percent of the survey takers perform them monthly. The youngest women (under 44) and the oldest women (over 65) were least likely to do so. "I'd like to see all those figures higher," says Dr. Osuch. "Even though the youngest women have the least risk of breast cancer, the earlier they start, the more likely it will become a lifelong habit."

Pap is important. Pap test rates for cervical cancer were excellent for survey takers in their thirties and forties, but older women aren't doing as well. Overall, three-quarters of the women reported having annual Pap tests, a frequency that meets and even exceeds most medical experts' recommendations. The most vigilant women were between 35 and 44; a solid 85 percent of them get annual Pap tests. "It's thrilling to see this rate of Pap-smear testing," says Dr. Osuch, "because invasive cervical cancer is preventable. Even for women who may have cervical cancer, if it's caught early, it can be treated locally without removing the whole cervix or uterus."

But, like mammography and breast self-exams, there was a disturbing downward trend in Pap test frequency for women age 65 and over. Only 65 percent of that age group are getting annual Pap tests. AMWA gynecologist Diana Dell, M.D., points out that it's a myth that only young women or sexually active women need the test. Even post-hysterectomy patients should be tested regularly.

SKIN CARE GETS A BIG VOTE

Most women use sunscreens, but only some of the time. An impressive 83 percent of survey takers say they use sunscreens and sunblocks. But only a fifth use them all the time. "This rate of use is probably better than among the general population," says Dr. Osuch, "but it's still disappointing.

"Even one sunburn can cause permanent damage that can lead to skin cancer. Melanoma of the skin is one of the most lethal cancers we see, and it's preventable. What's more, the incidence of melanoma is going way up, perhaps from the thinning of the ozone layer letting in more ultraviolet light. I'd like to see 100 percent saying they always use sunscreens."

The women over age 65 were the most likely to say they never use sunscreens or sunblocks—nearly a third of them never use it.

Tanning salons are still popular among some health-conscious women. The ultraviolet light from tanning machines may be even more dangerous than the sun's rays. So it was gratifying to see that a total of 78 percent of the survey takers said they never go to tanning salons. But when *Prevention* broke this figure down by women's ages, the results were a little more disquieting.

Some 40 percent of women ages 18 to 34 have visited a salon, and 30 percent of women ages 35 to 44 and 25 percent of women ages 45 to 54 have done so. Those are higher rates than we'd like to see. So it's an issue about which younger women must be educated. "Salons are dangerous," Dr. Osuch comments. "It's important to remind younger women that avoiding suntanning and salons prevents not only cancer but also wrinkles."

AIDS PREVENTION NEEDS ATTENTION

Women are more comfortable asking their dentists to take precautions against AIDS than they are asking their sexual partners. When women were asked what measures they're taking to protect themselves against AIDS, the survey indicated:

- Four percent of married women practice safer sex and insist on a condom, while 22 percent of unmarried women do so.
- Nine percent of married women have had an HIV test, compared with 24 percent of unmarried women.
- Only 3 percent of married women have asked their partners to have an HIV test; 14 percent of single women have.

AMWA's Dr. Guinan, who is also an AIDS specialist, comments, "I wish this many women across the country were taking these steps and insisting on safer sex! We want these figures to go up to 100 percent, but this is a good start."

Meanwhile, a huge 20 percent of women have asked their dentists or doctors whether they're taking precautions to prevent transmission of the AIDS virus. Dr. Guinan was ambivalent about that response. "When you consider that only one dentist in the country is known to have transmitted AIDS to a patient, you realize it should be a much lower priority than talking to your sex partner. But it's so much easier in society to talk about nonsexual than sexual things."

The most popular anti-AIDS measure is banking blood. More than a third of the women said that they would consider it, or have already done it.

COMBATING STRESS

Women rely mostly on exercising and sharing concerns to combat stress. Exercising was the most popular way to relieve stress (66 percent), and sharing concerns with a trusted family member or friend ranked a close second (65 percent). Praying was third (52 percent), while less than half (40 percent) set aside quiet time.

When *Prevention* analyzed these results by age, it found that women under 55 are far more likely to share concerns than are older women. More than 70 percent of women under 55 talk to trusted friends about their stressors, while 59 percent of women age 55 to 64 do so, and only 39 percent of women 65 and older are sharing concerns. Elizabeth Karlin, M.D., chair of AMWA's Women's Health Committee, says more women should reach out to others. "Studies show that sharing concerns is one of the most dramatic ways to improve health," she notes. Women under 55 are consistently more likely to report frequent or severe anxiety, mild or severe depression and general fatigue than are older women.

In every one of these categories, younger women do worse. Why? "We underestimate the pressures that are on young women today," says Dr. Dickstein. "If they're under 40, their biological clock is ticking: Should they have children? Should they worry about their careers? Relationships? Or perhaps they're taking care of the children—and aging family members." But as women reach their fifties, Dr. Dickstein adds, "many of those pressures are lessened and are in better control. Although for women in their fifties, their stressors may include home, full-time work, elderly relatives, grown children living at home, grandchildren and relationship losses."

WOMEN AND DOCTORS

More than three-quarters of the survey takers have primary care physicians. That's good news; it means that there's probably one person consistently overseeing each woman's health.

But here again there were some meaningful age differences. Younger women are far more likely than older women to tell us that they use their gynecologists as their primary care physicians. A quarter of the women ages 18 to 34 said they consider their gynecologists their primary care physicians, compared with 14 percent of the women ages 35 to 54, and even fewer in older groups. That's usually okay, says Dr. Guinan, "For the most part younger women are healthy. What they really need is reproductive health care, like contraception, sexually transmitted disease prevention and breast exams, which their gynecologists can do."

But she adds one caveat, "Gynecologists must understand that they are acting as primary care physicians, and they should ask about issues that are particular problems for young women, though not necessarily gynecological." These kinds of issues include dieting, nutrition and eating disorders, anxiety and depression and substance abuse. "And if there's any sign of these problems, gynecologists must know who they can refer them to for help," adds Dr. Guinan.

—*Cathy Perlmutter with Maureen Sangiorgio*

The American Medical Women's Association is a national association of women physicians and medical students. Founded in 1915, AMWA works to promote women's health and the role of women in medicine.

CREATING A HEALTHY LIFESTYLE

YOU'RE DOING EVERYTHING YOU CAN TO EAT RIGHT AND LIVE WELL. WHAT OTHER STEPS CAN YOU TAKE?

Even women who take care of their health need coaching about doing all the right things. When 16,500 readers of *Prevention* magazine took part in the *Prevention*/American Medical Women's Association (AMWA) Healthy Women Survey, they showed that they were on the right track for making healthy lifestyle choices.

But the survey also revealed the areas in which women need to improve. To be the healthiest you can be, check out what the survey says about things most women can do to fine-tune a healthy lifestyle.

FITNESS BOOSTERS

Explore the pleasures of exercise. Despite the preachings of some fitness gurus, pain does not equal gain. In fact, as AMWA physicians remind us, the more you enjoy exercise, the more likely—and the more often—you will do it. Here are some ideas that underscore the "pleasure principle."

- Play to your preferences. Think about an activity that you really love, any activity—it doesn't have to be fitness oriented. Then get creative, combining fun with a physical challenge. Love to shop? Fitness walk along your favorite shopping district before the stores open and preview the window displays. Got the travel bug? Sign up for a fitness-oriented vacation. Rather be doing crafts? Take a nature walk and collect pine cones, twigs and other found objects for your next project.

- Get active any way you choose. If you have an aversion to exercise, a fresh perspective may help, says AMWA obesity expert Susan Yanovski, M.D., of the National Institute of Diabetes and Digestive and Kidney Diseases. "In our field, we're getting away from prescribing specific exercises. Instead, we encourage our patients to develop active lifestyles." Variety is the key. Try all kinds of activities—bird-watching, gardening, playing Ping-Pong, horseback riding, social dancing. The best workouts aren't necessarily the ones that deliver the greatest calorie burn; they're the activities you enjoy most because you're more likely to do them.

- Socialize actively! Instead of a sit-down dinner party, throw a backyard badminton party (with light finger foods and fresh fruit or vegetable "cocktails" between sets). Or invite a few friends to join you on a nature hike and share a picnic lunch. Don't miss a step at holidays, either; create active celebrations with your family or friends.

- Remember: exercise doesn't kill time, it creates time. After the first week or so of beginning a regular exercise program, many people say that their energy and stamina surge to the point where they feel like they've gained more productive hours in a day. Consider, too, that by reducing your risk of heart disease, osteoporosis and other life-threatening diseases, regular aerobic exercise can add days, even years, to your life.

- Borrow an hour of early-morning snooze time. Before your

day begins, little can come between you and your workout. That may explain why morning exercisers tend to stick with their fitness programs better, says Dr. Yanovski. AMWA cardiologist Debra Judelson, M.D., notes, "When patients come to me and say they're always tired, I say, 'Get up early and take a brisk walk.' Inevitably, they come back and say, 'I feel great and have much more energy.'"

- Walk and talk. Time spent chatting on the telephone, over lunch or across a desk may provide an opportunity for fitness. Whether it's an intimate conversation with a good friend or a brainstorming session for an annual fund-raiser, consider talking while you walk.
- Join the resistance. Resistance training may offer the most benefit to older (post-menopausal) women—who, according to the study, seem to be most reluctant to working out with weights. Studies have shown that performing a few simple exercises three times a week improves seniors' mobility and flexibility dramatically in just eight weeks. In one study done with a group of people over 90, a couple of them even ended up throwing away their canes! Resistance training can also help strengthen and maintain bone, to ward off crippling osteoporosis. So, get pumping!
- Invest in a pair of one- or two-pound weights and a resistance band. For a more targeted workout routine using free weights, machines and/or barbells, refer to "Getting the Most Out of Your Muscle" on page 252, to help you burn fat and firm up your body.
- Hop on your stationary bike for resistance exercise that benefits the crucial hip area. "Just increase the resistance against which you're pedaling," says AMWA osteoporosis expert Sydney Bonnick, M.D., who heads osteoporosis services at the Cooper Clinic Aerobics Center in Dallas. "That strengthens the muscles of the upper hips and thighs so they pull on the bone, which is a good stimulus to bone growth." You can get the same effect on a bicycle outdoors by going uphill. However, bicycling doesn't strengthen the spine; for that, the impact of brisk walking or jogging does wonders.

NUTRITION BOOSTERS

You're doing a great job of trimming the fat. Now you need to tickle your taste buds. "If healthy eating is always a kind of drudgery—a prison of rice cakes and water—you're not going to last and you'll go back to the full-fat stuff!" says nutritionist and registered dietitian Evelyn Tribole, author of *Eating on the Run*.

To put flavor and fun on your plate:

- Buy the freshest vegetables you can find. "Vegetables right out of the ground are incredible," says food consultant Aliza Green, a chef with 15 years' experience in Philadelphia.

  But that heavenly flavor vanishes when veggies sit around. To get the most intense flavor, look for vegetables in season. Go to farmers' markets or to roadside stands, or find the supermarket in your area known for the best produce.

- Get acquainted with the new additions in the produce aisle. Have you had a plumcot—a sweet, tangy cross between a plum and an apricot? Or yellow fingers—rich, buttery-tasting potatoes the size of your fingers? New produce varieties can taste great.

- Experiment with unfamiliar herbs and spices, especially fresh ones. The flavor success of many healthy recipes depends on them. Many wonderful seasonings, such as cilantro, coriander seed, cumin and chilies, are acquired tastes. You need repeated exposures—and then you'll love them! Green's gentle but firm advice for trying a new herb or spice is, "Don't be afraid—give it a chance—have a little bit."

- Bet on basil! Green calls it the most-important, number-one, don't-live-without-it herb. She also says it's best when it's fresh: "It's practically worthless when it's dried!" Look for fresh basil in farmers' markets or the produce section of your supermarket. To store it, cut the fresh stems and place the "bouquet" in a glass of water. Cover it with a plastic bag and refrigerate. If stored properly, it keeps about a week. Make sure your refrigerator isn't too cold, because basil freezes easily.

- Break mealtime monotony with interesting breads. Round

out summer meals of salad or chilled soup with luscious slices of multigrain, pumpernickel, herb, raisin or sourdough breads. Supermarket bakeries now offer them fresh. And hearty whole-grain breads don't need butter to taste fabulous.

- Perk up bland meals with fat-free condiments from the gourmet aisle at the supermarket. Try mango chutney with plain baked chicken breast. Or coarse-grain mustard instead of mayo on a turkey breast sandwich.

GETTING MORE CALCIUM

Many of us need to bone up on calcium. Low calcium intake is almost certainly linked to osteoporosis, the notorious brittle-bone condition that can debilitate and kill. And few women are consuming enough calcium to prevent this. Some experts recommend getting 1,000 milligrams a day, with 1,200 milligrams for women under 25 (who still build peak bone mass) and 1,500 milligrams for postmenopausal women (whose bones lose calcium faster). To preserve strong bones:

- Make low-fat and nonfat dairy products and orange juice fortified with calcium your mainstays. "Unfortunately, most women are running at least a half-quart low on milk every day," says osteoporosis expert Doris Gorka Bartuska, M.D., director of the Division of Endocrinology and Metabolism at the Medical College of Pennsylvania in Philadelphia. And that's a source of concern. Low-fat and nonfat milk and yogurt and calcium-fortified orange juice are the top dietary sources of calcium. No other foods come close in terms of calcium availability and absorbability.

  Other foods considered "good" calcium sources come up short by comparison. Regular cheese is higher in fat. Cottage cheese, kidney beans and cooked kale or broccoli deliver much less calcium. Nonfat frozen desserts, including frozen yogurt, contain less calcium and more calories. The calcium in spinach is much less absorbable.

- Eat canned fish with the bones (like sardines or salmon) to help boost your calcium intake.

- Use a calcium supplement to make up whatever part of your daily quota you don't get from dietary sources.

For many women, getting all the calcium they need from food is a tall order, says Dr. Bartuska. A daily multivitamin/mineral supplement usually supplies just 200 milligrams or less—not nearly enough to make up the difference. Most women need to supplement with 500 milligrams or more a day, Dr. Bartuska explains. She recommends chewable calcium carbonate. It provides the most calcium per tablet and the chewing helps it dissolve for easier absorption. She suggests calcium citrate for women who find that calcium carbonate causes bloating or constipation.

Note: If you take more than 500 milligrams of supplemental calcium, divide the dosage between morning and evening to maximize absorption.

There's no reason to exceed 1,500 milligrams total calcium intake (food plus supplement) per day, because there really is no proof that more than that is beneficial. If you've had kidney stones in the past or you've been advised to avoid calcium, or if you are considering supplementation, discuss it with your doctor. To ensure optimum bone health, other factors—such as menopause (low estrogen), vitamin D status, lack of weight-bearing exercise, drugs that may drive calcium down, heredity and age—may need to be evaluated as well.

Those who aren't already taking a multivitamin/mineral supplement may want to consider doing so. "In a perfect world, you'd have perfect eating habits. But in the real world, it's not a bad idea to take a multivitamin/mineral supplement," says Elaine Feldman, M.D., director emeritus of the Georgia Institute of Human Nutrition at the Medical College of Georgia in Augusta.

In particular, Dr. Feldman advises supplements for women who are dieting, past middle age or sedentary. These women are likely to be consuming too few calories to get all the essential nutrients—even with the best intentions, she says.

Nutrition experts at Utah State University in Logan concluded it would be impossible to meet women's Recommended Dietary Allowances for all vitamins and minerals plus National Research Council diet guidelines on much less than 2,200 calories a day. Yet the average American woman may consume only 1,600 calories daily. But note the following tips.

- If you're of childbearing age, make sure your multivitamin/mineral supplement contains 400 micrograms of folate. This level has been shown to decrease the risk of neural-tube defects in developing fetuses. These brain and spinal-cord defects develop in the earliest weeks of pregnancy, before many women realize that they are pregnant. Other research indicates that folate may lower risks of cervical cancer caused by a strain of the human papillomavirus.

    Note: Dark green vegetables like spinach are rich in this B vitamin. But to get 400 micrograms, you'd need to eat about 1½ cups of boiled spinach a day!
- Tell your doctor what supplements you're taking. It's an important part of a health history, says Dr. Feldman.
- Choose a multivitamin/mineral supplement with about 100 percent of the Daily Value for iron, unless your doctor recommends more. In the absence of diagnosed iron deficiency (determined by a blood test), supplementing with higher doses of iron is considered unwise and may even be harmful, says Dr. Feldman. One theory now suggests that excess iron may contribute to coronary-artery disease in post-menopausal women.
- Buy only a six month (or less) supply of supplements at a time. The longer supplements sit on your shelf, the greater the chance the vitamins may deteriorate, advises Dr. Feldman.
- Don't use supplements as an excuse for skipping veggies, fruit, whole grains or other healthy foods. There are crucial substances in food that you can't get from any pill. Some you know about, like fiber. And some are just being discovered, like sulforaphane, a potential cancer fighter in broccoli and its relatives.

SLIMMING STRATEGIES

Many of us could benefit from fine-tuning our weight-loss programs. What do you do when a good exercise regimen and low-fat eating plan don't add up to your weight-loss goals? Two nutrition experts offered some of the following suggestions.
- Watch out for too-hefty portions of favorite low-fat or

nonfat treats. Tribole says she's now seeing "fat-free bingeing" in clients who treat reduced-fat foods as if they were calorie-free—which, of course, they aren't.

- Beware of the "fudge factor." This is the all-too-human tendency to underestimate how much you eat and overestimate how much you exercise. The "fudge factor" is extremely common, says Dr. Feldman. For example, researchers at St. Luke's–Roosevelt Hospital Center in New York City found that dieters who honestly believed they ate an average of 1,028 calories a day really were consuming an average of 2,081 calories a day—an extra 1,000 calories. Many also had a tendency to overestimate the amount of time they spent exercising.

  The best way to keep a close watch on what you're consuming is to keep a food diary. Log in every morsel that passes your lips. Sometimes, just committing this information to paper is enough to heighten your awareness of how much you're really eating. For assistance in evaluating your fat or calorie intake, ask your doctor to recommend a dietitian.

  As for keeping tabs on your exercise time, wear a watch and log the actual activity time. Do not mistake activity time for gym time; getting dressed, showering or chatting with friends doesn't count.

- Satisfy your sweet tooth—and your fat tooth—with this delicious mighty bite. Eating sweets was the habit the survey takers said they'd most like to break. But experts say the craving for sweetness usually goes hand-in-hand with a craving for fat. How do you satisfy both without sabotaging your diet? Suck on a butterscotch drop. For all that buttery sweetness, you only get about 25 calories and about one-tenth of a gram of fat (from the tiny amount of butter it contains).

  By delivering rich, sugary flavor in a measured morsel that takes about 15 minutes to dissolve in your mouth, butterscotch drops could help get you through your worst snack attacks feeling not so deprived. In the same 15 minutes, you could easily eat 1½ cups nonfat frozen yogurt for 360 calories or 1½ cups premium ice cream for up to 900 calories.

Remember to set healthy weight expectations. The question of ideal weight has been debated back and forth in medical journals and at scientific conferences. "The fact is, there's a broad range of body weights associated with health," says Dr. Yanovski, who is an obesity researcher at the National Institutes of Health. What's the best (healthiest) weight for you? That depends, say the experts. Standard height-and-weight charts can give you a rough range.

First determine whether you are an apple or a pear. One key indicator of whether your weight is healthy for you, says Dr. Yanovski, is where your fat is distributed. "Women whose fat is in a pear-shaped distribution—around the hips—are at a lower medical risk for complications of obesity, like heart disease, than women with weight around the abdomen and upper body."

To determine your waist-to-hip ratio, divide your waist size in inches by your hip measurement in inches. If that number is greater than 0.8, you have an apple shape and may be at a higher risk for medical complications of obesity than a pear-shaped woman of the same weight. Your doctor can help you determine your medical risk from overweight.

STRESS BUSTERS

Seek a little support from your friends and community. Several studies have shown that social contacts improve quality of life, reduce anxiety and depression and increase life span.

"Both psychologically and physiologically, there's something about sharing problems that helps us put them in perspective, makes us blame ourselves less and enhances our coping skills," says David Spiegel, M.D., a professor of psychiatry at Stanford University, who's a leading researcher in this field. If you don't have a strong social network, here's how you can reach out and develop one.

- Take "doing" classes. Listening to a lecture is not a great way to meet people, but taking a bridge class, cooking class, dancing class or language class is. They provide the perfect opportunity to interact with people who share interests with you and to expand your network of friends.
- Find a support group. Whatever your life situation or issue,

there's probably a group for you. Whether you've had your first baby after 35 or you're a home-based professional or you're looking for a new job, you can find a group of like-minded people. Check out the offerings in adult-education programs, hospitals and organizations of all kinds.

- Be a volunteer. It's old advice, but good advice. Just make sure the volunteer work doesn't keep you at home—like making telephone calls. The most life-enhancing kind of volunteer work, research indicates, involves direct contact. Some ideas: teach English, deliver meals to shut-ins, work at a homeless shelter. That kind of helping others offers not just friendship, but its own life-enhancing high as well.

—*Cathy Perlmutter and Holly McCord, R.D., with Maureen Sangiorgio*

MEDICAL TESTS THAT CAN SAVE YOUR LIFE

HEALTHY LIFESTYLE CHOICES ARE IMPORTANT, BUT THEY AREN'T THE WHOLE STORY. HERE'S THE LOWDOWN ON THE MOST IMPORTANT MEDICAL TESTS FOR WOMEN.

If every woman were routinely screened for breast cancer, some 15,000 lives would be saved each year. Screening for colon cancer could save many thousands of women's lives. Even simple things like having blood pressure and cholesterol levels measured and controlled regularly could prevent up to half of the 250,000 heart attack deaths and the 100,000 stroke deaths among women each year.

Besides making healthy lifestyle changes (like quitting smoking, eating a healthy diet and exercising regularly), following established guidelines for medical screening tests and self-exams is a key to prevention.

When the responses to the *Prevention*/American Medical Women's Association (AMWA) Healthy Women Survey were tabulated, it became obvious that most female survey takers are getting basic screening tests. The vast majority go for blood pressure checks and cholesterol level checks annually, for example.

But there were also some areas—particularly those specific to women's health—where these women (and maybe you, too) could be doing better. For example:

Breast self-examination rates are disappointing. Only 47 percent of the survey takers perform them monthly.

Older women need special encouragement to ensure they get annual mammograms. Only 74 percent of the survey takers ages 55 to 64 get annual mammograms. This, despite the fact that increasing age is the primary risk factor for breast cancer.

Annual Pap test rates aren't very good for mature women. Rates to screen for cervical cancer were good for women in their thirties and forties (around 80 percent), but dropped to 65 percent for women over age 65.

Why the gaps? Some of these screening tests are inconvenient or uncomfortable, so only the most motivated women go. Another obstacle is expense: Public and private insurances don't pay for every vital test, like bone scans for osteoporosis.

But motivation or cost is not the biggest barrier, asserts AMWA breast cancer expert Janet Rose Osuch, M.D., who is an associate professor of surgery at Michigan State University in East Lansing. She places most of the blame squarely on the shoulders of her fellow physicians. "Doctors are not doing a good enough job reminding women to get the tests they need," says Dr. Osuch.

She points to mammography as an example. "In research studies, the reason women most commonly cite for not having a mammogram is that their doctors didn't tell them to do it."

Indeed, a study by the Massachusetts Institute of Behavioral Medicine is one of many that bear her out. The researchers interviewed 630 women, half of whom had had at least one mammogram, though none of them were getting them as regularly as they should. In that study, the women who reported physician encouragement were four times more likely to have had a mammogram. In fact, doctor encouragement was more closely correlated with having a mammogram than any other factor, including age, education, income, health status or attitude.

It's not that physicians have bad intentions. Often, they're just too busy to address preventive-care measures with every patient. In fact, a national study recently found that the average time a doctor spent talking with each patient was a meager 11 minutes.

What's more disturbing is that many doctors are less likely to encourage senior women to get screening tests. In the study, for example, women age 55 and older were more likely than those between 50 and 54 to report that their doctors didn't suggest breast self-examinations or annual mammograms to them. Yet about 75 percent of women who get breast cancer are 55 or older. And the older a woman is, the greater her chances for developing the disease.

FINDING DR. RIGHT

One of the most important steps a woman can take to protect her health is to find a primary care physician who takes time to talk about preventive care and who is sensitive to women's health issues. "If a woman does not have a good primary care physician, it can jeopardize her health," says AMWA women's health expert Lila Wallis, M.D.

Dr. Wallis says that too many women rely on specialists, like gynecologists, for primary care. This is especially true of young women. Our survey found that more than a quarter of the women under age 34 consider their gynecologists to be their primary care doctors. That's better than not seeing a doctor at all, says Dr. Wallis, but women need someone with a wider perspective.

Dr. Wallis says that most women's best bet for primary care physicians are general internists with special training in women's health. "They're more likely to offer preventive counseling on many different health issues. Even their waiting rooms are more likely to have literature about screening tests."

Ideally, that doctor should be well-informed about women's health. That's a little tougher for a patient to investigate, though Dr. Wallis says if the doctor herself is a woman, she may be more attuned to women.

One big clue to whether a physician is informed about women's health is if she does careful breast and pelvic exams during the annual physical.

Another clue is whether the physician asks about issues that are particularly important to women at each stage of life. For example, Dr. Wallis says, young women should be asked about body image, eating disorders and calcium intake. For women in the middle years, it's particularly important to ask about multiple stressors, which could stem from caring for elders and children, sleep and weight changes and coping with menopause. For seniors, bone health, social contacts and abuse by spouse or by caregivers are examples of issues to which physicians should be sensitive.

Under Dr. Wallis's supervision, AMWA developed a comprehensive women's health curriculum that it offers to interested physicians. Women's health, they feel, combines internal medicine, obstetrics and gynecology, family practice and psychiatry. But, Dr. Wallis adds, re-educating doctors won't do the whole job.

"We need to teach women how to be responsible partners in their health care," says Dr. Wallis. "With health reforms on the horizon, physicians may spend even less time with each patient. So women need to be even more assertive."

How to do it?

Keep your own medical log. Are you the kind of person who thinks you had a Pap test a year ago, but when you check you find out it was in 1989? That's why it's a good idea to start a notebook in which you list every major screening test you've had or might need. (See "The Top 15 Tests for Women" below.) Next to each entry, write down the date on which you had the test. It's also a good idea to write down the results of the test. Call your doctor after each test to discuss it. (That practice has the added advantage of forcing the doctor to look at your test results.)

Take your log book with you when you visit your doctor. It's a good idea to discuss your screening schedule with your primary care physician at least once a year. Changes in screening guidelines or in your personal risk factors might suggest that your screening schedule needs updating. Says Dr. Osuch, "Most doctors are not going to get upset by a gentle reminder to talk about medical screening tests—they're going to be grateful. The patient is not just saying, 'Do you think I need a mammogram?' but also, 'I'm willing to go get one, and I'm asking for your expert advice.'"

THE TOP 15 TESTS FOR WOMEN

Which medical screening tests should you have regularly? Each woman's needs are different, based on her age, genetics, medical history and lifestyle. Use the following information to help you and your physician determine a screening schedule that's best for you. Keep in mind that these are general guidelines for women, approved by AMWA physicians. Admittedly, some may differ slightly from those recommended by other professional associations. Nevertheless, this list is a good starting point for your discussions with your physician.

HEART HEALTH

Heart disease is the leading cause of death among American women, killing half a million each year. By following the guidelines below, symptoms of heart disease can be detected early and reversed through lifestyle changes and/or medication.

1. Blood pressure check. A measurement of blood pressure taken with an inflatable cuff, known as a sphygmomanometer.

- **Once every year** if you are 19 to 40 years of age with no heart-disease risk factors and are not taking oral contraceptives.
- **Twice or more every year** if you are over 40, take oral contraceptives, have borderline-high blood pressure (140/90 or greater), have a personal history of high blood pressure or heart disease, are on blood pressure medication, have a family history of high blood pressure and/or heart disease, smoke, are very overweight, regularly take over-the-counter nonsteroidal anti-inflammatory medications (analgesics) or if your physician has recommended it for other reasons.

    Note: A healthy blood pressure reading should be less than 140 systolic over less than 90 diastolic.

2. Blood cholesterol test. A small blood sample is analyzed

at the doctor's office or in a laboratory, after a 12-hour fast (triglycerides are very sensitive to diet). This would include total cholesterol plus high-density lipoprotein (HDL) (good cholesterol) and low-density lipoprotein (LDL) (bad cholesterol) ratios in addition to your triglyceride level.

- **Once every year** at any age if you are in good health. "Even screening in childhood may be of benefit and should be continued lifelong," says AMWA cardiologist Debra Judelson, M.D.

- **Twice or more every year** if you have recently gained a great deal of weight, have become sedentary, have become ill, have borderline high cholesterol (about 200 to 240), have high cholesterol (above 240), are on cholesterol-lowering medication, have diabetes or kidney disease, have HDL levels below 35, have had your ovaries removed, have recently gone through menopause, have heart disease or symptoms of heart disease or if your physician has recommended it for other reasons.

  Note: Healthy readings for women should be approximately 160 for total cholesterol, 50 or higher for HDL, below 120 for LDL and below 110 for triglycerides.

3. Exercise stress test. Requires exercise on a treadmill while the heart is monitored externally.

- **One screening test**, possibly followed by tests every two to five years if you are over age 40, are over age 30 and have strong risk factors for heart disease (such as high blood pressure, diabetes, significant obesity, smoking or a family history of heart disease), have had your ovaries removed, have high cholesterol, have symptoms of heart disease or if your doctor has recommended it for other reasons.

  Note: For 40 percent of women who take the exercise stress test, the result is a false positive—in other words, it indicates problems when there are none. When the finding is abnormal, the physician refers a patient for more sophisticated tests, like a stress echocardiogram, involving exercise and an ultrasound, or a nuclear medicine test, involving an injection of radioactive material. If a woman is at a high risk for heart disease, a physician may skip the exercise stress test and go directly to the more sensitive tests.

BREAST CARE

Some 180,000 women in the United States were diagnosed with breast cancer last year; as many as 46,000 of those women died. But AMWA experts say that if all women followed the guidelines below, a third of those deaths could have been avoided.

4. Breast self-examination (BSE). The careful self-palpation of each breast, preferably done the week after a woman's menstrual period, to check for any unusual lumps or masses.

- **Once every month** if you are over age 16, the age by which most women's breasts are fully developed. Doctors say it's best to learn BSE when you're young, so it becomes a lifelong habit.

  Note: To learn the skill of BSE, ask your physician for guidance or check with your community hospital or woman's health clinic for classes or your local American Cancer Society office.

5. Breast examination by a qualified health professional. The visual examination and careful palpation of the breasts and underarms by a health professional. The practitioner should examine your breasts while you are sitting up and lying down, too.

- **Once every 2 to 3 years** if you are age 16 to 39 and have no risk factors for or symptoms of breast cancer.
- **Once every year or more frequently** if you are over age 40, have lumpy breasts that are difficult to self-examine, do not perform monthly breast self-exams, have risk factors for breast cancer (such as a family history of the disease, no children before age 30, breast biopsies that show a condition known as atypical epithelial hyperplasia or a personal history of breast cancer) or if your physician has recommended it for other reasons.

6. Mammography. Breast x-ray using low-dose radiation. The apparatus compresses the breast firmly between two plates, which may cause discomfort. Usually two or three views per breast are required for a complete screening.

- **One baseline test, followed by additional tests every one to two years** if you are between the ages of 40 and 49 and

don't have risk factors for or symptoms of breast cancer.
- **Once every year** if you are age 50 or older, have risk factors for breast cancer regardless of your age or if your physician has recommended it.

Note: Most physicians recommend that women schedule their mammograms for the week after their menstrual periods, to minimize discomfort.

There is controversy over whether most women under age 50 need regular mammograms. Some studies suggest that mammography in younger women doesn't help significantly reduce death rates. However, Dr. Osuch points out, even if that unproven contention is true, early detection through mammography does give younger women more treatment options, like breast-saving lumpectomy. Until there's more data, AMWA says, it's still a good idea for women to begin getting regular mammograms at age 40.

All suspicious lumps should be biopsied for a definitive diagnosis regardless of what the mammograms show. There is a 15 percent false-negative rate for mammography.

GYNECOLOGICAL CARE

Women are susceptible to a wide range of gynecological problems, ranging from vaginal infections and uterine fibroids to cervical abnormalities and ovarian growths. That's why careful annual pelvic examinations, along with the screening tests described in this chapter, are an essential part of a woman's annual physical exam. With early detection, most gynecological problems can be treated successfully.

7. Pelvic examination. A manual examination by a qualified health professional of the vaginal area to check for any abnormalities of the uterus and ovaries. Usually, the doctor places—carefully and gently—two gloved fingers in the vagina while the other hand presses firmly on top of the abdomen.
- **Once every year** if you are over age 18.

8. Pap test. After inserting a speculum into the vagina and opening it to reveal the cervix, the doctor takes a scraping of cells from the cervix and the cervical canal and smears them

on a slide. The sample is sent to a laboratory to examine for signs of cervical cancer.

- **Once every year** if you are over age 18.

    Note: Cervical cancer has been linked to certain strains of the human papillomavirus. This virus can be transmitted through sexual intercourse. But any woman can develop cervical cancer at any age, regardless of sexual activity. "I've seen cancer of the cervix in nuns," says Dr. Wallis. Seniors still need to be tested regularly, even if they don't have a partner. This is true even after a hysterectomy if the cervix is left intact. (If your cervix has been removed, you still need Pap smears, but not as often.)

    The Pap test's reliability depends on the skill of the medical professional and the laboratory that analyzes the slide. Seek a board-certified health practitioner for your test.

9. **Transvaginal ultrasound.** An ultrasonic probe is inserted into the vagina, transmitting images of the uterus and ovaries to a monitoring screen. It's sometimes used as a screening tool to detect changes in the lining of the uterus and the ovaries that might suggest cancer.

- **One screening test, possibly followed by others at the recommendation of a physician** if you are at or past menopause and may be at risk for endometrial cancer. May also be used for women of any age who have a strong family history (in your immediate family—mother, sister or daughter) or other significant risk factors for ovarian cancer.

10. **Endometrial tissue sample.** A thin instrument is inserted through the vagina and cervical opening to remove a tiny tissue sample from the lining of the uterus. Also called an endometrial biopsy or aspiration, the procedure can cause cramping.

- **One screening test, possibly followed by others, at intervals recommended by a physician** if you're past menopause and are considering or currently taking hormone-replacement therapy, are taking tamoxifen, eat a very high fat diet, have a history of infertility, have a history of not ovulating, are very overweight, have a family history of endometrial cancer, exhibit abnormal uterine bleeding or if your doctor has recommended it for other reasons.

Note: Endometrial sampling should be performed by an experienced physician, to avoid damage to the uterus.

COLON CANCER PREVENTION

Colon cancer is the third leading cancer among women, after breast and lung cancer. More women are affected by colon cancer annually (56,000) than men (53,000). But the following screening recommendations could help nip those cancers in the bud. These tests can help detect precancerous changes and early cancer, which can usually be easily treated.

11. **Digital-rectal exam.** With a gloved finger, a physician feels inside the rectum for abnormalities.

- **Once every year** if you are age 40 or over.

12. **Fecal occult blood test.** A stool sample is usually brought to a physician's office, hospital or clinic for analysis. (The stool sample could also be obtained in the doctor's office.) The test seeks blood as a possible symptom of colorectal cancer.

- **Once every year** if you're age 50 or over.

   Note: This test has been criticized because of the high rate of false positives (wrongly indicating a possibility of cancer) and false negatives (it misses the cancer when it's really there). But it's important to remember that, while a positive result may not mean cancer, it can indicate ulcers, hemorrhoids or other problems. For a definitive diagnosis of colorectal cancer, more sophisticated tests are required (see below).

13. **Sigmoidoscopy.** A thin, hollow, lighted tube is inserted into the rectum and lower part of the colon to look for precancerous polyps and remove them before a cancer develops. Flexible sigmoidoscopes are preferred because they cause less discomfort than rigid scopes.

- **Once every three to five years** if you are age 50 or over, without colorectal cancer risk factors or symptoms.
- **More than once every three years, at the discretion of the physician,** if you have a personal history of colon polyps, chronic inflammatory bowel disease or colorectal cancer; a family history of colon polyps or colorectal cancer (espe-

cially if a member of your immediate family—a parent, sibling or child developed colon cancer before age 50); symptoms of colorectal cancer (such as diarrhea, constipation or both; blood in the stools; very narrow stools; unexplained weight loss; or frequent gas pains and general stomach discomfort); a feeling that the bowel does not empty completely; a history of breast, endometrial or ovarian cancer or if your physician has recommended it for other reasons.

BONE HEALTH

One in two women will develop fractures from osteoporosis in her lifetime, and complications of hip fractures account for 50,000 deaths every year. "There's no reason we can't prevent most hip fractures and deaths from osteoporosis if we combine early detection and treatment," says AMWA osteoporosis expert Sydney Bonnick, M.D.

14. Bone scan. The scans are performed by machines that use low-dose radiation. The woman sits or lies on a table with the machine's energy sources above and/or below her; depending on the technology, the painless procedure may take five minutes to a half-hour.

- **One baseline screening test** just before menopause or very early in menopause; one more test a year to 18 months after menopause. In specific cases, more follow-up tests may be required. Older or younger women may also require testing, depending on their risk factors for osteoporosis (family history, steroid use, low-calcium diet or sedentary lifestyle) or if their physicians have recommended it.

    Note: A bone scan can show women who are approaching menopause whether they are at risk for osteoporosis and should take estrogen or other medication (like salmon calcitonin or etidronate), to prevent further bone weakening. It also provides a baseline measurement, so that a year after menopause, a repeat scan can determine whether you have lost too much bone and need to begin medication or adjust your current dosage.

    Several different technologies are available for measuring bone density, including Dual Energy X-ray Absorptiometry, Dual Photon Absorptiometry, Single Photon Absorptiometry, Quantitative Computed Tomography and Radiographic Absorptiometry. All of the techniques are capable of detecting low bone mass and diagnosing osteoporosis, according to Sandra C. Raymond, executive director of the National Osteoporosis Foundation. She points out that "some experts believe that for predicting fracture risk, the specific bone at risk for fracturing should be measured."

It's not always easy to find a facility for a bone-density test. The National Osteoporosis Foundation suggests checking with a local academic health center, a major hospital or the local branch of the American Medical Association.

Even major medical centers may not perform tests accurately. "It's a problem all of us recognize and are trying to improve," says Dr. Bonnick. In the meantime, ask the technician whether he has had several years of experience with bone scans. And make sure the physician will be reviewing the test and providing a written interpretation—don't settle for a computer-printout-based diagnosis. Raymond emphasizes that "a bone-mass measurement should be performed in the context of a total medical assessment by a qualified physician."

AIDS PREVENTION

There are many powerful reasons for women—and their partners—to be tested for human immunodeficiency virus (HIV). That's because transmission of the AIDS virus in the United States goes back to 1977.

15. HIV test. A blood sample is taken for analysis. At an anonymous test site, results are returned in 10 to 14 days. Private physicians may return results sooner.

- One screening test with follow-up tests at least three to six months after last possible exposure to the virus; if you had a blood transfusion between 1977 and 1985; if you have had sexual intercourse since 1977 with any partner whose sexual, transfusion or drug-use history since 1977 is uncertain or if you have ever injected drugs with shared needles.

Note: For the vast majority of people, an HIV test at least three months after the last possible exposure indicates whether HIV is present. However, in very rare cases, the telltale antibodies to HIV don't show up in the blood until six months after the last exposure. We suggest taking a test at three months and continuing to abstain from sex or to practice safer sex (limiting activity to nonpenetration or careful and consistent use of condoms) until a test after six months from last possible exposure.

Many people are reluctant to get an HIV test through their physicians because they are concerned about their anonymity. Fortunately, there are anonymous test sites in every state. They never take names, identifying clients only through a number. To locate these sites, call your state health department and ask for the HIV/AIDS department. Or call the Centers for Disease Control and Prevention toll-free national AIDS hotline at 1-800-342-AIDS. (Spanish speakers can call 1-800-344-SIDA).

—*Cathy Perlmutter with Maureen Sangiorgio*

HOME REMEDIES FOR WOMEN'S PROBLEMS

EVERY WOMAN NEEDS TO SEE A DOCTOR
ON A REGULAR BASIS, BUT NO WOMAN WANTS
TO RUN TO THE DOCTOR FOR EVERY LITTLE THING.
HERE ARE A FEW THINGS THAT WOMEN
SAY WORK FOR THEM.

As sure as the monthly menstrual cycle, women face certain health snags at each stage of life: premenstrual breast tenderness, menstrual cramps, vaginal infections, hot flashes and episodes of anxiety or depression. Of course, not every woman suffers the same problems or to the same degree. But most feel some sort of twinge at one time or another.

What are the most common complaints? And which home remedies and medical self-care measures do women find most effective in helping them manage these problems?

The Healthy Woman Survey conducted by *Prevention* and the American Medical Women's Association (AMWA) gleaned some fascinating answers from among its 16,500 responses.

One of the most provocative and unexpected findings involves the role of fitness. For every problem addressed here, women who exercise at least three times a week report greater success with self-care remedies than women who exercise less often. The physicians we talked with couldn't explain that correlation. But one lesson seems obvious: Regular, moderate exercise makes almost everything better. Here are other findings, as well as practical advice, concerning women's most troublesome health problems.

DEALING WITH BLADDER INFECTIONS

According to our survey results, bladder infections are the number-one problem; 46 percent reported experiencing them.

The burning and pain on urination, the urgency to urinate frequently, the lower-back pain and sometimes even blood in the urine—they're all symptoms that cannot and must not be ignored, or women run a risk of kidney damage. Fortunately, the vast majority of survey takers (81 percent) said they consulted a health professional within a few days of experiencing these symptoms.

A family doctor, internist or gynecologist can diagnose and treat bladder infections. Usually, all that's required is a three- to five-day treatment with antibiotics. For women with recurrent infections, doctors may prescribe a birth control method other than a diaphragm or occasional use of antibiotics, especially after sexual intercourse. If it's menopause that has triggered the bladder infection, estrogen cream can help. Ask your doctor.

Here are some things you can do on your own for a bladder infection.

Drink plenty of water. This was judged to be the most effective home remedy. Virtually all the women who'd had a bladder infection tried it. Some 82 percent of those pronounced it good treatment. Doctors advise women to drink six to eight glasses of water daily to flush the bacteria out of their systems and dilute nutrients that bacteria consume.

Drink cranberry juice. Again, the vast majority of women with bladder infections tried this remedy, and 59 percent reported favorable results. There is research that gives a little support to this practice; studies have shown that cranberry juice (as well as blueberry juice) helps prevent bacteria from adhering to the walls of the bladder. Some scientists suggest that the juice is considerably more effective in preventing recurrent bladder infections—or in nipping early infections in the bud—rather than in healing a raging infection. The acidity in the juice may actually irritate an infection that's in full swing.

Follow a low-caffeine diet. Only 10 percent of our survey takers tried it, but of those, 57 percent said they found it helpful. Doctors say that, in sensitive people, the lining of the bladder may become irritated by coffee.

BANISHING VAGINAL INFECTIONS

The second most common health problem in our survey— vaginal infections—plagued some 40 percent.

Doctors divide vaginal infections into two categories, notes AMWA gynecologist Diana Dell, M.D. The first kind, she says, is the overgrowth of something that normally lives in the vagina in small quantities. That usually means *Candida*, a form of yeast, or *Gardnerella*, a bacteria. The other kind is infection caused by agents that don't normally live in the vagina, like *Trichomonas*, a protozoan; *Neisseria gonorrhea* and *Chlamydia*, sexually transmitted bacterium; and human papillomavirus, a virus.

Unfortunately, the different diseases can be devilishly hard to tell apart, since all can cause similar symptoms: vaginal discharge, burning pain, itching and sometimes an unpleasant odor. Yeast infections are probably the easiest to recognize, says Dr. Dell, because there's often a characteristic cottage-cheese-like discharge.

Vaginal infections are a problem that our survey takers act on promptly. Nearly 70 percent consulted a health professional within days.

It's important to see a gynecologist or family doctor soon, because certain infections can damage the fallopian tubes, impairing fertility. A doctor can prescribe an appropriate treatment.

Here are some things you can try at home.

Use an over-the-counter antiyeast vaginal cream. These antifungal agents performed well. About 70 percent of our survey takers rated their effectiveness as "good."

If you have any doubt about whether your infection is really a yeast infection, head for a doctor right away. But if you're certain it's a yeast infection, it's okay to purchase the product without checking with a doctor, says Dr. Dell. If there's no significant change in your symptoms after the first three days, see your doctor; you may have another type of infection that requires prescription medication.

Eat yogurt. More than half (56 percent) reported good results with this home remedy. Preliminary studies have hinted that eating yogurt containing active cultures of *Lactobacillus acidophilus* may help combat yeast infections, but these results haven't been confirmed yet. Not all brands of yogurt contain active (or live) cultures, though, so read their labels.

Take a salt or vinegar sitz bath. Not too many women tried baths, but many who did (52 percent) said they found them helpful. A sitz bath is a shallow bath in lukewarm water—water that's too hot may make symptoms worse. Low-pressure douching may also help reduce the number of microorganisms in the vagina and soothe the area, says Dr. Dell. Adding a little vinegar to the water helps to increase the acidity of the vagina, making it less hospitable to some microorganisms.

GETTING RID OF MILD DEPRESSION

A third of our survey takers told us they'd experienced mild depression. But we found that women weren't as prompt to seek professional help for emotional problems as for physical ones. Only 42 percent said they'd consulted a health professional at all for mild depression, and a quarter of the women said they'd waited several years before getting help. "It's tragic that women delay or avoid medical treatment for depression," says AMWA president Leah J. Dickstein, M.D., a psychiatrist. "Depression is one of the most treatable of medical illnesses we have today."

If you're feeling down, and the mood persists for several weeks, talk to your primary care physician first, to rule out physical causes like infections or endocrine disorders.

Your next step should be to talk to a counselor—a therapist, psychologist or psychiatrist. The latest research suggests that combining approaches like cognitive and behavioral therapies is as effective as antidepressant medications for mild depression. Cognitive therapy means learning to identify negative thoughts and replace them with positive thoughts.

If symptoms persist or worsen, you may have severe depression and need medication. Of all the mental health professionals, psychiatrists are best trained to treat serious depression.

If your depression is of the mild, fleeting sort, here's how to send it on its way.

Exercise. A huge number of women tried this approach for mild depression and anxiety, and more than three-quarters (77 percent) said the results were good. Dr. Dickstein wasn't surprised: She recommends moderate exercise for depressed patients after they have been cleared by their physicians to do so. Exercise increases energy levels, relieves tension and improves feelings of control. And the exercise may even alter brain chemistry to enhance chemicals that make us feel better.

COOLING OFF HOT FLASHES OR NIGHT SWEATS

Hot flashes, a menopausal symptom, tied for third place with mild depression. A sizable 60 percent had consulted a health professional, most of them within days or weeks of noticing the problem.

Hot flashes (or night sweats, as they're called when they happen at night) are caused by a widening of the blood vessels near the skin surface, probably triggered by hormonal fluctuations. They're often a woman's first symptom of menopause. They tend to occur with the onset of what's supposed to be the most restful part of sleep, REM (rapid eye movement), says Dr. Dell, so many menopausal women who experience fatigue and irritability may be having chronic sleep deprivation. During the daytime, hot flashes often come on when a woman drinks something hot, takes a hot shower or imbibes alcohol.

If the problem is distressing, it's important to talk to your gynecologist or internist, says Dr. Dell. Hormone-replacement therapy is a good option for some women; it not only alleviates symptoms of menopause but it also helps prevent osteoporosis and cardiovascular disease. For women who cannot take estrogen, there are prescription products geared toward relieving hot flashes that you can discuss with your doctor.

There are also a few things you can do on your own.

Get moving. Sixty percent of women with menopausal symptoms rated this approach "good." "It really helps with a wide variety of symptoms that women experience in midlife," says Dr. Dell.

Take vitamin E. Half the women who took vitamin E reported a cooling of their symptoms. So far, though, there's no firm scientific evidence of vitamin E's effectiveness. "Until more data are available to provide guidelines for vitamin E administration, interested women might be advised to consult with a qualified nutritionist, who also can determine whether vitamin E might be contraindicated," says Fredi Kronenberg, Ph.D., physiologist at Columbia University College of Physicians and Surgeons in New York City.

ENDING MENSTRUAL CRAMPS

Twenty-nine percent of our survey takers said they'd experienced menstrual cramps. For a third of those women, the problem was severe enough that they saw a health professional. Menstrual cramps are probably caused by a release of prostaglandins, hormonelike agents that cause the uterine muscles to contract painfully.

A gynecologist, internist or family doctor may prescribe effective medication, but if cramps aren't very severe, women can ease them at home.

Take ibuprofen. This was judged the most effective remedy for cramps—60 percent rated the results "good." Yet fewer women tried it than tried aspirin, which wasn't judged as effective. Ibuprofen is a nonsteroidal anti-inflammatory drug (NSAID) that stops prostaglandins from forming. Research has found that ibuprofen is more effective than aspirin or acetaminophen in treatment of "mild" menstrual cramps, and physicians consider it the medication of choice.

Move that body. Is there anything exercise isn't good for? More than half of the women (54 percent) considered moderate exercise good medicine for menstrual discomfort.

Take calcium. Of those who tried it, 34 percent rated calcium a good treatment. Calcium does play a role in how well muscle functions, and the uterus is made of muscle. In one very small study, women who took 1,300 milligrams of calcium for about two months reported fewer aches and pains during menstruation than when they took only 600 milligrams of calcium per day for the same period of time. The study is far from conclusive, so the researchers are now doing a larger follow-up, says James Penland, Ph.D., research psychologist with the U.S. Department of Agriculture (USDA).

Try aspirin. More women tried aspirin than ibuprofen, but less than half as many (29 percent) reported pain relief. Aspirin is a mild antiprostaglandin—not as powerful in that regard as ibuprofen, says Houston endocrinologist Shahla Nader, M.D.

CHASING AWAY FATIGUE AND LETHARGY

More than a quarter of the women (27 percent) had experienced lethargy. That didn't surprise AMWA women's health expert and past president Lila Wallis, M.D. "In my experience, the most common cause of general fatigue among women is overwork and frustration. Women have a dual role: Working and taking care of their families. That's exhausting by itself. And if they don't like their work, if it doesn't engage all of their capacities, they are more likely to suffer fatigue. Frustration is exhausting."

The second leading cause of tiredness she sees is depression. One clue: "Many people who are depressed have early-morning wakening and exhaustion—feelings of paralysis and being unable to move when they should be bright and active."

Fatigue can have physical causes, too, Dr. Wallis notes. An important clue is easy fatigability. "That's different from feeling lethargic all the time. Fatigability means you do just a little work but quickly become tired. There can be many different causes—anemia, heart disease, thyroid disease and other endocrine disorders, including estrogen deficiency." Easy fatigability may be from fever and a number of infections.

Another possibility is chronic fatigue syndrome (CFS). CFS is a little-understood immunological disorder characterized not just by persistent fatigue, but often by recurrent sore throats, joint and muscle pain, low-grade fevers, unusual headaches and other symptoms as well.

Dr. Wallis advises women to see a physician promptly if lethargy or fatigability lasts longer than a week or so. She suggests women consult board-certified internists, since they are trained to diagnose different conditions and can refer patients to subspecialists if needed.

DEALING WITH PAINFUL OR FIBROCYSTIC BREASTS

A quarter of the women who filled out our survey told us their breasts were fibrocystic and/or painful, and nearly 80 percent of those had consulted health professionals, most of them promptly.

"Lots of people have breast tenderness and find things that relieve their symptoms," says Dr. Dell. "It's not really a disease and it doesn't mean you have a higher risk of cancer—it's a very common and benign condition. But you should talk to your doctor, especially if there's a new and unusual tenderness, to make sure there's no underlying mass."

Our survey takers also report one home remedy that works for them.

Try a low-caffeine diet. A whopping 65 percent of women who cut back on caffeine rated its results "good." "We don't know if caffeine makes breast symptoms worse," says Dr. Nader, "but cutting back does seem to help some people."

ENDING FREQUENT OR SEVERE ANXIETY

Worrying is a normal part of life. But if we worry all the time about unlikely scenarios, then we could be facing an anxiety disorder. Experts at the Anxiety Disorders Association of America (ADAA) say that anxiety has gone too far if it's excessive or unrealistic and lasts six months or more. General anxiety disorder can even translate into physical symptoms: trembling, muscle soreness, restlessness, fatigue, shortness of breath, heart palpitations, insomnia, sweating, irritability and difficulty concentrating. Since so many illnesses have these symptoms, it can be difficult to diagnose.

If anxiety has gotten out of hand, see a physician for a complete physical first. Like depression, our survey takers didn't seek help as promptly as they should have—while 52 percent went to a professional within weeks, 28 percent say they waited "years."

After a checkup, a physician may recommend a psychotherapist. Behavior and cognitive therapy can make a big difference in reducing anxiety. Severe cases may require medication.

Here are a few home treatments that work.

Banish caffeine. This really seemed to make a difference. A sizable 71 percent of women who cut back on caffeine to reduce anxiety pronounced the results "good." Scientists say caffeine does alter brain chemistry and can increase anxiety levels.

Try a relaxation technique. Our survey takers didn't rate these, but they're known to be helpful in reducing moderate anxiety. They include things like progressive muscle relaxation, yoga, massage and meditation. The ADAA also advises regular, moderate exercise, like brisk walking.

DEALING WITH PREMENSTRUAL SYNDROME

While 21 percent of our survey takers have experienced PMS, only a third (33 percent) of these consulted health professionals—and a substantial number of those women waited years to get help. That's not surprising, since the exact causes of PMS are unknown and treatments are controversial.

The symptoms, however, are well-known: breast swelling and tenderness, nausea, abdominal bloating, diarrhea or constipation, increased thirst or appetite, joint and muscle pain, anxiety, acne, food cravings, tension or migraine headaches, fatigue, sadness, sinusitis, sleep changes and mood swings. These all occur in the last half of the menstrual cycle, about two weeks before the onset of menstruation.

"Once women understand that the symptoms are part of PMS and they will live through it, they can do many things to help themselves," says Dr. Nader. If some of these symptoms are severe, a doctor might be of help. But so far, there's no proven overall treatment for PMS.

Here are some things that work for some women.

Try a low-sodium diet for premenstrual breast tenderness and bloating. Sodium increases fluid retention, possibly increasing pain in the breasts for some women. Low-sodium diets were rated "good" against breast tenderness by 57 percent of our survey takers. For premenstrual bloating, 61 percent rated it "good."

Exercise. More than half (54 percent) rated exercise a "good" defense against PMS. There is scientific research suggesting that exercise may help, possibly from an increase in "feel-good" endorphins in the brain.

You could try vitamin B_6. While a few women find this vitamin helpful, most of our survey takers didn't rate this remedy as good. There are scientific studies on B_6 and PMS, but they're small and contradictory. Also, high doses of vitamin B_6 can be toxic; so if you do take it, stay under about 10 milligrams a day to be safe.

GETTING RID OF VAGINAL DRYNESS

A problem encountered by a fifth of our readers, vaginal dryness can have many causes. Pregnancy, emotional stress, surgery, medications (like ulcer and blood pressure drugs) and menopause are among the most common culprits. Vaginal infections and douching can also reduce lubrication.

Vaginal dryness is very treatable; yet only 45 percent of our survey takers who encountered the problem consulted health professionals, and 20 percent of those women waited "years."

The treatment of choice for menopausal women is estrogen, either in pill or cream form. There's also much that a woman can do to help herself. We didn't ask our survey takers about any specific home remedies, but here are some ideas.

Try water-soluble lubricants without fragrances. Several commercial products are available. Ask your pharmacist to direct you. Avoid petroleum jelly; it can be difficult to remove, mask symptoms of infection and deteriorate condoms. For longer-term use, doctors recommend vaginal moisturizers.

Have sex. This helps keep the vagina healthy and moist. Be patient—and teach your partner to slow down. Lubrication may simply take longer for comfortable coitus.

TURNING OFF URINARY INCONTINENCE

Eleven percent of our survey takers say that they experience urinary incontinence—a highly treatable problem.

Most people don't need drugs or surgery; simple self-care measures have a good track record, with no harmful side effects. But a doctor's diagnosis is essential. "Start with a family physician, and if he doesn't help, keep looking until you find a knowledgeable physician or allied health professional who takes your symptoms seriously and offers a comprehensive treatment plan," says Katherine Jeter, Ed.D., founder and director of Help for Incontinent People (HIP) and clinical assistant professor of urology, Medical University of South Carolina. For more information on urinary incontinence, write HIP at P.O. Box 544, Union, SC 29379.

Here are a few tried and true home remedies.

Try Kegel exercises. These exercises helped nearly half (47 percent) of the women who tried them. This is in line with expert estimates that most people with incontinence can be helped by Kegels and may avoid surgery or medication. (If you don't know how to do Kegels, ask your doctor to provide instruction or to direct you to someone who can teach you.)

Banish caffeine. Of those who had experienced urinary incontinence, cutting back on caffeine seemed to help. Fifty-three percent rated this remedy "good."

—Cathy Perlmutter with Maureen Sangiorgio and Gloria McVeigh

THE PROCESS
OF THE "PAUSE"

IT'S BEEN CALLED THE CURSE, AND YOU'VE
PROBABLY CURSED IT YOURSELF. BUT WHAT
HAPPENS WHEN IT STOPS? HERE'S A DETAILED LOOK
AT WHAT GOES ON INSIDE A WOMAN'S BODY
AS SHE APPROACHES MENOPAUSE.

So you've been feeling a bit tired lately. Maybe it's because you've been waking up a few times at night and having difficulty getting back to sleep. Or it's possible you don't feel quite well—nothing you can put your finger on, just feeling a bit down or irritable; maybe things just seem to upset you more easily these days. And come to think of it, your periods have changed a bit. Nothing remarkable; in fact, it's hardly noticeable. But your cycle is a bit longer or shorter and the bleeding somewhat lighter or heavier than usual.

But you're only in your early to mid-forties, maybe just your late thirties. It *couldn't* be the beginning of menopause, could it? Yes, it could.

TIMING VARIES

While in rare cases a woman's periods just suddenly end one day, most women find that the process of the Pause averages between 2 and 10 years, and can sometimes take as long as 15. One woman started having irregular cycles when she was 36. She was having a period every two or three weeks and they were lasting 10 to 14 days. It seemed as if she was bleeding all the time. When she had her hormone levels tested, they were all over the map. She had a series of D and Cs—a scraping of the uterus frequently done when there is irregular bleeding with no known cause. Her gynecologist hoped that removing the top layer of cells from uterine lining would address the cause of the bleeding and it would stop. When one doctor did label her symptoms menopause, she left his office in a huff. She could not believe he would even intimate such a thing. Finally, when she was 48, her periods stopped completely. For her, menopause was a difficult and drawn-out process.

Just as each woman experiences pregnancy differently, we each go through the Pause in our own fashion. Some women breeze through pregnancy and then further infuriate the rest of us with a three-hour labor and delivery. Others have no problems in the early stages of pregnancy, but end up spending the last three months in bed or requiring a C-section. And some women remain sick from the moment they conceive and are further tormented by postpartum depression. With menopause, women range from having virtually no symptoms except the cessation of their periods to suffering through symptoms that severely interfere with day-to-day living.

RIDING THE HORMONAL ROLLER COASTER

Many of our reactions, both to pregnancy and to the Pause, have to do with the intensity of hormonal changes and our sensitivity to them. To begin with, we each have unique levels of hormones coursing through our bodies, causing menstrual cycles ranging from 26 to 36 days. In addition, our different diets, exercise patterns and life experiences make us more and more unlike one another as we age. Add to this the different ways in which the hormonal changes take place during this period, from abrupt drops and surges to a gradual tapering off of hormone production, and you can see how the process of the Pause can be infinitely variable.

Furthermore, some of us are more sensitive to our fluctuating hormones than others. The same absolute hormonal change that creates symptoms in one woman will hardly be noticed by another. And a level of symptoms experienced by one woman may cause her to seek medical intervention, while another with the same physical symptoms might grin and bear it.

Finally, the ease or difficulty with which we are visited by the Pause is further affected by certain factors, such as stress, diet, smoking, genetic differences and individual or cultural attitudes toward menopause. Japanese women, for example, don't have hot flashes; they have stiff shoulders. Mayan women express virtually no physical complaints at all. In contrast, women in a number of African tribes report complaints very similar to those of Western women.

THE PMS CONNECTION

Unfortunately, women who are the most likely candidates for problems with menopause are those who have experienced pre-menstrual syndrome (PMS) or postpartum depression. These are the women who end up being most sensitive to hormonal fluctuation.

"At 16 I'd come home from school because I'd be terribly depressed and I'd have such bad cramps I'd feel sick. And I remember they always told me: 'As you get older, it gets better.' Then they said, 'When you have kids, it all goes away.' And now I'm going through menopause and I'm still complaining about it."

It appears that 10 to 15 percent of women breeze through menopause with virtually no discomfort.

"I'm 52 and, to me, menopause really never was a big issue. I don't have my periods anymore. That stopped when I was 49. First, the timing of my periods was weird, they didn't come on time, but I never bled like some women. I never really had any problems. I occasionally have hot flashes, but by no means do I pay much attention to it."

"I'll be 48 next week. I'm just beginning menopause because every once in a while I miss a period. I also find that I have to exercise more to keep from gaining weight and I don't think it's because I've changed the way I've been eating, but that's about all I've noticed."

Another 10 to 15 percent of women experience symptoms so severe that they are incapacitated.

"Though I am normally even-tempered, I started to have psychotic experiences. I felt enraged, out of control. I was having hot flashes that felt like panic attacks every twenty minutes—day and night. I couldn't work. Most of the time, I couldn't even be around people."

"I've been a person who always felt well. But over the last five or six years, it's been yuck. I've even thought, 'What's the purpose of living?' be-

cause the quality of my life has been so bad—fighting constantly at work, with myself, with my body."

Women who experience a difficult menopause are often dismissed as neurotic or hypochondriacal. Unfortunately, many of us accept this label, especially if we do not know others who are suffering similarly.

"I used to think that women who had problems with menopause had the problem up in their heads. I knew it would be a breeze for me. Boy, was I ever surprised when I had these vicious hot flashes and unbelievable mood swings. It really taught me humility."

What are symptoms women commonly experience during the Pause? They include night awakenings, headaches, joint pains, unusual skin sensitivities, fatigue, irritability, moodiness, memory loss, mental sluggishness, hot flashes and night sweats. Some women also feel a lack of sexual desire, lack of vaginal lubrication and pain with intercourse. The good news is that you are unlikely to get *all* of these symptoms. The bad news is that none of them is fun. But remember, symptoms for most of us are mild, not sufficient to disrupt the daily routine seriously, especially once we realize that they are a response to the Pause and nothing more.

"It's so subtle, it really sneaks up on you. I had a hard time sleeping at night. I would get hot flashes and wake up drenched. And my sexual interest did go down a bit."

DON'T EXPECT DRAMATIC ENDINGS

Maybe the best way to explain why we experience symptoms is first to describe the process our bodies undergo during our reproductive years, and then how it changes as we enter the Pause.

"It's like making popcorn," says Jordan Horowitz, M.D., a San Francisco obstetrician and gynecologist. "Imagine the eggs as corn kernels and the hormones as heat. During puberty the eggs are all there. But it's not until the hormones are turned up that periods begin. Most young women are prone to irregular ovulation for a while, much like the first kernels of popcorn that go off intermittently. In the middle of reproductive life, like the middle of the popcorn analogy, we see regular ovulation and regular 'popping.' But as you have fewer kernels left, they again pop more irregularly. In fact, just before all the kernels have popped, there may be a quiet moment when you think everything's finished. Then suddenly a few more kernels pop. That is what happens as you get close to menopause. You may have a few months without ovulation and suddenly you'll ovulate again, until finally, everything that is going to pop has popped. And then you have reached menopause."

THE HORMONIC SYMPHONY

Now let's see how hormones figure into this popcorn analogy. Basically, your hormones regulate one another in a complex feedback system resembling a thermostat. When the temperature in your house reaches a certain low level, the thermostat signals the heater to turn on. Once the temperature is high enough, the thermostat turns the heater off. Your hormones signal each other in a similar way. There are actually a number of different hormones involved in the menstrual cycle, but for the sake of simplicity, we'll stick with the major players: estrogen, progesterone, follicle-stimulating hormone (FSH) and luteinizing hormone (LH).

Let's imagine a hypothetical 28-day cycle. On day 1, you start bleeding. At this point, estrogen and progesterone are at their lowest level. Once these hormones reach this low level, the thermostat turns on and signals the pituitary to begin producing FSH, which encourages the follicles in the ovary to ripen. A follicle is an egg surrounded by a layer of hormone-producing cells.

Initially, FSH causes a number of follicles to develop, but generally only one, the dominant follicle, called the Graafian follicle, will mature to ovulation. (One way we get twins or triplets is when more than one egg matures.) As the follicles are developing, they each secrete estrogen. Among other things, the estrogen causes blood to be brought to the uterine lining to prepare it for the implantation of the egg.

For the first 12 days of the cycle, FSH and estrogen levels are rising. Once the estrogen level is high enough, the thermostat signals the pituitary to stop producing FSH and to start secreting more LH. This midcycle surge of LH causes the egg to be released from the Graafian follicle. This is called ovulation and occurs at about day 14.

The empty follicle is now called the corpus luteum, or yellow body. The yellow body secretes its own estrogen and progesterone. Progesterone is the hormone that matures the uterine lining created by the estrogen and prepares it for pregnancy. Another thermostat begins working, and when the progesterone reaches a sufficiently high level, it signals the pituitary to shut off production of LH.

Even though FSH and LH have been shut off, the corpus luteum keeps pumping out estrogen and progesterone until about day 22, when it runs out of steam. If fertilization occurs, the fertilized egg begins secreting hormones of its own. If not, levels of progesterone and estrogen just keep decreasing. With this rapid decline of estrogen and progesterone, the blood vessels in the uterine wall (which has been prepared for the implantation of the fertilized egg) go into spasm and contract. This causes the uterine lining to break down and the blood cells and mucus that make up the lining are shed, and bleeding begins.

Now you are back to day 1, when the low levels of estrogen and progesterone trip the thermostat and signal the pituitary to begin releasing FSH—and the cycle begins again.

APPROACHING MENOPAUSE

As you approach menopause the cycle changes in a number of ways. First of all, as you age, you have fewer follicles left and those you have are often insufficient in quality to make it to ovulation. FSH levels rise higher and higher in an attempt to get the follicles to respond in order to produce a good egg. (It's kind of like turning up the heat, in the popcorn analogy, to get those last kernels to pop.)

It is the high level of FSH that ultimately determines the hormonal diagnosis of menopause. Unfortunately, FSH testing is often not diagnostically helpful because many women experience uncomfortable symptoms long before their FSH level rises to any degree. And by the time your FSH level rises above 40, the official determination of menopause, you are likely to have sufficient symptoms and your periods should be irregular enough that the test probably only confirms what you already know. After menopause, this FSH level will stay high and will drop only slightly over the years.

What you have during the Pause, those two to ten years before your periods stop, is disequilibrium. When your hormones are in balance, everything works well and you feel fine. When they are out of balance or when estrogen drops below a certain level—one that is unique for each woman and detected by her brain—you experience symptoms.

Your body responds to the withdrawal of estrogen. In a sense, your body is hooked on estrogen, much as a drug addict's body is hooked on heroin. Your central nervous system and other bodily functions have become accustomed to operating with certain levels of estrogen. When the estrogen drops below this comfort level, called the estrogen set-point, you experience symptoms just as the drug addict does when heroin is withheld. However, once you adapt to the lowered levels of estrogen (like after a drug addict has withdrawn from a drug), symptoms stop.

The problem is that you are not being withdrawn from estrogen in a steady and gradual manner. For example, in some months during the Pause you may have a "good" ovulation, and your estrogen level surges. This is like interrupting a drug addict's withdrawal program with a fix from time to time. The additional estrogen creates new receptors that produce symptoms when they are again deprived of estrogen as levels descend further.

COMMON PATTERNS

While we each go through the Pause in our own unique manner, there are a couple of fairly common patterns of hormone imbalance that can produce uncomfortable symptoms.

In the first pattern, estrogen levels are too high in relation to progesterone levels. This commonly occurs in midcycle as FSH and LH levels have been turned up in an attempt to stimulate one follicle to ovulate. Because the follicles are substandard, a number need to be stimulated, each one producing estrogen. This estrogen surge can lead to midcycle breast tenderness, headaches, nausea and some bloating. You may also have heavy bleeding, or it may take a lot longer than the usual 14 days to produce one good egg, thereby extending the cycle.

A second common pattern occurs when progesterone levels are higher in comparison to estrogen levels. In this case, estrogen declines more rapidly than progesterone. Furthermore, the relatively higher levels of progesterone actually turn off estrogen receptors. This diminishes the unusable estrogen, causing the estrogen levels effectively to dip below the set-point. When this occurs, we see such symptoms as PMS, mood swings, memory loss, food cravings (especially for sweets) and hot flashes.

As hormones continue to taper off, it is not uncommon for the proper balance between them to be regained for some time (although at reduced levels); you may find yourself in a honeymoon period, where symptoms decline for a few months or even a few years. For example, as the number of good follicles dwindles, fewer are left to produce estrogen, and this midcycle surge of estrogen quiets down. The relatively high levels of progesterone subside when you hit months in which you do not ovulate—called ovulatory cycles—because there is no corpus luteum to produce progesterone in the second half of the cycle.

It is this break in symptoms that often causes women to doubt that menopause is really upon them. One woman experienced this hiatus and concluded: "It can't be my hormones, because I'm just fine now. It was probably just stress." A couple of months later she began wondering all over again.

Finally, as you progress further toward menopause, fewer and fewer follicles are capable of ovulation—the final stages of the popcorn analogy. As estrogen levels continue to decrease further, you may drop below the estrogen set-point for a greater portion of the month. Initially, it may just be the last week of the month; then it is the last half of the month. Finally, women who are sensitive to this estrogen set-point may be symptomatic most of the time.

However, after a period of time, with no more ovulations and no more intermittent surges of estrogen, you adapt to the lowered levels of hormones, and symptoms disappear permanently.

PREMATURE AND SURGICAL MENOPAUSE

Natural menopause generally begins for women during their forties, but it can start earlier. Most women *complete* menopause between ages 45 and 55. The age at which your mother went through menopause is a fairly good indicator of your probable age at menopause. However, certain factors can result in an earlier transition. Women who have never been pregnant and those who have had their uteruses removed, as well as women who have been vegetarians or have been malnourished or anorexic for extended periods, are apt to go through menopause one to four years earlier than the average age. But smoking, as it turns out, is the major cause of an early menopause. Tobacco not only induces premature aging in all areas, it has a toxic effect on the ovaries.

About 1 percent of women go through what is termed *premature ovarian failure,* meaning that their periods stop completely before their 40th birthday. Ovarian damage from radiation or chemotherapy, or from certain autoimmune disorders and genetic abnormalities, is the most common cause.

Missing periods, even for an extended time, is not the same as premature menopause. Physical and emotional stress can and will affect your menstrual cycles. We know that anorexia nervosa—undereating to the point of extreme thinness—and unusual athletic training such as marathon running, or even changing time zones, can inhibit menstruation. Emotional stress such as a traumatic divorce or the death of a loved one can have the same effect. Generally, however, menstrual cycles will begin again once the stressful situation has ended.

Some women enter menopause as a result of an oophorectomy, the removal of the ovaries. This is called a surgical menopause. If just the uterus is removed, a woman still goes through a natural menopause at the appropriate time, but she may not recognize it right away because, without a uterus, she no longer has periods and cannot use a change in her menstrual cycle as confirming evidence.

When the ovaries are removed, a woman goes through an abrupt menopause. Her FSH and LH levels rise dramatically within a very short time as all of the hormones produced by her ovaries are cut off overnight. As a result, she is likely to experience exaggerated symptoms—everything from intense hot flashes to a precipitous drop in sexual desire.

Despite a reduction in function, the ovaries continue to produce hormones long after menopause is completed. This is one of the reasons you do not want to have your ovaries removed unless absolutely necessary. Along with the adrenal glands, the ovaries produce androgens. One of the androgens, called testosterone, is primarily responsible for your sex drive.

Androstenedione, another androgen produced in both the ovaries and the adrenals, is converted into estrogen largely in our fat cells. Our fat cells act as miniature factories, changing androgens into estrogen. Women with a little extra fat have more estrogen. This is one reason why thinner women tend to experience more symptoms during the Pause. With age, this process of converting androgens to estrogen in the fat cells gets more and more refined. So even after you have gone through menopause, you are not necessarily hormonally depleted. Many women continue to produce sufficient hormones to live perfectly comfortably on every level. Others experience sexual problems or are more likely candidates for heart disease or osteoporosis in later life.

A NEW BEGINNING

Once a natural menopause is reached, or at least within a couple of years after the last menstrual cycle, most women will have adapted to a lowered level of estrogen and, except in rare cases, most non–sexually related symptoms will have ceased. In fact, after menopause most women start to feel great. And they report fewer symptoms, both physical and psychological, than at any earlier time in their lives.

> "One thing I've noticed is a difference in my energy level. It's incredible. There are no ups or downs like I used to have as I went through my cycle getting ready for my period. It's just leveled out. That's the thing I've noticed most; it's the best."

Menopause is like a tunnel. Some women flow through effortlessly. Others bounce back and forth off the walls. But eventually everyone gets through. The one thing to keep in mind during this time is that there is a light at the end of the tunnel. Menopause does conclude and positive changes await us at the other side.

—*Lonnie Barbach, Ph.D.*

FACING UP TO MENOPAUSE

YOU REMEMBER WHEN WOMEN ONLY WHISPERED ABOUT THE CHANGE OF LIFE. THESE DAYS YOUNGER WOMEN INFORM THEMSELVES AND HEAD OFF POTENTIAL PROBLEMS.

Your girlfriend called the other day and you still can't get the conversation out of your mind.

"I've noticed some changes in my body lately," she said. "And I can't help wondering if I'm starting."

"Starting what?" you asked, half distracted by thoughts about your upcoming vacation.

"Menopause."

Menopause! That sure caught your attention. Here was your best friend—who is only a few years older than you—talking about a health issue you didn't think you had to worry about yet. You knew it would happen to both of you eventually. But not now. Not so soon. Neither of you are even 50 yet. Menopause was something meant for your mother and your great aunt. It's something for . . . for older women.

THE MEANING OF MENOPAUSE

For most women, menopause is a landmark of aging, says Ellen Klutznick, Psy.D., a psychologist in private practice in San

Francisco, who specializes in women's health issues. How women respond to it varies greatly.

While women who've already gone through menopause often see it as a new beginning, younger women who aren't there yet tend to feel more anxious about the transition, says Dr. Klutznick. "They are worried about how they are going to feel when they are 50 and about feeling old. They see it as aging," she says.

First, menopause marks the end of a woman's reproductive years. "The biological clock is ticking away for a lot of these younger women, and it's frightening," says Dr. Klutznick. For them, menopause is about the loss of their fertility, and in a society that places great emphasis on youth, beauty and reproduction, this can be difficult, she says. The loss of the potential to have children can be hard even for women who are finished having children or for those who never planned to, agrees Brian Walsh, M.D., director of the Menopause Clinic at Brigham and Women's Hospital in Boston. "They have lost the ability to choose. A door has been closed," he says.

Women are also concerned about how menopause will affect their physical appearance—they're worried that their bodies and skin won't be the same, that their breasts will sag and their faces will wrinkle and their waists will thicken, says Dr. Klutznick. And all of that is tied to their sexuality, she says. They worry that when they walk into a bar or restaurant, men won't look at them—they'll be eyeing the younger women in the room or the football game on television, she says. Aging in a youth-worshiping society makes some women feel invisible and devalued, says Dr. Klutznick. It is not that the women physically feel old, but they worry that society sees them as old. Women in this age group will ask her, "What do I have to look forward to but getting old? Who's going to want me?"

UNDERSTANDING MENOPAUSE

Literally speaking, menopause refers to a woman's last period. Technically, to be menopausal, a woman must not have menstruated for an entire year. The average age for menopause in the United States is 51, although women can go through it earlier. About 1 percent of women experience menopause before age 40.

Women who have their ovaries removed during a hysterectomy become menopausal virtually overnight, says Joan Borton, a licensed mental health counselor with a private practice in Rockport, Massachusetts, and author of *Drawing from the Women's Well: Reflections on the Life Passage of Menopause.* They often feel as if they've been propelled into menopause without any preparation. Women who have undergone chemotherapy can also go into early menopause.

In natural menopause, a woman's final period is surrounded by a number of years in which other physical changes occur. This is what is known as the climacteric or perimenopause. It generally begins several years before menstruation ends, says Dr. Walsh. During this time, women can experience a whole range of physical changes, including hot flashes, night sweats, sleep difficulties, vaginal dryness, skin changes, hair loss, mood swings, depression and weight gain. Hot flashes, often the symptom of most concern to women approaching menopause, affect approximately 75 to 85 percent of postmenopausal women.

All of these changes, including the cessation of the menstrual period, is triggered by decreasing levels of estrogen, one of several hormones produced by the ovaries. As a woman ages, her ovaries do, too; they shrink in size, stop releasing eggs and produce less estrogen.

YOUR RISKS DOWN THE ROAD

Estrogen also boosts bone quality and strength, so its decline at menopause can place women at increased risk for osteoporosis—a disease in which bones become brittle and fragile. Osteoporosis results in an estimated 1.5 million fractures per year. One-third of all women over 65 experience spinal fractures, and one in three women in their nineties, hip fractures (compared to one in six in men). Overall, between 25 to 44 percent of women experience fractures after menopause because of the disease.

The decrease in estrogen that accompanies menopause increases the risk of heart disease, the number-one killer of American women. That's because estrogen is a natural protector against heart disease. Without it, women and men are equal in their efforts to avoid heart disease. This means a woman's risk for heart attack and stroke go up after menopause. Before the age of 65, one in nine women will experience a heart attack, according to the American Heart Association. After 65, that rate skyrockets to one in three.

PLANNING AHEAD FOR MENOPAUSE

You can't avoid menopause. But there are some things you can do now, before you get there, that can make the whole experience a little easier. Menopause doesn't have to be a trying time, and it doesn't have to make you look and feel older. Here's what you can do.

Get a move on it. Exercise is one of the best things women can do ahead of time in order to fare better during their menopausal years, says Dr. Walsh. Exercise places stress on the bones, increasing their density and strength. Women's bones lose density after menopause—at the rate of about 4 to 6 percent in the first four to five years after menopause. So the stronger they are to start off with, the better. Weight-bearing activities, such as walking or running, are best, experts say. Exercise also helps keep cholesterol levels down, offering protection against heart disease.

Eat right. Get on a nutritious diet low in saturated fat, says Dr. Walsh. This will help reduce cholesterol and reduce the risk of heart disease, he says, both of which go up after menopause. Experts recommend that you keep your fat intake to 25 percent or less of the total calories you consume.

Keep an eye on PMS. If you have premenstrual syndrome (PMS) keep a log of your symptoms and pay attention to any changes. Sometimes PMS symptoms become far more intense as women enter menopause, says Dr. Klutznick, and they can serve as a signal for you that you're becoming menopausal.

Some possible changes you might notice are PMS symptoms that last longer than usual or a feeling that your mind is "fuzzy," she says. If you notice changes, tell your doctor. She can perform a simple blood test called the follicle-stimulating hormone (FSH) test, which measures the amount of FSH in your blood. Before menopause, your body produces enough FSH to help follicles develop and trigger ovulation. At menopause, however, you have fewer follicles and it takes more FSH to get one to mature and ovulate. So your body pumps out more of it than it use to. If your test shows a high FSH level, above 40 say, that means you are officially in menopause.

Quit smoking. If you stop smoking at a younger age, that can help you experience a gentler menopause, says Dr. Walsh. Smokers are more likely to have menopausal symptoms than nonsmokers are, he says. Smokers also have a tendency toward lower bone mass, putting them at greater risk for osteoporosis. Smoking can cause you to experience menopause earlier, experts say. They think its because nicotine may somehow contribute to the drop in estrogen. So stopping now could delay it a bit.

Get your calcium now. While the decrease in bone mass accelerates at menopause, it *begins* around age 35. After age 35 women lose 1 percent of their bone mass per year. So it's important that you consume enough calcium. The current Recommended Dietary Allowance for adults is 800 milligrams of calcium, but some experts suggest 1,000 milligrams a day for premenopausal women, and 1,500 milligrams for post-menopausal women.

Unfortunately, most women consume only about 500 milligrams a day through diet. You can come closer to protective amounts by adding low-fat and nonfat dairy products, canned fish with the bones (like salmon) and tofu to your daily diet. For example, one serving of low-fat milk gives you 300 milligrams of calcium and one serving of low-fat yogurt contains 415 milligrams. Three ounces of canned sockeye salmon contains 203 milligrams of calcium, and a half-cup of raw tofu contains 258 milligrams.

Another way to increase your calcium intake is through supplements. The amount that you should take and the type of tablet you use—calcium carbonate, calcium lactate or calcium citrate—will depend on your individual health needs, so consult your doctor.

Know your cholesterol level. Get your cholesterol levels checked, says Dr. Walsh. Menopause can cause the level of high-density lipoproteins (HDLs), or good cholesterol, to decrease and the level of low-density lipoproteins (LDLs), or bad cholesterol, to rise. So the better your cholesterol profile before menopause, the better. Experts say the best measurement to use is your total cholesterol/HDL ratio. A ratio less than 3.5 is considered low, a ratio between 3.5 and 6.9 is moderate and a ratio over 7.0 is high.

Talk to your mom. Women often follow the same patterns as their mothers, says Dr. Walsh, particularly if they have similar health experiences. So ask your mom about when she started menopause and what it was like for her.

WHEN THE TIME COMES

If you think you may be entering menopause, or if you're there already, here are some things you can do.

Get support. "The most valuable thing is gathering together with other women," says Borton. By talking with other women, either one-on-one or in support groups, you can learn about various symptoms and gather information about the doctors and health care professionals other women go to, like and recommend, she says. "Talking with other women and sharing experiences helps women feel supported and not so isolated," agrees Dr. Klutznick. One option is to join a support group. Call your local hospital to find out about groups in your area. Or, talk to other women.

Find the right doctor. Menopause will bring lots of physical changes and lots of questions, particularly about hormone-replacement therapy (HRT). HRT is recommended to help replace missing estrogen and keep bones strong. But it is also controversial, mainly because it may increase your risk of certain cancers. "The key is to get a doctor to work *with* you, one who will honor your decision," says Borton. Ask your friends about their doctors. And don't be afraid to "shop around" until you find a doctor you like.

Find a mentor. Find a woman 10 to 15 years older than you who's been through menopause and whom you admire, says

Borton. "Spend time with older women exploring with them what it is that holds meaning in their lives," she says. "Numbers of us have felt that doing this has helped us cross the threshold into seeing ourselves as older women and embracing it in a way that feels really wonderful." In addition to identifying women who can serve as mentors in your day-to-day life, look for older women in the public eye who you can follow and learn from, she says.

Stay lubricated. The decrease in estrogen that women experience with menopause can cause vaginal dryness. The elasticity and size of the vagina changes, and the walls become thinner and lose their ability to become moist. This can make sex painful or even undesirable, says Dr. Klutznick. Surveys indicate that this happens in 8 to 25 percent of postmenopausal women. While premenopausal women can generally lubricate in 6 to 20 seconds when aroused, it can take one to three minutes for a postmenopausal woman.

Women can stay lubricated by using water-based vaginal lubricants, such as K-Y Jelly, Replens and Astroglide, which are available over the counter, says Dr. Klutznick. Steer clear of oil-based lubricants such as petroleum jelly; studies indicate that they don't dissolve as easily in the vagina and can therefore trigger vaginal infections. Hormone-replacement therapy can also help alleviate the problem, says Dr. Klutznick.

Stay sexually active. Women who stay sexually active experience fewer vaginal changes than those who don't. Sexual activity promotes circulation in the vaginal area, which helps it stay moist. For women without partners, masturbation helps promote circulation and moistness in the vagina, she says.

Keep it cool. The hot flashes women experience during menopause can range from warm sensations to burning hot ones in which women become flushed and sweat. It can help to dress in layers and to keep the environment cool, experts say. Some women suck on ice cubes and drink cold liquids or visualize themselves walking in the snow or swimming in a clear lake. Hot liquids and spicy foods can trigger hot flashes, so keep these to a minimum. Experts don't completely understand what causes hot flashes, but they think that the decline in estrogen somehow upsets the body's internal thermometer.

—*Elisabeth Torg*

OUTSMART
OVARIAN CANCER

NOW YOU CAN CHANNEL YOUR CONCERN
INTO POSITIVE ACTION WITH THIS
MAXIMUM-PROTECTION PLAN.

My wife Gilda was afraid of cancer all her life," recounts Gene Wilder in a public-service ad. "And even with wonderful doctors, no one discovered she had ovarian cancer until it was too late. . . ."

The ad, sponsored by a renowned cancer-treatment center, goes on to caution women: "If you have vague symptoms, like abdominal bloating, clothes that feel tight, backache and sudden fatigue, don't worry, they're normal. But if they don't go away—and especially if you have a family history of ovarian cancer—see your doctor right away."

Well-intentioned as it may be, this ad sent an untold number of healthy women into a state of near panic. After reading that ad, a number of women dashed to their gynecologists and insisted on pelvic exams, sonograms and CA-125 blood tests (just as the ad advises).

IN SEARCH OF BETTER
SCREENING GUIDELINES

What's the bottom line? *Should* every woman who notices these vague and common symptoms be concerned about the possibility of ovarian cancer and get tested? And more important, haven't better screening guidelines been established that can detect ovarian cancer in its very early stages, before these symptoms develop?

In our search for answers, we spoke with leading experts at America's best cancer centers and research institutions. Several commented that, while the public-service message delivered by Wilder, widower of the late "Saturday Night Live" comedienne Gilda Radner, is technically accurate, it is horribly misleading.

"Suggesting to a woman that if she has abdominal bloating, she should see her doctor right away because it could be ovarian cancer is like saying if you have a headache, it's time to see a neurosurgeon because you probably have a brain tumor," says Michael Muto, M.D., head of the Familial Ovarian Cancer Center at Brigham and Women's Hospital in Boston.

Nearly every woman has stepped into pants that she can't

A MATTER OF RISK

Risk Raiser

Using talcum powder. Several studies have linked frequent use of talc around the genital area with an increased risk of ovarian cancer. A recent study conducted by Daniel Cramer, M.D., Sc.D., associate professor of obstetrics and gynecology at Brigham and Women's Hospital and Harvard Medical School in Boston, and his colleagues found that women who used talc for genital hygiene on a daily basis for many years, particularly during their childbearing years, have an up to threefold increased risk for ovarian cancer. While cause and effect has not been established, Dr. Cramer suspects that contamination of the vaginal area with talc may allow particles to reach the ovaries through the uterus and fallopian tubes, which may cause inflammation within the ovaries, contributing to the eventual development of ovarian cancer.

While the study concluded that only a small percentage of ovarian cancers arise in this manner, a regular habit of applying talc directly to the genital area or using it as a dusting powder for underwear, sanitary napkins or diaphragms was discouraged by the study's authors. Although not enough women had used cornstarch powder to comment on its safety, it generally produces less inflammation and is likely to be safer for occasional use.

Risk Reducers

Having children. We know that a woman who has had one full-term pregnancy has a 40 percent lower risk of ovarian cancer than a woman who has had no preg-

snap. "But the percentage of women who have these symptoms and have ovarian cancer is very, very small," notes William Hoskins, M.D., chief of Gynecologic Oncology at Memorial Sloan-Kettering Cancer Center in New York City.

Besides, treating ovarian cancer after symptoms develop is more difficult.

Detecting ovarian cancer before symptoms erupt is the best

nancies. With each additional child, a woman's risk drops even further, by 14 percent.

Breast-feeding. In addition to all of the goodies a baby gets by being breast-fed, Mom benefits, too. Each month of breast-feeding a baby reduces her risk of ovarian cancer. Breast-feeding for a total of 12 to 24 months can reduce risk by about one-third.

Eating foods high in beta-carotene. Researchers at Ohio State University noted a link between a high intake of beta-carotene-rich foods, such as carrots, sweet potatoes and dark, leafy greens, and a reduced risk of ovarian cancer. Although this was a small study—213 women—its findings were consistent with several larger studies. Eating three medium carrots every five days was associated with a lower risk of ovarian cancer.

Taking oral contraceptives. See "Should You Take Birth Control Pills?" on page 68.

Exercising. Mounting studies suggest that regular exercise may help prevent colon and breast cancer. Now a collaborative study between the National Cancer Institute and the Shanghai Cancer Institute in China provides some evidence that women who held jobs requiring high physical activity may have a reduced incidence of ovarian cancer. Women who sat for long periods of time on the job or expended little energy at work had an increased incidence of the disease. While the researchers acknowledge that the jury is still out, a physically active lifestyle has so many other benefits that regular exercise seems prudent.

bet; at this early stage, women with ovarian cancer have an 80 to 90 percent survival rate, according to the American College of Obstetricians and Gynecologists. But, to date, there are no established screening guidelines for ovarian cancer, as there are for, say, breast cancer or cervical cancer.

Organizations like the American Cancer Society and the National Cancer Institute (NCI) argue that, because ovarian cancer is rare, mass screening of all women is not economical. The average woman has a 1 in 65 chance of developing ovarian cancer over her lifetime as compared with a 1 in 8 probability of getting breast cancer.

An even more compelling argument against mass screening is that the best available tests are unreliable. The CA-125 blood test, in particular, is notoriously inaccurate. Since the only way to confirm cancer is through a surgical biopsy, mistakenly abnormal results on a CA-125 blood test too often lead to unnecessary surgery.

WHAT'S A WOMAN TO DO?

Obviously, this is another area of women's health where medical research is sorely lacking. The question is, What's the best you can do to protect yourself now?

HOW DO YOU FIND A QUALIFIED DOCTOR?

If you know or suspect that you are at risk for ovarian cancer, it's important to seek consultation with a physician who specializes in the prevention, detection and treatment of women's cancers, a gynecologic oncologist. To locate this specialist, send a self-addressed envelope (6" x 9" or larger) stamped with $1.25 in postage to the Society of Gynecologic Oncologists, 401 North Michigan Avenue, Chicago, IL 60611, and ask for referral information. They'll send you their membership directory, which provides names, addresses and telephone numbers of board-certified or board-eligible gynecologic oncologists in your area.

First, nearly every expert we consulted said to keep your concern in perspective. The fact is, ovarian cancer is a relatively uncommon disease. "There will be approximately 182,000 new cases of breast cancer diagnosed this year and 22,000 new cases of ovarian cancer," Dr. Muto explains.

"This is not a disease we should be in a panic about," agrees Susan Harlap, M.D., epidemiologist at Memorial Sloan-Kettering Cancer Center. "The vast majority of women are not at risk and needn't worry."

Of course, some of us may be at higher risk. And it's important for us to know that so we can channel our concern into positive action.

FOR WOMEN AT HIGH RISK

Overwhelmingly, our experts agree that the number-one risk factor for ovarian cancer is a family history of the disease. Primarily, a woman who has at least one documented case of ovarian cancer in an immediate relative—a mother, sister or daughter—is considered at high risk. Having an aunt or grandmother with ovarian cancer ups her risk, too, but not to the same degree.

It's important to note, however, that having a family history of ovarian cancer doesn't mean you're born with a time bomb ticking inside. It means that there's a chance you may have inherited a flawed gene that could make you more vulnerable to the disease. Unfortunately, there's no way to tell whether you've inherited the gene. Not yet, anyway, though Dr. Muto anticipates that within the next five years genetic testing will make it possible to do just that.

In the meantime, if you know or suspect that anyone in your family has had ovarian cancer, make an appointment with a women's cancer specialist (a gynecologic oncologist) for a risk assessment.

Cancer specialists say many women mistakenly believe their families carry hereditary ovarian cancer. "It sometimes turns out that the relative had another type of cancer that spread to the ovaries. Once you put the pieces together, it really isn't ovarian cancer," says Neil Rosenshein, M.D., director of the Division of

Gynecologic Oncology at Johns Hopkins University Medical Center in Baltimore.

Another consideration is that few cases of ovarian cancer are hereditary—only 5 percent, says Dr. Rosenshein. Having an immediate relative with ovarian cancer doesn't mean it's genetic or hereditary. It could be just chance. Short of obtaining permission to see your relative's medical records (which is definitely worth the effort if you're in doubt), the only clue that you may be dealing with a hereditary disease is the age at which your relative was stricken.

Familial ovarian cancer tends to strike women ten years

THE BEST TESTS...AT LEAST FOR NOW

Screening for ovarian cancer is a terribly imperfect science. That's why the National Cancer Institute (NCI) is planning clinical trials to help evaluate the lifesaving value of the following tests. Until the results are in, here's what we know.

Pelvic exam: a basic and essential tool in screening all women for ovarian cancer. In this exam, a physician inserts one finger into the vagina and presses on the abdomen with the other hand to palpate the ovaries and feel for abnormalities. Another variation is to perform a pelvic exam, as described above, with one finger in the vagina and another in the rectum. According to Conley Lacey, M.D., head of Gynecologic Oncology at the Scripps Clinic and Research Foundation in La Jolla, California, this allows for a more thorough assessment of the ovaries. Effectiveness depends, to a very large degree, on the experience and training of the physician and on the woman's build (excess abdominal weight can interfere with accuracy).

Transvaginal ultrasound: useful, in combination with the pelvic exam, to screen women at high and above-average risk. Also used to assess women whose pelvic exams are inadequate or suspicious. In transvaginal ultrasound (also called sonogram), a probe is inserted into the vagina and high-frequency sound waves are

sooner, on average, than nonfamilial ovarian cancer. Also, a family tree strewn with multiple cases of ovarian cancer suggests a familial pattern.

Experts agree, the highest hereditary risk is reserved primarily for women who have either two or more immediate relatives with documented ovarian cancer or one immediate relative and multiple distant relatives (aunt, grandmother or other) with the disease.

Apparently, too, a woman has an elevated risk of developing ovarian cancer if her family tree is laden with ovarian cancer plus breast cancer or her family tree has a preponderance of colon

bounced off the uterus and ovaries; the resulting image is transmitted to a monitor for viewing. The test can detect an enlarged ovary, which may suggest cancer. But it's far from foolproof. As William Hoskins, M.D., chief of Gynecologic Oncology at Memorial Sloan-Kettering Cancer Center in New York City explains, not every enlarged ovary is cancerous. Unfortunately, determining whether it is requires a surgical biopsy. Because of that—and the high cost of the exam (about $300)—transvaginal ultrasound is reserved as a tool for women at risk for ovarian cancer.

CA-125 blood test: too troublesome to use for screening. This blood test, which screens for antibodies produced by cancer cells, is notoriously inaccurate. It misses about half of the early ovarian cancers it should detect, says Dr. Hoskins. And according to an NCI study, it sometimes suggests cancer in women who are disease-free; pregnancy, endometriosis, pelvic inflammatory disease, uterine fibroids, even menstruation can skew the test results. Besides, CA-125 has never been approved by the Food and Drug Administration for use as a screening test; its only approved usage is for assessing recurrences in women treated for ovarian cancer, points out Michael Muto, M.D., at Brigham and Women's Hospital.

cancer along with any of these cancers: ovarian, endometrial (uterine), lung, pancreatic or prostate.

But, some experts agree, just one immediate relative is enough to nudge you into the high-risk category. Often, however, it can be difficult to prove what a relative had was really ovarian cancer. In our opinion, unless you can prove beyond a

SHOULD YOU TAKE BIRTH CONTROL PILLS?

Birth control pills interrupt ovulation, just as pregnancy does, which appears to be a plus in preventing ovarian cancer. Even using the Pill for as little as one year can reduce your risk. After four years of use, risk is reduced by almost 50 percent. That's roughly the same degree of protection as having three full-term pregnancies, says Neil Rosenshein, M.D., director of the Division of Gynecologic Oncology at Johns Hopkins University Medical Center in Baltimore.

Is that reason enough to suggest taking oral contraceptives as a preventive?

"That depends," was the consensus of our cancer experts. For some women, it's definitely not an option. The health risks for certain women (such as those with known heart disease, high blood pressure, active liver disease or a personal history of breast cancer, stroke or phlebitis) outweigh the health benefits, according to Paul Blumenthal, M.D., M.P.H., director of Contraceptive Research Programs at Francis Scott Key Medical Center in Baltimore. Likewise, the Pill is not advised for women who smoke, especially if they're over 35.

But for those who can safely take the Pill and are at high risk for ovarian cancer, "oral contraceptives are certainly a strategy to consider," says Dr. Rosenshein. "I personally have prescribed them for young women with a strong family history of ovarian cancer."

William Hoskins, M.D., chief of Gynecologic Oncology at Memorial Sloan-Kettering Cancer Center in New York City, agrees. "The use of oral contraceptives

reasonable doubt that it wasn't, you would be wise to take a cautious approach.

Being cautious means continuing to see a qualified gynecologist—preferably a gynecologic oncologist—for periodic checkups. As a woman's cancer specialist, a gynecologic oncologist has specialized training and experience to help you decide on a

for two years or more does appear to significantly decrease the risk of ovarian cancer as well as endometrial cancer—and the benefits are lifelong. I think it's reasonable to recommend them for primary prevention in high-risk women."

Whether child-free or infertile women (who are considered at above-average risk) should take the Pill for prevention is hotly debated, however. "Right now, I'd be a little reluctant to recommend birth control pills for someone who doesn't need them for contraception just because that person is in the moderate-risk category," says Dr. Hoskins. But he feels that women should be given the facts about oral contraceptives' protective effect. Conley Lacey, M.D., head of Gynecologic Oncology at Scripps Clinic and Research Foundation in La Jolla, California, agrees. "I think it is something this woman needs to consider in her overall health care. You need to tell her that she may be able to reduce her risk of ovarian cancer by as much as 50 percent. Then she can make a decision about using this as a preventive measure."

It's also unclear whether women over 40 who are at high or above-average risk can benefit from the protection of birth control pills. Despite this, several experts admitted that it's reasonable to recommend the Pill to women up to age 45 who are at risk.

For women at no increased risk, a decision to take oral contraceptives should be made strictly because of a need for contraception and not to prevent ovarian cancer, agree our experts.

personal action plan. (See "How Do You Find a Qualified Doctor?" on page 64.)

According to the cancer specialists we interviewed, the best advice for women at high risk would be to have a pelvic exam and/or a transvaginal ultrasound every six months beginning between the ages of 21 and 25. (See "The Best Tests . . . At Least for Now" on page 66.)

Dr. Rosenshein usually alternates these two tests at six-month intervals for his high-risk patients. Conley Lacey, M.D., head of Gynecologic Oncology at the Scripps Clinic and Research Foundation in La Jolla, California, tailors the tests to each individual. He gives his high-risk patients a pelvic exam every six months and makes liberal use of transvaginal ultrasound, particularly in women who are difficult to examine because of anxiety or excess body weight or when the pelvic-exam findings are suspicious.

FOR WOMEN AT ABOVE-AVERAGE RISK

Although heredity represents the most significant risk factor for ovarian cancer, 95 percent of the women who develop the disease do not have a family history of it.

The search for reasons has led researchers to identify other possible risk factors. Two groups of women have emerged with above-average risk: women who have not had children and have not taken oral contraceptives, and women who have had breast cancer.

How many ovulations you have during your reproductive years appears to be a critical issue in determining ovarian-cancer risk, explains Dr. Rosenshein. If you ovulate continually until menopause, without interruption by pregnancy, breast-feeding or the use of oral contraceptives, your ovaries are subject to monthly hormonal stimulation. This, experts believe, may increase cancer risk to the ovaries.

A woman who has had breast cancer is considered to be at increased risk for ovarian cancer as well, for reasons that are not exactly yet known.

Like breast cancer, ovarian cancer is an age-specific disease, meaning that it's more likely to occur as you get older. The chance of developing ovarian cancer takes its biggest jump between the ages of 50 and 65, from about 28 cases per 100,000 to 54 cases per 100,000, and peaks around age 70 to 74 with 60 cases per 100,000 women. A woman at above-average risk (because of either uninterrupted ovulation or previous breast cancer) needs to be aware that advancing age may compound her risk.

If you fit the risk profile described here, take your concerns to a gynecologist (preferably a gynecologic oncologist) and discuss an action plan that's right for you. In addition to an annual pelvic exam, some of our experts offer their patients transvaginal ultrasound and suggest that it may be wise to have one once a year, beginning at age 35, as a precaution. However, they are quick to add that, while transvaginal ultrasound is a valuable tool, it is not perfect. It can detect enlargements of the ovaries, but it cannot tell if they're from cancer or not. So in coming up with a plan that's right for you, it's a good idea to discuss with a gynecologic oncologist the pros and cons of transvaginal ultrasound.

FOR WOMEN AT NO INCREASED RISK

Each of our experts emphasizes the importance of regular gynecologic care for women who are at no increased risk for ovarian cancer, since neither CA-125 nor transvaginal ultrasound is an appropriate test for the general population. A careful pelvic examination at the time of a Pap test (to detect cervical cancer) should be performed by a qualified physician or health professional once a year beginning at age 18 (or sooner if a woman is sexually active).

"I urge women to have a pelvic exam and Pap test every year without fail, never to miss a mammogram and to examine their breasts every month," advises Dr. Muto.

—*Toni Donina, Toby Hanlon and Emrika Padus*

NEW RELIEF
FROM THOSE
CURSED CRAMPS

AS MEDICAL SCIENCE ADVANCES, PAINFUL PERIODS ARE BECOMING A THING OF THE PAST. HERE'S A GUIDE TO THE BEST SELF-CARE AND PRESCRIPTION PAIN STOPPERS.

Some women experience only a mild twinge. But many women suffer, doubled over in lip-biting silence, month after month. Usually, the pain is of mild to moderate intensity, which is bad enough. But occasionally, women swear their menstrual cramps are on a par with labor pains. (In fact, both are precipitated by the same body chemicals.)

Today, thank goodness, there's more to do than plug in the heating pad; leading gynecologists recommend a plan of action that can often halt your menstrual misery even before you feel the first twinge.

THE PROSTAGLANDIN CONNECTION

Researchers aren't completely sure what causes painful periods, but most believe that hormonelike substances called prostaglandins are behind the problem. In addition to regulating other functions in your body, prostaglandins stimulate your uterine muscles to contract. In fact, doctors actually use prostaglandins to induce labor in pregnant women, says Toni Harris, M.D., chief of the Division of Gynecology at the University of California, Davis.

Before your period begins, the production of prostaglandins naturally rises. This makes the uterine contractions stronger— probably to help your body push the menstrual fluid out of your uterus, experts say. These contractions may be so mild that you don't feel them at all. But in some women, they can be very intense. The intensity may have to do with the amount of prostaglandins the women produce, researchers think. Indeed, studies suggest that the menstrual fluids of women who have cramps contain higher levels of prostaglandins than the menstrual fluids of women who don't.

Now, here's the good news. Prostaglandin production can be blocked with a common over-the-counter medication: ibuprofen. In fact, doctors used to prescribe ibuprofen specifically for painful periods before it was available over the counter. (If you have kidney problems, ulcers, nasal polyps or asthma, please consult your physician before self-medicating.)

To get the most benefit from ibuprofen, though, you have to take it correctly, says Susan Ballagh, M.D., director of the Stanford Women's Group at Stanford University Medical School. "Always anticipate the pain and try to get the medication on board before cramps begin, because ibuprofen works much better at preventing pain than it does in removing the pain once it's started," she says.

If your periods are regular or you have body signals like breast tenderness or bloating, it's easy to figure out when you're about a day away from your next period. That's when you begin taking ibuprofen at the dosage recommended on the label—two 200-milligram tablets every four to six hours—and continue that for about two days after you begin bleeding (or for as long as your cramps usually last).

Some women who have more severe pain might want to consider adjusting the dose to a maximum of three 200-milligram pills four times a day (with meals, to avoid side effects). That's equal to the dose used when ibuprofen was available only as a prescription, says Joanne Piscitelli, M.D., head of the Division of General Obstetrics and Gynecology at Duke University Medical School in Durham, North Carolina. "But make sure you're limiting it to the couple of days around your periods," she adds.

Ibuprofen may cause side effects, like stomach upset and diarrhea—even stomach bleeding—in some people. That may be doubly troublesome to women who commonly experience stomach problems along with their menstrual cramps. But you can usually avoid that by taking your dose along with meals and by strictly limiting the number of days you take it. To be safe, watch for dark stools, which signal abdominal bleeding, and report them to your doctor. (If you have stomach ulcers, you should avoid taking ibuprofen. Talk to your doctor about alternatives.)

TAKING THE NEXT STEP

If you don't find relief after three cycles on the above regimen, see your doctor for a pelvic exam. "If it's normal and there's no reason to suspect that there's a hidden cause for your menstrual cramps, the next step would be to consider taking low-dose birth control pills," Dr. Piscitelli says. Your doctor may even advise you to continue taking ibuprofen for added protection.

WHEN PAINFUL PERIODS SIGNAL SOMETHING ELSE

Painful periods may occasionally signal a serious problem, such as endometriosis (a condition linked to fertility problems), pelvic inflammatory disease or fibroid tumors, says Toni Harris, M.D., chief of the Division of Gynecology at the University of California, Davis. The good news is that these conditions are simple to detect, if you're alert to their symptoms. Here's what to look for.
• Fever
• Vomiting
• An unusually painful period
• Pain that's located on the sides of the pelvis, instead of centrally over your pubic bone
• Foul-smelling discharge
• Unusually painful intercourse
• Pain that starts more than a day or two before your period and continues to the end or beyond

While it's often said that menstrual pain should subside with age and after childbirth, don't worry if yours doesn't, Dr. Harris says. "But if you have a period that is really unusually painful—out of step with gradual changes you've been experiencing—you should definitely seek a medical evaluation." You should also schedule an appointment if self-care measures fail to provide relief.

Today's commonly prescribed combination birth control pills (containing estrogen and progesterone) help reduce the amount of prostaglandins you produce by preventing ovulation and thinning the lining of the uterus. Some older studies suggested that oral contraceptive use may increase your risk of breast cancer. More recent, higher-quality studies have refuted that evidence, Dr. Harris says.

"The low-dose pills are remarkably safe. They even have some significant health advantages, like helping to lower incidence of ovarian cancer and endometrial cancer, lower incidence of pelvic inflammatory disease and fewer ectopic pregnancies," she says. Women who have a history of heart attack, stroke, high blood pressure and blood clots in their legs or lungs or who have already had breast cancer, though, should avoid taking oral contraceptives.

If you are unable or unwilling to take the Pill, or if after three cycles on it your cramps still don't subside, your doctor may prescribe any one of a number of nonsteroidal anti-inflammatory drugs (NSAIDs) that work as prostaglandin inhibitors—like ibuprofen, but more powerful. They're prescribed for short-term use—for the day before your period begins and for the first day or two after you start bleeding. While they require less-frequent dosing than ibuprofen, these NSAIDs are more likely to cause side effects.

You may have to go through a couple of two-cycle trial runs to find a prescription NSAID that relieves your cramps and that you can tolerate, Dr. Ballagh says. It's extremely rare for prescription NSAIDs not to work for simple menstrual cramps, she adds.

SELF-CARE OPTIONS TO CONSIDER

Unfortunately, the research on self-care remedies for menstrual cramps is sorely lacking. Very often, women must rely on information from other women about what works for them. Our experts suggest that the following, while scientifically unproven, may have some merit in both preventing and easing those monthly woes.

Relax away the pain. There are dozens of good reasons to practice some form of stress management. Preventing and easing menstrual cramps may be one of them.

"Some studies suggest that elevations in stress hormones can increase your perception of pain," explains Dr. Ballagh. "So stress reduction around the time of your period may somewhat reduce your experience of the cramping."

Dr. Harris theorizes that prostaglandins may play a role, too. "There may be a stress component that either alters prosta-glandin production or makes the uterus more sensitive to prostaglandin levels," she says.

Whatever the case, Dr. Harris often recommends medication together with relaxation techniques, such as yoga and medita-tion, to maximize pain relief.

Exercise. As a stress reliever, of course, exercise just can't be beat. Plus, there may be another reason it helps to ease men-strual pain. "Exercise does increase the level of endorphins— your body's natural painkillers—and that may have an effect on menstrual-cramp pain, but we don't know for sure," says Chris-tine Wells, Ph.D., professor of exercise science and physical ed-ucation at Arizona State University in Tempe and author of *Women, Sport and Performance.*

So even if you're not feeling up to speed, try to stay active (unless, of course, you have severe nausea or vomiting). If you feel weak in the legs, try something easy, like moderate walking, if you can.

"Sometimes, attacking the problem rather than lying on the couch and being a victim really makes a difference," adds Dr. Harris. Take it easy for the first 15 minutes of your workout. Then pick up the pace, if you feel good enough. If you don't, complete your workout at your warm-up pace.

It's also a good idea to avoid heavy lifting and intense ab-dominal work on "crampy" days. It's okay to do resistance training when you have cramps, but don't choose that time to increase weight or add new, unfamiliar exercises. Plus, heavy lifting puts stress on your abdominal muscles, which may ag-gravate your cramps. For that reason, give yourself a couple of days off from stomach crunches and other belly-busting exer-cises, too.

Curl up. Practice the Child's Pose. "Yoga can help you relax," says yoga expert Mary Pullig Schatz, M.D., medical staff president at Centennial Medical Center in Nashville and author of *Back Care Basics*. "Certain poses—particularly forward bends—also allow a gentle compression of the pelvic organs, which may also have a soothing effect."

She recommends the Child's Pose for cramp relief. It requires no particular yoga training. But if it causes you any back or hip pain, you should refrain from doing it. Kneel on the floor, sitting back on your heels, arms at your sides. Bend over and rest your chest on your thighs, keeping your arms alongside your torso. Place your forehead on the floor, or turn your head to the side. Inhale deeply through your nose, exhale through your nose and pause a second or two before you inhale again. Hold the pose for as long as you're comfortable (up to several minutes).

If you're at all uncomfortable, try placing folded or rolled-up towels under your ankles to prevent excessive stretching, under your buttocks if you have trouble sitting back on your heels or beneath your head for cushioning or if you can't rest your head on the floor. If you feel any knee pain, place a rolled-up sock in the bend of each knee to create more space.

Consider making love. The effects of sex can be pain-relieving or pain-promoting. Some women say sex is their favorite cramp reliever. Others report that sex makes their cramps even worse—and there may be reasons for this. There are prostaglandins in semen, Dr. Ballagh explains. Plus, during an orgasm, your uterus contracts, which can heighten menstrual pain.

"Nevertheless, some women may actually experience heightened orgasm with the additional cramping," she adds. And your body does release post-orgasm endorphins, which are natural pain relievers.

The bottom line: Listen to your body and do whatever works best for you.

—*Lisa Delaney with Holly McCord, R.D.*

HOW TO GET MORE
FROM YOUR
OB-GYN VISIT

CAN YOU, SHOULD YOU, ASK FOR MORE FROM
YOUR DOCTOR IN THESE TIMES OF HEALTH-CARE
CUTBACKS AND REFORMS? YES!

Women need to understand the power of their dollar now more than ever," says Eddie Sollie, M.D., author of *Straight Talk with Your Gynecologist.* "Women's health is doctors' big new focus, and they are scrambling to provide these services because it represents income." If your doctor isn't able to give you the services outlined here, find one who can. Remember, you're paying for the visit, so make sure you're getting what you want and need.

MORE PREVENTIVE HEALTH

Just because you think of your gynecologist as your primary care doctor doesn't mean your doctor knows that. "Be very clear about telling your ob-gyn that she is the only doctor you see. That way the two of you can work together to give you the preventive and primary care you need," advises Richard U. Levine, M.D., vice-chair of the Department of Obstetrics and Gynecology at Columbia Presbyterian Medical Center in New York City.

What should you expect in the way of expanded health care? Ask your doctor specific questions—and get specific answers. "I have lots of patients who ask, 'Can I call you if I have a sore throat?' Unless the doctor has an idea of what you want, need or expect, how can she provide it?" asks Mary Jane Bovo, M.D., an ob-gyn in private practice in New York City who treats "as much strep as vaginitis."

Your ob-gyn might provide you with some of the following extra-curricular health services.

- Blood testing to track cholesterol as well as screening for anemia and kidney disease
- Blood pressure testing to screen for early signs of heart disease or high blood pressure
- Blood sugar screening to detect diabetes (if you have recurrent yeast infections, get a blood test for diabetes; diabetes or a prediabetic condition can change the acidity of the vagina, allowing yeast to proliferate)
- Thyroid testing
- Vaccinations such as measles, mumps, rubella (a combined vaccine), hepatitis B, tetanus and influenza
- Skin test for tuberculosis
- Urinalysis to screen for disorders of the urinary tract and kidneys as well as for diabetes
- Osteoporosis and joint assessment for early signs of arthritis
- Occult fecal blood test to screen for colon abnormalities from polyps to cancer
- Electrocardiogram or stress test for heart function

And don't just stick to strictly medical issues. "Ask your ob-gyn about smoking-cessation programs (ob-gyns can prescribe the nicotine patch), adoption, nutrition, weight loss, counseling on sexuality, vitamins, stress, sleep problems, mental health, even self-defense courses," says Ramona Slupik, M.D., assistant professor of obstetrics and gynecology at Northwestern University Medical School in Chicago. "A good gynecologist is an expert in the whole range of women's health issues. I may not treat everything, but I should know how to refer."

MAKE THE MOST OF EACH APPOINTMENT

Whether this is your 1st—or your 101st—appointment with the gynecologist, a little preparation can help you get more from the visit.

"State the reason or reasons for coming in when you make the appointment. That way the office manager can schedule you for the amount of time you need," says Dr. Levine. If you're going to need more time to talk to the doctor after the exam, say so. Don't expect a lot of extra time if you tack additional health problems on at the end of an office visit. (The average annual checkup takes about 25 minutes, estimates Dr. Slupik, which doesn't give you a lot of free time for discussion.) If a certain health problem is a concern, mention it when you make the appointment.

If you want to be seen on time, show up on time. Call to find out if the doctor is running late or to let the office know that you are going to be late.

Bring as much information about yourself as possible to the appointment. Have you called the doctor since your last visit? For what problems? Since your last appointment, have there been any changes in your health? How many urinary-tract or yeast infections have you had? Have you had any repeated viral illnesses or persistent symptoms? Has there been any change in the family history? (If your mother has had breast cancer or ovarian cancer, or your father has suffered a heart attack from elevated cholesterol, your doctor should know in order to screen you properly.)

Have you seen any other doctors? Are you taking any medications? (A good primary care doctor keeps a woman's health care from becoming fragmented, keeping tabs on the whole picture—the interaction of different health problems, treatments and drugs.)

Address any health concerns you have about your contraceptive method. Successful contraception is not only what works but what is healthiest. If you're on the Pill, your doctor should check your blood pressure every six months to detect changes. If you're using a diaphragm and have recurrent urinary-tract infections, she should check the size—you may need a smaller diaphragm. If you're using an IUD, ask about taking an iron supplement—women with IUDs sometimes lose twice as much blood during menstruation.

If this is a first appointment or a visit for a second opinion, bring your records, x-rays or test results with you. Know where your tests were done: If your doctor knows the lab, she'll be able to assess the quality of your results.

Write down your questions before your appointment. Make a copy of them for the doctor to review as you talk together. In a study at the University of Dayton in Ohio, researchers found that patients who wrote their questions down left their appointments feeling less anxious about their medical conditions and more at ease with their doctors.

"Writing down questions increases the accuracy and the detail of information you give to, and receive from, your doctor," says Dr. Slupik.

Come prepared to discuss your emotional well-being, too. The American College of Obstetricians and Gynecologists states that a physical exam should include an emotional history. "It sounds basic, but the medical establishment is just waking up to the fact that total women's health encompasses sexual and mental health issues, too," says Gay Guzinski, M.D., chief of benign gynecology and ambulatory obstetrics and gynecology at the University of Maryland at Baltimore.

"My patients are not walking reproductive systems—they're people with love lives, work lives, family lives, social lives," says Dr. Levine, who not only asks questions pertaining to these areas but also looks for clues in a patient's body language, speech and dress.

How do you take the initiative and bring up something that's been bothering you? The best way, according to Dr. Guzinski, is to say, "I have a problem with my sexual relationship. Is this something you can discuss with me, or can you refer me to someone else?" Rather than be detailed about the problem, this approach allows you to voice your concern and gives your doctor the option of discussing it with you or referring you to someone, such as a psychologist or sex therapist.

GETTING MORE FROM A PELVIC EXAM

Preparation is the key to getting top-quality information from your annual pelvic examination.

Before the exam, you should:

- Schedule the exam when you're not having your period—menstrual fluid can obscure a test sample. However, if unexplained bleeding is your worry, or if symptoms (say, of a vaginal infection) crop up during your period, make the appointment when you are bleeding, so the problem can be directly evaluated.
- Refrain from sexual intercourse at least 12 hours before—ejaculate or contraceptive creams can obscure test results.

- Avoid douching for three days beforehand (douching washes away the loosened cervical cells that are collected for a Pap smear).
- Empty your bladder at the doctor's office. A full bladder can block the doctor's view of the cervix. It can also make the exam more uncomfortable. (On the way to the bathroom, remember to ask if a urine sample is needed.)
- Ask if you have a choice of speculums. Speculums exert pressure to hold vaginal walls apart and rarely cause discomfort. But if you have felt discomfort in the past, you can ask for a smaller size—the Pederson speculum is a half-inch narrower than others. Some doctors also have both metal and plastic speculums. "I think metal ones insert more easily and comfortably," says Dr. Sollie. "Plastic ones can pinch." On the other hand, some patients prefer single-use disposable plastic ones.
- Release tension as you lie on the examining table by first contracting, then relaxing the vaginal muscles and the muscles of the inner thighs.
- Tell your doctor if you are at all nervous or apprehensive about pain. She can insert the speculum more slowly or lubricate it.

Before the exam, your doctor should:
- Touch you on the arm or leg to establish contact. "No doctor should launch right into a pelvic exam without any preamble," says Dr. Bovo.
- Ask your preference about draping. The physician or nurse may place a cloth or paper drape over your knees, but you may prefer to do without the drape so you can see what's taking place as the doctor examines you.

During the exam, you should:
- Open your knees as wide as you can. The farther apart your knees are, the more relaxed your vaginal opening is.
- Lightly rest your hands on your abdomen. Stretching arms back behind your head tightens the abdominal muscles and may increase any exam discomfort.

During the exam, your doctor should:
- Talk you through the exam. "The doctor is in a key position to give a woman positive feedback," notes Dr. Guzinski.

"Phrases such as, 'I'm examining your outer genitalia; everything looks normal,' can be very reassuring to patients."

- Announce the taking of a Pap smear. Again, this is done to prepare you for the movement of the sampling instrument you will feel inside. "My patients definitely feel the brush-type sampler," says Dr. Levine. "The bristles are a bit rougher, and the endocervical [inner cervical] canal is more sensitive." Your doctor should also warn you that you may experience a small amount of pink-tinged discharge after sampling with the brush. Also, if the cervix is irritated (which could happen if you have a mild infection), you may also have some blood-tinged discharge after a Pap smear.

MORE HEALTH DATA FROM A PELVIC EXAM

A pelvic exam is more than just a Pap smear. Ask your doctor to:

- Screen you for sexually transmitted diseases, such as chlamydia and genital warts
- Look for signs of vaginal infections, especially bacterial vaginosis
- Check for tampon or contraceptive injuries (scratches from plastic inserters can become infected: nonoxynol 9—the active ingredient in the sponge, diaphragm creams and spermicidal condoms—can cause irritation)
- Assess your estrogen status (any menstrual irregularities caused by excessive exercise or dieting can decrease estrogen levels)

Any of these can be done at the same time as a Pap smear.

MORE HEALTH FOR YOUR PARTNER

If you have a sexually transmitted disease, chances are high that your sexual partner is infected, too.

In the case of yeast infections, genital warts, trichomoniasis and chlamydia, he may not have symptoms but may harbor the bacteria or virus in his penis or ejaculate and thus be able to reinfect you. To break this cycle of reinfection, many ob-gyns are treating couples.

"Many men don't have a urologist to consult and may delay getting treated. If I see both partners, I know the couple is being treated at the same time," says Dr. Bovo.

The couples approach also discourages a woman from sharing her medication with her partner, a common cause of disease recurrence. (Partners sharing medication may feel better and the symptoms may seem to have gone away, but neither one will have received the entire course of medication necessary to clear the infection.) Sexually transmitted diseases aside, ob-gyns can also counsel couples on contraception, preconception care, conception and sexual problems.

MORE EFFECTIVE DISEASE CURES

Up-to-date ob-gyns are offering more effective drug treatments to clear infections. More effective means more rapid results, with fewer side effects and better cure rates. Get involved: Ask your doctor exactly which medication will be prescribed for your condition and why.

A common bugaboo for women, urinary-tract infections can now be cleared with a once-a-day regimen using a drug called lomefloxacin (such as Maxaquin), an improvement over the twice-daily schedule for conventional drugs.

With an estimated four million cases occurring annually, chlamydia is the most common sexually transmitted disease in the United States. A ten-day, twice-daily regimen of the antibiotic doxycycline has been the common method of treatment. But now there's azithromycin, which can be given as a one-time dose to clear the infection. The same drug, also in a single-dose strength, was found to be effective in treating urethritis and cervicitis (infections of the urethra and cervix), most commonly caused by chlamydia or gonorrhea.

Despite the availability and effectiveness of over-the-counter preparations for yeast infections, these are not always effective. If your infection doesn't clear or if it recurs, check with your doctor about getting a prescription antiyeast drug. These generally work within two weeks.

The most effective treatment for bacterial vaginosis is still under debate. What no one is disputing is that this vaginal infection should be treated promptly in both partners. Studies have linked bacterial vaginosis with increased risk of pelvic inflammatory diseases, inflammation of the fallopian tubes and infertility. Current treatment options include a vaginal gel form of metronidazole (MetroGel-Vaginal) and clindamycin phosphate vaginal cream (Cleocin).

MORE RAPID DIAGNOSIS

Many more ob-gyns are doing in-office testing. The upshot for you—speedier diagnosis, which means more rapid relief and cures.

The newly approved Amplicor Chlamydia Trachomatis test can diagnose chlamydia in both men and women from a urine sample in four hours, compared with a week for other methods. The Uri-Three diagnoses urinary-tract infections in 18 hours: Conventional methods take up to three days. Any ob-gyn with pH paper and a microscope can detect the higher alkalinity of the vaginal discharge as well as the "clue" cells that signal the presence of bacterial vaginosis, a form of vaginitis now thought to be as common as yeast infections in women.

MORE CONTROL
OVER YOUR PATIENT RECORDS

Many more ob-gyns are encouraging their patients to get involved with their health care—right down to their test results and records. Here are a few things you can do.
- Ask for a copy of your Pap smear. "The availability to you of your Pap test results is the touchstone of a doctor's philosophy—how far she is willing to empower patients," notes Dr. Sollie. "If your doctor refuses your request because the Pap test is 'too hard for you to understand,' recognize that this doctor is trying to exert control over you." If you don't understand the terms, you can ask. Perhaps the reason more doctors don't offer to let their patients have their records is that "doctors think patients will get hysterical if they see bad news," says Dr. Bovo.
- Don't let your doctor charge you to get your results. Labs

send Pap-smear reports in triplicate—you should be able to have one of the copies. Or, at the very least, you can borrow the results so you can have a copy made for your own files. Be wary of offices that charge excessive processing fees for records—it may be a tactic used to discourage patients from getting their results.

- Do keep other test results as well. Start a medical file to piece together a picture of your weight, blood pressure, cholesterol levels, infection cultures, contraceptive changes and Pap-smear results over time.
- Do specify if you'd like certain details added to your chart. For instance, if you're a DES daughter, be sure that there's a note in your file to mark that fact on every Pap smear you get. (Daughters of mothers who used this antimiscarriage drug while pregnant in the 1950s and early 1960s often exhibit dysplasia or abnormal cell changes.)
- Request that you be telephoned to inform you of the results of any tests. If you get a letter with test results and have questions about them, you can't call the doctor until the next day. Another practice that should be abandoned is sending the results on a postcard. "The mail carrier doesn't need to know that you've had a Pap smear," says Dr. Sollie.

READING YOUR RESULTS

You're not supposed to be a medical expert, but you can scan your test results for these key items.

- Is your name spelled correctly? If you're Ann Smith and you get a result for Anne Smith, you may have someone else's results. Labs screen thousands of Pap and other tests monthly.
- Does your correct Social Security number appear on the form? It's another double-check that you're getting your own results.
- Is your doctor's name on the report? If not, there's been a mix-up.
- For a Pap smear, check the "specimen adequacy" (also labeled "smear quality"), which indicates whether cells from the exocervix (the outside of the cervix) as well as from the

endocervical (inner cervical) canal were sampled. Look for the words "endocervical cellular component present" or "smear satisfactory" or "optimal". If the smear isn't considered optimal (the terms "suboptimal" or "unsatisfactory specimen" will appear on the lab report), doctors are obligated to repeat the test at no extra charge.

• Read the Pap-smear diagnosis. If your lab uses the class system—in which results are categorized from classes I to IV—ask your gynecologist to translate the diagnosis into words. If your lab uses the newer Bethesda system, which uses descriptions, be sure to ask about any phrases or terms that you do not understand.

—Stephanie Young

DENTAL CARE FOR WOMEN ONLY

THE PHASES IN A WOMAN'S LIFE CAN AFFECT HER DENTAL HEALTH. HERE'S WHAT TO DO ABOUT IT.

Maybe you've noticed it—red, tender gums and tiny, painful sores in your mouth during your menstrual cycle. Gums that bled every time you brushed your teeth when you were pregnant or a constantly dry mouth when you hit menopause, despite your strict daily routine of brushing and flossing.

Researchers don't know all the reasons why, but changes in a woman's body—especially hormonal changes—may affect her oral health. "There definitely are some physical changes that occur when you have higher hormone levels," says Rita D. Zachariasen, Ph.D., professor of physiology in the School of Dental Hygiene at the University of Texas Health Science Center in Houston. "The hormones may make it easier for bacteria to grow, which can lead to gum problems."

"Many women and their dentists have reported this connection for years," says Barbara J. Steinberg, D.D.S., professor of dental medicine at the Medical College of Pennsylvania in Philadelphia. "More research is needed to explain exactly what's going on." But there's little dispute that some women's oral health suffers during menstruation, pregnancy, menopause and oral-contraceptive use.

"With proper care and attention, though, a woman can maintain a healthy mouth for a lifetime," Dr. Steinberg says.

Here's the complete guide to dental care from a woman's perspective—the symptoms you need to look for in different life stages and how you can avoid serious problems.

MENSTRUATION: WATCH GUM HEALTH

During your menstrual cycle, you may develop gingivitis—red, swollen, sore gums that tend to bleed when you brush. The increased sensitivity of your gums may set the stage for bacteria to invade—and that could mean a case of full-blown gum disease. But if you're especially scrupulous about brushing and flossing, your symptoms should disappear once your period is over. If you have severe pain or if the symptoms don't disappear with your period, it's time to see your dentist.

Canker sores—ulcers that form inside your mouth—and fever blisters (caused by an oral herpes virus) also tend to erupt more frequently at this time. No one's really sure why, but luckily, there are effective treatments that can help stop the pain and speed healing. For canker sores, your dentist may prescribe a topical anesthetic or recommend an over-the-counter product. Fever blisters may be treated by an antiviral medication prescribed by your doctor.

PREGNANCY: TELL YOUR DENTIST

You may be more susceptible to gum problems when you're pregnant, especially if you have a history of gum disease or poor oral health habits. "Pregnancy gingivitis—experienced by 60 to 75 percent of all pregnant women—may be mild to moderate in nature or can progress into severe gingivitis," Dr. Steinberg says.

Pregnancy-related oral care problems can be prevented or

controlled with good oral hygiene habits. Notify your dentist when you find out you're pregnant, because he may schedule more frequent cleanings, reinforce brushing and flossing habits or recommend products like oral irrigators or mouth rinses that will help ensure you're getting a good cleaning at home.

To save you and the developing fetus from unnecessary drugs or x-rays, your dentist can schedule elective procedures during the second trimester, when the fetus is less vulnerable (and you're likely to be more comfortable) than in the late stages of pregnancy. Or, if possible, he may delay them until after you deliver, especially if you have a history of miscarriage.

If there's an emergency, though, there's little danger to the fetus from the low doses of radiation used in dental x-rays, Dr. Steinberg says. And wearing a lead apron will further insulate your baby from exposure. Your dentist can also use as little local anesthetic as possible, to limit the fetus's exposure to chemicals, and substitute safer drugs for those drugs known to be harmful to the fetus.

ORAL CONTRACEPTIVES CALL FOR SPECIAL PRECAUTIONS

Women taking oral contraceptives are also prone to gingivitis, perhaps because the hormones in birth control pills cause the body to mimic pregnancy. If standard dental cleanings don't improve the condition, your dentist can prescribe a mouth rinse that's highly effective against bacteria. For severe gum problems, a number of antibiotics can help. Many of these drugs aren't recommended if you're pregnant.

If your dentist prescribes an antibiotic, make sure you tell him you're on the Pill, because some antibiotics can weaken the effectiveness of oral contraceptives—especially low-dose formulas. You may need to rely on another form of birth control until your next period.

Dry mouth—also called xerostomia—can be a side effect of birth control pills (it's sometimes reported in pregnant women, too) and a serious threat to oral health. Without lubricating saliva, the soft tissue in your mouth can become dry and cracked, and tooth decay can accelerate.

To avoid this problem, Dr. Steinberg says, take sips of water frequently, especially when you're speaking. Help stimulate saliva flow by brushing regularly or chewing sugarless gum or sucking on sugarless candies. And avoid caffeine, tobacco, alcohol and salty, spicy or acidic foods. They'll further irritate a dry mouth. If these methods don't work, your dentist may prescribe an artificial-saliva product.

Although it's rare, oral contraceptives may cause complications if you need to have a tooth removed. Elevated hormone levels can keep your blood from clotting, causing "dry socket"— a painful condition that delays healing. To reduce your risk, your dentist may schedule extractions during days 23 through 28 of your cycle, when you're not taking the pill.

MENOPAUSE: YOUR DENTIST CAN HELP

Dry mouth and gingivitis, which can be treated with the methods already described, may also be encountered during menopause. You may develop "burning mouth" or notice changes in your sense of taste—foods may taste particularly salty or spicy. You may even have minor, stress-related jaw pain. While those problems may be annoying, there's no need to be concerned unless your pain is severe or prolonged. If this happens, see your dentist—it could be a sign of a more serious problem.

It's well-established that after menopause, your risk of developing osteoporosis—a disease that leaves your bones thin and brittle—increases. But whether postmenopausal loss of bone also affects your jaw, and thus, your chances of keeping your natural teeth, is controversial. Several studies have investigated the issue, with differing results. Researchers continue to grapple with the issue. The best advice for now is to follow your doctor's recommendations for minimizing bone loss and osteoporosis. He might suggest eating foods rich in bone-building nutrients like calcium and vitamin D, including low-fat dairy foods and vegetables like broccoli and kidney beans. Your doctor may even recommend a daily 500- to 1,000-milligram calcium supplement.

—*Melissa Meyers Gotthardt with Beth Higbee*

DON'T HAVE
A STROKE!

WE ALL KNOW ABOUT THE DANGERS
OF CANCER AND HEART ATTACK. YET MOST OF US
ARE SURPRISINGLY UNINFORMED ABOUT
STROKE—ONE OF THE LEADING CAUSES
OF DEATH IN WOMEN.

Lois Douthey had been feeling somewhat tired, but with three small children—twin boys who were barely two and another son in kindergarten—the Dallas homemaker didn't think much of it. Then one morning, Douthey, 29, woke up with blurry vision and numbness on the side of her face. As a trained nurse, she knew something was terribly wrong.

"The last thing I remember is lying down on a hospital bed and falling asleep," she says.

When the doctors examined her shortly afterward, they discovered that she'd had a stroke. A blood vessel in her head had burst without warning, causing bleeding into her brain. The damage that resulted left her unable to speak or to move the right side of her body.

"It was like there was this imaginary line down the center of me," she recalls. "One side was fine, but the other had no feeling at all."

Thanks to intensive rehabilitation, Douthey, now 47, has since regained all her abilities. But she is still shocked that the stroke happened at all. "I was so young," she says. "It was the last thing in the world I expected."

THE UNRECOGNIZED THREAT

Most women are aware of the risks that cancer and, to some extent, heart disease pose to their health. But for some reason, stroke—the third leading cause of death in American females—gets scant attention. A 1991 Gallup survey found that 97 percent of respondents were unable to recognize stroke's warning signs. And a survey by the American Heart Association showed that 42 percent of respondents couldn't name a single risk factor associated with it.

What's more, the little bit of information the public does have about stroke is misleading. Most people tend to think of stroke as a disorder that threatens only the very old. But while it's true that the majority of stroke patients are older adults, roughly a third of them are under age 65. Doctors predict that this year alone, 58,000 women between ages 30 and 64 will suffer a stroke.

The lack of public awareness about stroke can be dangerous, even deadly, health-care advocates say. Most patients don't show up at the emergency room until 24 hours after experiencing stroke symptoms, according to the National Stroke Association. In the past, that delay might not have made much of a difference. But today, many types of stroke can be treated, either with new surgeries or experimental drugs. And patients who get prompt care have a greatly improved chance of recovery.

"Stroke is an acute disorder, but it is treatable, even preventable," says Patricia Grady, Ph.D., assistant director of the National Institute of Neurological Disorders and Stroke in Bethesda, Maryland. "People should think of a stroke as a brain attack in the same way that they think of a heart attack."

TYPES OF STROKE

Cathy Pille's "brain attack" occurred when she was 34. Pille, a Minneapolis legal secretary, was at her desk when she got the most excruciating headache of her life. Shortly afterward, she lost consciousness, and her co-workers called an ambulance.

"I was lucky," says Pille, who walks with a cane and can't move her left arm and hand. "I could have lost my life."

Pille, now 41, suffered what doctors call a hemorrhagic stroke, one of the two major types of stroke. (In general, stroke means a sudden disruption of blood flow to the brain, which causes cells to die.) Hemorrhagic strokes occur when blood seeps from a hole in a blood vessel wall into the brain, or the area surrounding it, called the subarachnoid space.

The other type, an "ischemic" stroke, occurs when blood flow to the brain is blocked by a clot in an artery. Many ischemic strokes are preceded by "mini-strokes" known as transient ischemic attacks. Mini-strokes, which have symptoms similar to those of a stroke, generally last a minute or two and are caused by either a temporary blood clot or the narrowing of an artery leading to the brain.

While older women are more likely to have an ischemic stroke, younger women tend to suffer the hemorrhagic variety. Particularly common is a subtype called a subarachnoid hemorrhage (SAH), which results from malformed blood vessels or an aneurysm, a weakened blood vessel wall that may rupture.

Doctors say that about two-thirds of all SAHs occur in women. No one knows exactly what accounts for the gender difference, but there's speculation that some combination of estrogen and progesterone may weaken the major blood vessels, says Lawrence Brass, M.D., director of the stroke program at the Yale University School of Medicine.

Although there are still gaps in medical knowledge, doctors have learned a great deal in recent years about what causes stroke. Research has found that a number of factors—including high blood pressure, smoking, family history and ethnic background—can greatly increase a person's risk.

The jury is still out on other possible contributors. A handful of studies have suggested that estrogen-replacement therapy, which is often used for postmenopausal women, might increase the risk of stroke, reports Dr. Brass. But other research shows contrary findings. Scientists at the University of Washington, in Seattle, for instance, reported that estrogen cut a woman's chances of having a hemorrhagic stroke by half. Further research is under way.

THE DIRE CONSEQUENCES

Although debate on the cures and causes of stroke is sure to continue, there's no disagreement that its consequences can be devastating. About 150,000 Americans die of stroke every year. Of the 350,000 stroke victims who survive, an estimated two-thirds suffer permanent damage, including paralysis, impaired speech or thought process, memory loss and distorted vision.

Dianna Van Stelle of Bloomer, Wisconsin, is just one of those statistics. She was 41 in 1990 when she had her stroke, which doctors say was the result of a congenital heart defect she didn't know she had. "I was cleaning up after supper, and I began to feel a little dizzy," she recalls. She headed into the living room to rest, and before she knew it, she was out cold.

REDUCING THE RISK

The latest research shows that a number of factors put people at higher risk of stroke. These findings can help women gauge their risk—and determine what they may be able to do to lower it.

Hypertension. High blood pressure damages the artery walls, making them more likely to harden or rupture. Exercise, limiting alcohol and keeping weight down may help control high blood pressure.

Cigarette smoking. A study shows that women who smoke more than 25 cigarettes a day have nearly a threefold risk of stroke from a clot and an almost ten times greater risk of stroke from a burst blood vessel. Women who quit can cut their risk nearly to that of a nonsmoker in just two years.

Oral contraceptives. The old high-dose pills increased a woman's risk of stroke, but the jury is out on today's low-dose versions. Several studies suggest an increase in risk, while others have found a significant risk only in women who smoke as well as take the Pill. Women who use oral contraceptives, smoke and have migraines appear to have an even greater chance of having a stroke.

Race. Incidence of stroke is higher in African Americans and Hispanics, but as yet there's not a clear understanding of all the factors involved. Doctors do know, however, that African Americans are more prone to high blood pressure, which increases their risk.

Pregnancy. Stroke is 13 times more common during pregnancy. Because of changes in blood consistency, some pregnant women are more prone to developing blood clots, says Stephen Oppenheimer, M.D., director of the Cerbrovascular Program at the Johns Hopkins Uni-

Van Stelle's life has not been the same since. She walks with a cane, has trouble seeing and is frequently forgetful. She's much more dependent on her husband and has lost a great deal of her vitality and zest. "The worst part was not being able to go back to a job I loved," says the former junior-high-school music

versity School of Medicine in Baltimore. Pregnancy-related high blood pressure may also predispose women to stroke.

Diabetes. Women with diabetes are five times as likely to have a stroke as nondiabetic women. However, the National Institutes of Health reports that people with diabetes who closely monitor their glucose levels and inject themselves with insulin have fewer diabetes-related complications, including stroke.

Heart disease. Women with coronary artery disease have an increased risk of ischemic stroke, studies have found. A heart attack may result in the formation of clots within the heart, which can break loose and travel to the brain, resulting in an ischemic stroke.

History of transient ischemic attacks (TIA). If left untreated, a third of the people who have a TIA or mini-stroke will have a stroke within five years. Small doses of aspirin—as little as one-tenth of a tablet—have been found to diminish that risk. The anticlotting drug Ticlid, approved by the Food and Drug Administration, is slightly more effective, but has been associated with potentially serious side effects. Some may also benefit from a carotid endarterectomy, a surgical procedure that clears out the carotid artery running to the brain.

For more information contact:

- American Heart Association, 7272 Greenville Avenue, Dallas, TX 75231.
- National Institute of Neurological Disorders and Stroke, Building 31, Room 8A-06, 9000 Rockville Pike, Bethesda, MD 20814.
- National Stroke Association, 8480 East Orchard Road, Suite 100, Englewood, CO 80111.

teacher. "I still ache for it, but I had to tell myself, 'I can't do this anymore. I'm disabled.' "

Disability following a stroke depends on the part of the brain involved and the extent of the damage. "If an artery in the top part of the brain is blocked, you're more likely to lose the use of a hand, arm or leg," says Edward Diethrich, M.D., medical director of the Arizona Heart Institute in Phoenix and author of *Women and Heart Disease*. "If there's damage to an artery going to the base of the brain, you'll have problems with respiration." Dr. Diethrich notes, however, that any type of stroke can affect any area.

Beyond the physical problems wrought by stroke, there are emotional ones as well. Studies suggest that many female stroke patients experience a decline in sexual function, says Elliot Roth, M.D., a director of the stroke program at the Rehabilitation Institute of Chicago. "It could be related to changes in self-image that occur when some women are faced with a physical disability," he says. "And depression is a potential problem as well."

Roberta Parkinson, 45, of Chicago, experienced severe depression after having a stroke last year. Though she suffered no physical disabilities, Parkinson had trouble remembering—a fact that she found terribly frustrating. "Emotionally, I was a mess," she says.

Parkinson began seeing a therapist, who prescribed an antidepressant, and since then, she's been feeling much better. Her memory has improved, and she's back at work full-time.

NEW TREATMENTS

Fortunately, great strides have been made in treating stroke, especially in recent years. "The old dogma in neurology was that once the brain was damaged, there was nothing to do except try to adapt to it through rehabilitation," says Steven Warach, M.D., a neurologist at Beth Israel Hospital in Boston. "That's an incorrect attitude now."

The current thinking is that the first six hours immediately following a stroke are a critical time. Even though brain cells die when their blood supply is cut off by a stroke, the surrounding tissue is often still alive. New treatments try to spare as many brain cells as possible and quickly restore blood flow to the area. "There is a window of opportunity between the onset of the stroke and the time of irreversible brain damage," says Dr. Warach.

Treatments vary, depending on the type of stroke a person suffers. For some hemorrhagic strokes, surgery is often the treatment of choice. For certain types of ischemic strokes, neurologists work with a small arsenal of experimental drugs. At half a dozen medical centers around the country, researchers are getting good results with clot-busting drugs such as tPA and urokinase.

Doctors also are studying different ways of administering these medications. At Oregon Health Sciences University in Portland, six of seven patients who had urokinase delivered into their brains within about 18 hours after suffering a stroke showed significant improvement. "Our most astounding case was an 18-year-old woman who was in a coma for 48," says Wayne Clark, M.D., director of the stroke treatment program there. "We used urokinase to dissolve her clot, and within a month she was back in school."

Other new drugs hold similar promise. Scientists are optimistic about agents known as glutamate receptor antagonists, which may prevent permanent brain damage in stroke patients. Other potentially beneficial treatments include nitroglycerin and substances called lazaroids, which may be able to restore damaged brain tissue. If these treatments pan out, they could significantly improve the prognosis for stroke patients, doctors say.

Great advances, too, have been made in the area of rehabilitation. "We realize now that the sooner rehabilitation therapy begins, the better the chance that patients will regain their functions," says Barbara J. Browne, M.D., attending physician at Magee Rehabilitation Hospital in Philadelphia. She explains that rehabilitation often starts within the first 72 hours after the stroke. Intensive therapy, tailored to help patients compensate for the deficits that resulted from stroke, includes exercises to help patients walk, talk, swallow, even dress themselves and use the toilet.

With rehabilitation about 70 percent of stroke patients will be able to care for themselves. As many as a third of all patients will recover enough that they will be able to return to work. And the most fortunate will improve as dramatically as Lois Douthey, the Dallas woman whose recovery is virtually complete.

Though her doctors had predicted permanent impairment, Douthey believes that hard work and determination helped her defy the odds. "Sometimes, my hand might feel a little numb, or I'll be a bit forgetful, and I'll think that maybe that's a result of my stroke," she says. "But no one else really notices anything."

Douthey's children are grown now, and she's returned to full-time work. She maintains a healthy lifestyle, but remains acutely aware of the warning signs of stroke. "You never think it can happen to you," she says. "But it can."

—*Leslie Laurence*

FEMALE HEARTS AT RISK

THINK OF HEART DISEASE AS A MEN'S PROBLEM, DO YOU? WELL, GUESS AGAIN. IT'S THE NUMBER-ONE KILLER OF WOMEN.

Lois zealously eliminates every gram of cholesterol from her husband's favorite dishes, has convinced him to give up smoking and has surprised him with a membership in a health club for their anniversary. So the 52-year-old homemaker is stunned when her doctor tells her that she, not her husband, Dan, will soon face coronary bypass surgery.

Allison, a 39-year-old financial analyst, lies on the table in a New York City hospital emergency room as waves of unbearable chest pain sweep over her. Tucked into her green leather shoulder bag among her keys, lipstick and appointment book are packets of birth control pills and cigarettes. With her unusually strong family history of heart disease, this combination is potentially deadly. But no one ever warned Allison.

Formerly a strong swimmer, Joan, 63, must now be content to paddle slowly up and down the pool. Her enlarged heart has grown so weak that it can't keep up with the demands of much exertion. Early medical treatment could have allowed her to remain active longer, but her family doctor scoffed at her complaints of chest pain for years, telling her, "It's all in your head."

Like most American women, Lois, Allison and Joan lived their lives without giving much thought to their hearts. They had no reason not to assume their hearts were fine.

For years women, and too often their doctors, as well, have shared these assumptions. Health-care books, articles in women's magazines, even television commercials convey the impression that heart disease strikes men, not women. "I worried about my husband's cholesterol, but now it's down to 168," exults a woman in a TV commercial about the joys of switching to vegetable shortening. "My husband eats right, works out and he's feeling great," says another beaming TV commercial wife, shown picking up her husband at the gym.

It's now becoming clear that these assumptions fly in the face of reality. Although the rate of heart disease in the United States has declined in recent years, it is still the number-one killer of American women, far outranking stroke, lung cancer and even the disease most dreaded by women, breast cancer. But women remain largely unaware of their risk. Repeatedly, they voice their fears about breast cancer, never dreaming of a threat that looms much larger.

Since this threat to their lives has been so widely overlooked for so long, even now many women remain unaware of how vulnerable their hearts are. Sometimes this can be tragic, as many of these risks can be avoided or their impact lessened. What's more, although the past few decades have been marked by dramatic progress against heart disease, these innovations have been denied to many women. Such potentially lifesaving procedures as coronary bypass surgery, in which a new blood supply to the heart is created; balloon angioplasty, in which narrowed coronary arteries are dilated to allow the flow of more blood; and thrombolytic therapy, the administration of "clot busters" to minimize damage after a heart attack, are all performed far less frequently on women than on men. While experts argue among themselves whether this is scientifically justified, the fact remains that as a woman, it's less likely these procedures will be offered to you.

Even though there is now a new awareness of heart disease in women, other problems that affect women's hearts remain too often overlooked: irregular heart rhythm (known also as arrhythmia), mitral valve prolapse and congenital heart defects, all of which more often affect, or manifest symptoms in, women than men.

CORONARY HEART DISEASE: THE "MALE" DISEASE?

Each year 240,000 women in the U.S. die from heart disease. Heart disease is the second leading killer of U.S. women over the age of 40, second only to cancer; by age 55 heart disease assumes the lead. By comparison, 90,000 women die annually from stroke, 41,600 from lung cancer and 40,500 from breast cancer. These other devastating diseases must not be overlooked, but the numbers make it clear that, for women, preventing heart disease is of utmost importance. Still, polls repeatedly show that when women are asked to rank their biggest health worry, cancer comes out on top, with heart disease listed far below.

Faced with this threat, the best way for a woman to safeguard her heart is through knowledge. You must learn about the changing risks that may damage your heart over the course of your life.

As you age, your risk of heart disease increases. Typically, women develop heart disease 15 to 20 years later than men, although once they reach menopause, their rate of heart disease begins to climb. Once past the age of 65, every woman is a candidate for heart disease, no matter what her state of health. She may be a nonsmoker, exercise and qualify as a health-food "nut." At this stage of life, her heart becomes as vulnerable to heart disease as her male counterpart's.

YOUNG WOMEN— "IMMUNE" FROM HEART DISEASE?

The fact that older women have a higher risk of suffering a heart attack than younger women contributes to another dangerous belief: that only the older women are in jeopardy. While it's true that heart attacks usually kill elderly women, young women are not necessarily immune. An estimated 6,000 U.S. women under age 65 die each year of heart attacks, and nearly a third of them are under age 45.

In fact, heart disease in middle-aged women is far from uncommon; they are seen daily in cardiology clinics across the country. There are many reasons that a middle-aged woman is at risk for developing heart disease. She may have diabetes, a factor more strongly related to heart disease in women than in men. She might have gone through menopause early, resulting in a loss of estrogen—which may turn out to be the most important contributor to the development of heart disease in women. Or she may have inherited abnormal blood cholesterol levels.

Some women can appear deceptively robust, like Linda, a nonsmoking gym teacher who suffered a heart attack in her early fifties. In her gym shorts, with her whistle hanging around her neck, she once seemed the very picture of good health. But her body harbored two hidden time bombs. The first was hyperlipidemia, a metabolic disorder that results in abnormal levels of blood cholesterol. The second was that her ovaries had been removed years earlier, propelling her body into premature menopause.

Although it's unusual for a woman under the age of 45 to suffer a heart attack or develop heart disease, it happens more often than most doctors suspect. Sometimes the risk factors go unrecognized until it's almost too late. That was the case with Randi, a 35-year-old mother of two who was unaware that she had hyperlipidemia. When she complained to her doctor of chest pain, he brushed her worries aside. He did reluctantly order a treadmill exercise test, a measure commonly used to help diagnose heart disease. But because he ordered a type that is less accurate when used on women than on men, Randi's results were interpreted as normal. Randi's doctor told her she was "too nervous" and that if she worried less, her symptoms would disappear.

Fortunately, she saw another doctor who used a more sensitive version of the test. The results clearly showed that two of her coronary arteries were seriously blocked. If her condition had remained undiscovered, she most likely would have suffered a major heart attack.

If you're a young woman suffering cardiac symptoms for which there is no other explanation, it's up to you to make certain your doctor investigates the possibility of heart problems, because heart disease is so rarely suspected in young women. It may save your life.

SOCIETY'S RISKS TO WOMEN'S HEARTS

Over the years, women's place in society has changed, in many ways for the better. However, there has been one dangerous change: In recent years, more and more women have taken up smoking, a deadly habit for a woman's heart.

Stress also poses a risk for women and their hearts. Although the link between stress and heart disease is not as clear as the connection between smoking or diabetes and heart disease, some studies show that stress can present risks to your general health and to your heart. Some say that women's new roles in the workplace may lead to heart attacks, but this is not necessarily so.

As we discover more about stress, it appears that it's not the typical hard-driving Type-A personality that contributes to heart problems, but the anger, frustration and powerlessness which may be unhealthy. Women trapped in dead-end jobs or workplace discrimination may be the ones who find their emotions tied up in knots, under just the type of stress that may contribute to damaging their hearts.

HEART ATTACK: HIGH RISK FOR WOMEN

Some studies have found that when women suffer heart attacks, they fare even worse than men. Research has shown that a woman's first heart attack is more likely to kill her, or to be followed by a second attack. A major study at the University of Massachusetts Medical Center in Worcester found that more than double the number of women suffering a heart attack died within six weeks. Studies have also shown that women are less likely than men to survive over the long term.

But, the picture is not completely bleak. Most of the time, women do survive heart attacks. Even if they recover, however, they tend to suffer more than men from such symptoms as disabling chest pain. This makes them less likely to be able to return to work or enjoy their lives fully. Mary, a supervisor for a high-tech computer company, had a heart attack when she was 57 years old. Afterward, she still suffered chest pains, which forced her to quit her job. Her pains persisted, even after coronary bypass surgery and despite her use of a variety of cardiovascular medications. Although her case was extreme, it's not uncommon for women to be plagued with chest pain and other symptoms even after the physical causes of their heart problems appear to have been resolved.

The feminist revolution not withstanding, women in our society are still burdened with running the household and taking care of the children. These responsibilities don't disappear if a woman has a heart attack or undergoes heart surgery. Many women feel compelled to be up and about managing the household when they should rest. Or they may try to return to their jobs outside the home too early because they can't afford not to or feel anxious about losing their hard-won place on the corporate fast track.

Congenital heart defects are a hidden danger that women face more often than men. Although such heart defects are usually diagnosed in childhood, a significant number remain hidden until adulthood. Unless treated, some may cause irreversible damage to the heart.

A "GENDER BIAS" IN HEART DISEASE?

Coronary bypass surgery is now one of the most common operations in the United States, and the risk for the procedure has decreased sharply over the years. Still, despite some three decades of experience, studies nationwide persist in showing that coronary surgery remains riskier for women than men. This is also true of balloon angioplasty and similar interventional procedures used to treat coronary artery disease (also known as coronary heart disease). While experts debate the reasons, these dangerous discrepancies for women persist.

"Can't I count on my doctor to recognize a heart problem?" you might very well ask. The unfortunate answer to this is "Sometimes, but not always." The truth is that while women have mistakenly believed they're not vulnerable to heart problems, this belief is often shared by their doctors.

Although women visit doctors more often than men, their problems are often given short shrifts, especially when it comes to their hearts. Not so long ago, doctors were taught to respond differently to women. If a medical student approached an instructor to discuss the case of a woman with chest pain, he or she would almost always be told to dismiss it. "She must be psychosomatic. It's all in her head" was the standard line. Studies have shown that when doctors are asked to diagnose women with chest pain, the problem is more likely to be attributed to "psychiatric" causes.

A major reason that doctors may tend to ignore women's cardiac problems is that consciously or subconsciously, women are viewed as less important than men in the economic marketplace. Also, because women develop heart disease later in life than men, a doctor may erroneously assume that the snowy-haired woman seated before him cannot withstand the rigors of surgery. It's true that coronary bypass surgery is riskier for women than men, but by not being objectively evaluated a woman may be denied a potentially lifesaving treatment.

That women's hearts are treated differently than men's can be seen in the rate and type of diagnostic tests performed on women. In 1991, major studies at the Oregon Heart Institute in Portland and the Brigham and Women's Hospital in Boston revealed convincing evidence that doctors treat women with heart disease less aggressively than they do men. These studies, involving tens of thousands of women, showed that they were, at most, half as likely as men to undergo cardiac catheterization, a common diagnostic procedure required before treatments like balloon angioplasty and coronary bypass surgery.

Not all studies support the contention of gender bias. A study that compared the treatment after heart attacks of 2,473 patients in Boston found that women were as likely to receive balloon angioplasty as men. This study also found that although men were more likely to be referred for coronary bypass, the difference was very slight.

Over the years, some studies have intimated that coronary bypass surgery and other "aggressive" treatments may be overused. If these procedures are indeed being performed too often on men, women certainly don't want to fall into the same trap. Still, the sharp difference between the way men and women are treated has generated an important discussion.

OUR UNDERSTANDING OF HEART DISEASE

Such treatment differences may not be surprising when you consider that coronary heart disease has been viewed as a man's disease, from the early days of modern cardiology. Our modern understanding of coronary disease was shaped, in part, in the 1950s, when pathologists examining the corpses of young Korean War soldiers discovered, to their amazement, the fatty streaking that is the first step on the path to clogged arteries. Since then, coronary heart disease has been perceived as a male problem. In the ensuing years, this emphasis on men has not only persisted, but has helped to shape our national health policy.

A major example is the Framingham Heart Study, the nation's largest continuing study of coronary artery disease, which began in 1948. While women were included in this major study, the early results concluded that chest pain in women was not a serious problem. Even though this was later found to be wrong, the damage had been done. "The myth that 'women don't get heart disease' had taken root," says Nanette K. Wenger, M.D., a cardiologist and professor of medicine at Emory University School of Medicine in Atlanta. But, she notes, times are changing. "Years ago, older women were less visible. There were fewer of them, they had retired from the work force and they had fulfilled their family duties. Heart disease in women was not perceived as a major problem. But now that the life span of women has increased, and they live on average six to seven years longer than men, we are seeing a tremendous change."

The emphasis on men and heart disease has also meant that far less clinical research has focused on women; some believe that potential treatments may have been overlooked. "If we had a disease like breast cancer and most of the research had been done on men, we would not use the male model and say, 'Oh, let's see how we can adapt it to women.' We would want to take a fresh approach," says Erica Frank, M.D., of the Stanford Center for Research and Disease Prevention at the Stanford University School of Medicine.

This male perspective has also shaped the methods by which drugs are tested in this country. Cardiovascular drugs, the medications that control blood pressure, reduce cholesterol and ease the symptoms of heart disease, are of particular concern because they're prescribed for women as often as for men, yet have been tested almost exclusively on men. Traditionally, women have been excluded from medical research because of the concern that if they're young, they might become pregnant, or if they're older, they most likely have developed other diseases, which will complicate the results.

"The argument is spurious. It says we cannot study women because they are so different, but yet they should take medicines developed on the basis of work done on men," says Florence Haseltine, M.D., a founder of the Society for the Advancement of Women's Health Research in Washington, D.C. "You can't have it both ways."

Some promising developments, however, have emerged. At the National Institutes of Health (NIH), which directs America's taxpayer-supported scientific and medical research, the Women's Health Initiative, a $625 million, ten-year research project on the health problems of older women, is under way. As the first female director of the NIH, Bernadine Healy, M.D., a cardiologist, has pledged to include women in the NIH's medical trials.

"There has been a general awakening to the fact that all too many articles published in the medical research literature and publicized by the mass media have been based on studies of men," notes Dr. Healy. "This is unfortunate as coronary heart disease is the major killer of both men and women."

The NIH has also pledged to include members of minority groups in clinical studies. The vast majority of medical research in heart disease has targeted not just men, but white men. If information on how heart disease affects women is slim, information on how heart disease affects women of different racial groups, such as blacks and Hispanics, is far more scant.

Because of this past lack of emphasis on heart disease in women, women are only now discovering the importance of caring for their hearts. The urgency extends not only to older women, who make up the majority of heart disease patients, but to younger women as well. The most "heartening" news of all is that women of all ages can benefit from taking care of their hearts.

—*Fredric J. Pashkow, M.D., and Charlotte Libov*

PART TWO

SEX AND THAT SPECIAL
MAN IN YOUR LIFE

SECOND CHANCE
FOR ROMANCE

HAS THE SPARK IN YOUR RELATIONSHIP SPUTTERED?
REKINDLE THE FLAME WITH THESE SIMPLE EXERCISES.

Remember what it was like when you first fell in love? You were the best, your partner was the best and the world was alight with your fire. Nothing was too good for your baby, no challenge too great for your love. Remember?

Harville Hendrix, the founder and director of the Institute for Relationship Therapy in New York City, does. In fact, he has devoted much of his life to pinning down these memorable yet elusive emotions in an effort to identify exactly how lovers who've grown apart can reawaken those loving feelings. And, remarkable though it may seem, he has pieced together the puzzle—to a point. The rest is up to you.

Love is essentially mysterious, after all. Yet your history, actions and motives—all of which contribute to the intimacy within your relationship—are not. And neither are your lover's. Hendrix believes that you have to consider these variables when you examine your relationship. These are the things, he says, that hold the key to making love last.

GETTING TO THE HEART OF THE MATTER

In contrast to the classical views of romantic love, which attribute its source to external forces—such as the perfect man or woman—modern psychologies of love trace its origin to the human mind. In other words, while we might think that our romantic feelings are triggered by the person we've fallen for, psychologists today tell us that these feelings are really the product of our own desires.

Here's Hendrix's hypothesis: You project what you need from a romantic relationship onto another person—the man or woman you choose to love. And the closer that person comes to fulfilling your needs, the easier it is to credit him or her with unmet attributes as well—to pretend that he is communicative or she is creative, even when he or she is not.

Unfortunately, says Hendrix, author of two best-selling books on relationships—*Getting the Love You Want* and *Keeping the Love You Find*—the longer the relationship lasts, the harder it is to maintain the fantasy and the more disillusioned you become. You start to yearn for more. And you won't be able to get more until you understand that you alone have the power to reactivate your passions; your lover cannot. Rekindling the flame you used to share starts with you—and the following exercises.

In the 20 years since he began his practice, Hendrix has developed a series of simple exercises to enliven a relationship that has lost its luster. They work in two significant ways—by prompting each of you to gain a more accurate image of the other and by forcing each of you to take responsibility for communicating your needs and desires to the other. Regardless of how dispassionate or angry you feel when you're performing them, they will foster intimacy.

The romance probably fizzled out of your relationship because it became old hat, and you stopped showing each other that you care. Now you must reverse the process—you must share a little tenderness to conjure up those warm feelings again. Although it seems backward, it does work.

Before you start, you both need to do a little homework, says Hendrix. First, confirm your willingness to do the exercises by writing down the following statement (or something similar): "Because our relationship is very important to us, we are making a pact to take time to get to know ourselves and each other and to create new and interesting ways to communicate and show our feelings. We agree to do all the exercises in a careful, conscientious manner."

Hendrix also suggests that, before you start, you both understand that the information you gather while doing these exercises is meant to enlighten you and your partner about each other's needs. Sharing this information in no way obligates you to meet those needs.

And remember, above all, that regardless of whom you are with, a lasting relationship requires equal parts commitment, time and work. Remember, too, that the romance you miss so much may be right where you originally found it—in your lover's arms.

The following three exercises correspond to exercises 9, 10 and 11 in Hendrix's book *Getting the Love You Want*. Perform the first and third exercises together; do the second separately. The whole series should take about two hours to complete.

Exercise 1: Re-romanticizing. Your partner cannot read your mind. So by sharing specific information about what pleases you and by agreeing to please your partner regularly, you can bring back some of the intimacy into your relationship.

"The object of this exercise is to re-establish feelings of closeness and pleasure, which, in turn, will set the stage for heightened intimacy later on," says Hendrix. "When couples increase the number of times a day they act lovingly toward each other—regardless of how they feel—they begin to feel more loving toward each other."

1. Identify what your partner is doing now that pleases you. On a separate sheet of paper, complete this sentence in as many ways as you can think of, being specific and positive and focusing on events that occur with some regularity: *I feel loved and cared about when you. . . .*

Examples: Fill my coffee cup when it's empty . . . let me read the front page of the paper first . . . kiss me before you leave the house . . . sit close to me while we're watching TV . . . bring me surprise presents . . . massage my back.

2. Recall the romantic stage of your relationship. Are there caring behaviors that you once did for each other but are no longer doing? On a separate sheet of paper, complete this sentence: *I used to feel loved and cared about when you. . . .*

Examples: Wrote me love letters . . . brought me candy and flowers . . . held my hand as we walked . . . made love to me more than once a day . . . whispered sexy nothings into my ear.

3. Identify some caring behaviors that you have always wanted but never have received or asked for. These behaviors may reflect your mental picture of the perfect partner or they may be things you experienced in a prior relationship. Whenever possible, provide specifics (such as how often, how long or how much) about your request. On a separate sheet of paper, complete this sentence: *I would like you to. . . .*

Examples: Take a shower with me . . . massage my feet for 30 minutes without stopping . . . sleep in the nude.

4. Indicate how important each caring behavior is to you by rating it from one to five, with one being very important and five being not so important; your partner should do the same.

5. Exchange lists. Examine your partner's lists and put an *X* by any items that you are unwilling to do. All remaining behaviors should pose no conflict. Then, beginning the next day, fulfill at least two of your partner's desired behaviors; your partner should do the same. Add more items to your list as they occur to you. And when your partner performs a caring behavior for you, acknowledge it with an appreciative comment. Fulfill these activities regardless of how you feel about your partner and no matter how many loving gestures your partner extends to you.

Exercise 2: Surprise! The positive feelings that were kindled by re-romanticizing efforts often die out after a few months, primarily because the caring behaviors become too predictable to hold their charm. This is perfectly normal. The purpose of this exercise, then, is to strengthen the staying power of your caring by adding unanticipated pleasures to the mix.

1. Make a list of the things you'd be willing to do for your partner that would be especially pleasing for him or her—behaviors above and beyond those requested by your partner in Exercise 1. Don't guess. Create your list from memories of specific events that have made your partner happy or from hints or comments that your partner has made. Keep this list hidden from your partner at all times.

2. Select one item from your list and surprise your partner with it this week. Continue to do this on a weekly basis. Be sure to surprise your partner at random times so that it will be difficult for him or her to anticipate the treat.

3. Record the date when you give each surprise. On a separate sheet of paper, keep track of the surprises you receive from your partner. And don't forget to say thanks for each surprise.

Exercise 3: Forever fun. This last exercise is meant to inject a little fun into your relationship. "Most of the activities people tend to write down as caring behaviors are fairly passive, 'adult' activities," says Hendrix. "Couples tend to forget how to have fun together. Yet, when they do have fun, they become sources of pleasure for one another, which intensifies their emotional bond."

1. On a separate sheet of paper, list high-energy and exciting activities that you'd like to do with your partner. Include activities that are characterized by body contact that is physically pleasurable. Examples might include bicycling, dancing, tickling, wrestling, showering together and having sex.

2. Share your lists and then compile a third list that combines the two.

3. Choose one activity a week to do together.

4. Perform this exercise regardless of whether you or your partner are reluctant to do so (which may occur if your relationship is rife with conflict). It's important that you fight your natural inclination to maintain your composure and experiment with this brief return to childhood.

—*JoAnn Jones*

WHEN DESIRE FADES

PASSION SEEMS SUCH A FLEETING THING. WHEN IT DOESN'T FLY AWAY ON ITS OWN—WE LET IT GO. HERE'S HOW YOU CAN COAX IT BACK.

Every morning during their three-week vacation in Greece, Anna Behringer and her husband, George, would wander from their whitewashed cottage into a nearby village to shop, eat a leisurely lunch and stroll down to the beach to spend the day. "We would lie there in the warm sand, then cool off in the blue waters of the Aegean," she recalls dreamily. "It was an incredibly sensuous time."

And every afternoon, Anna and George would walk back to their cottage, shower off the sand and sweat and make love. "Every afternoon," Anna emphasizes. "Like we were in our twenties, not our forties. For three weeks, all we focused on was pleasure."

But three weeks back into "real life," Anna found that her sex drive had slipped into park. Sex had settled again at the bottom of her priority list, after kids, business meetings, bill paying, housecleaning and, all too often, reruns of "Roseanne."

"In our real life, a month or two can go by before we realize, hey, we haven't had sex," says Anna, a writer. "All those things I have to do—cooking, shopping, working, taking out the garbage—intrude into my head, which is where sex starts for me. Sometimes at the end of the day, it's hard for me to turn off stress and get in tune with my body again."

Anna's experience with sexual desire—as hot and steamy as a locker room one week, as elusive the next as a cab in the rain—isn't uncommon among women. Passion is a fragile thing, sensitive to everything from changes in hormones to changes in climate. It is, as sex therapist Michael Seiler, Ph.D., associate director of the Phoenix Institute in Chicago and coauthor of *ISD: Inhibited Sexual Desire*, describes it, "a psychosomatic experience," a shivery response by your body to some delightful tickle in your head.

This response is easily triggered by a tryst with a new lover, a weekend getaway with an old one or a partner who brings you breakfast in bed and cleans up afterward. And what kills it? It doesn't take much. Any child under 18, a ringing telephone, a new boss or a husband who eats breakfast in bed and leaves the kitchen for you to tidy. Any or all of these things can turn a sex life that once seemed like a chapter from the *Kama Sutra* into one from *The Tibetan Book of the Dead*.

But even the most lifeless libido can be resurrected. It probably won't happen in one enchanted evening. And it most certainly will require some soul-searching on your part. Mostly, though, it necessitates that you and your partner have a few good heart-to-hearts—where good sex always starts.

WHO KNOWS WHAT'S NORMAL?

No one—not even the experts—has a definite idea how often the average American woman desires sex—or, for that matter, what's normal when it comes to female libido. We know from national surveys how often the average American has sex: about 2.8 times a week. But most experts put little stock in this figure.

"I've never seen 0.8 of a sexual encounter," says Judith Seifer,

Ph.D., R.N., president of the American Association of Sex Educators, Counselors and Therapists. According to statistics, between 11 and 48 percent of sexually active individuals experience a decrease in libido at one time or another, and 70 percent of those reporting it are women.

By one estimate, about a third of all women rarely, if ever, experience a spontaneous interest in sex—though this doesn't mean they don't get in the mood once they're sexually stimulated by a partner. They just don't arrive at the party first.

So when it comes to sex drive, statistics—good or bad—aren't particularly illuminating. Most experts agree that a normal sex drive is what feels normal to you, whether you want sex once a day, once a week or once a month. But what drives most people to a sex therapist is a change in their libido—going from wanting sex a few times a week to wanting it once a month or not at all. At times, your endocrine system is the culprit—when your hormones drop during menopause, for instance, or when your body produces hormones after childbirth. But when the thrill is gone, it's likely that the problem is in your head.

ANGER BETWEEN THE SHEETS

Somewhere in the first five years of her marriage, Karen McManus lost her desire. She and her husband, Mark, had married at age 20 and put each other through college—but Karen got her degree in between giving birth to two children, 18 months apart. And while it was hard for both of them, it was Karen who had to juggle carpooling, shopping and cleaning with calculus homework and chemistry labs. "For the longest time, I thought I was the one who was abnormal," she says. "I thought, 'How come he wants it three times a week and I want it three times a year?' I was angry. I felt like I was doing all the work. I didn't even want to try making love because I felt numb from the neck down."

Many experts believe that this kind of unresolved anger in a relationship is the primary cause of decreased sex drive. The anger may come from anywhere—"He never tells me he loves me" or "He never picks up his dirty socks." But in a two-career family, it often comes down to division of labor.

A woman who has a career and works "the second shift"—as a full-time mother and/or housekeeper—may feel her sexual desire evaporate not just because she's so busy, but because her partner isn't willing to pitch in with the vacuuming, says Dr. Seiler. The operative phrase here is "isn't willing," you can fill in your own household chore.

"For a woman, sex isn't about how he touches her breasts or her clitoris. It's how he touches her psyche—how he relates to her within the context of their relationship," says Dr. Seiler. "Feeling connected and cared for is what turns women on most."

TOO STRESSED FOR SEX

Stress is an integral part of life. It comes with birth and death, beginnings and endings, rises and falls in fortune—and it may be your libido's second-biggest enemy. Though they seem like polar opposites, a death in the family and the birth of a baby are equally likely to drive sexual desire into a dark corner, at least temporarily. In fact, says Dr. Seiler, "I most often see couples disconnect sexually when they get engaged, get married or have a baby. Those are very complicated psychological changes within a relationship and that's where a lot of couples lose it."

The fact is, many couples are so busy with work, the house and the kids that they don't have time to pay attention to each other. And they gripe that their passion for each other fluttered off suddenly like a canary fleeing its cage. "But in reality, it didn't go—they went," says Sandra Scantling, Psy.D., assistant clinical professor of psychiatry at the University of Connecticut and coauthor of *Ordinary Women, Extraordinary Sex.* "We leave the passion behind when we focus too much of our attention on things that aren't related to the pleasure we feel with our partners."

As a result, pleasure sinks to the bottom of a long list of "must dos." Indeed, we often lose our sense of what gives us pleasure to begin with. We don't take time to smell the roses or the pheromones, those mysterious scents men and women secrete that some scientists believe trigger sexual attraction. In fact, we may not get close enough to our partners to get even a whiff, says Dr. Scantling. Just think about the average American "good-morning kiss"—a one-second peck on the cheek during which both partners are thinking not of each other, but of all the things they have to do that day.

FEAR OF FLYING

Sexual desire—and good sex—flourishes only when a woman feels safe, secure and sure of herself and her partner. If sex makes you anxious, you'll want it about as much as you want an IRS audit.

Women who have suffered through hurtful relationships are often fearful that their partners will simply repeat history and, consequently, they're afraid to trust. Some are self-conscious about their bodies. "Women in our society often feel bad if they don't meet the cultural standards of beauty and, as a result, don't feel sexual," says Leslie Schover, Ph.D., clinical psychologist at the Center for Sexual Function at the Cleveland Clinic.

Other women are afraid of letting themselves be swept away by their own passion. "They think, 'What's he going to say if I yell, scream, moan or wet my pants?,' " says Seifer. "Fear is a profound inhibitor of sexual desire; it's hard to let go if you're inhibited."

Still others fret that they're not doing it right, as if each sexual encounter were a pop quiz that counted toward a final grade. Sex becomes an exercise in technique with the big O—orgasm—as the passing grade. Many women are also afraid to discuss their sexual needs with their partners because they don't want to be turned down, humiliated or ignored. "When we ask and don't get a response, we stop asking and talking, and we withdraw," says Dr. Seifer. "Then we wonder why sex doesn't happen anymore."

GETTING IT BACK

No matter what has driven the desire away, if you once felt those erotic urges, you can feel them again—but don't expect miracles overnight. "There are no 'three easy steps to a better sex life,' " says Dr. Schover. "Sexual desire is complex; what helps one person may not do anything for the next." With this caveat in mind, take note of the following suggestions from the experts for re-igniting your sexual fire.

Talk it out. If your passion was extinguished by a previous relationship or a sexual problem, try explaining this to your partner. "Sexual intercourse rarely occurs without verbal discourse," says Dr. Seiler. But like many people, you may find it easier to have sex than to talk about it. And if discussions about relationship problems often end in shouting matches or frustrated silences, you may be avoiding discussions about sex as well as sex itself. To make talking it over easier, you need to set a few ground rules.

Don't cast blame. One way to avoid messy, unproductive arguments is to avoid putting your partner on the defensive. Use "I" messages rather than "you" messages. Although the bottom line may be the same, there's a big difference between saying, "I feel overwhelmed and alone when I have to cook, clean and take care of the kids when I come home from work" and "You never do anything around the house." One is a simple statement describing how you feel; the other is a blanket accusation.

Be explicit. Tell your partner exactly what you want—in bed and out. Your biggest turn-on might be seeing your partner voluntarily cleaning the bathroom. Or it might be a certain way he touches your breasts. Or both. Tell him.

Choose neutral territory. The bedroom might not be the best place to discuss problems, especially if it has become your battleground. "Find a nonsexual moment to discuss your sexual concerns," suggests Dr. Seifer. San Francisco psychologist Lonnie Barbach often suggests couples talk things over during a long, relaxing car ride. "There's nobody else in the car, and there's privacy—no phone and no distractions," says Barbach. And unless you're used to doing it in the back seat, the car has no association with your sex life.

Practice listening. Once you've selected the time and place, take turns talking and listening. If you're the talker, make a short statement, maintaining eye contact with your partner, if possible. Afterward, your partner should repeat, in his own words, what he heard you say. Then it's his turn to talk—and yours to listen.

Keep talking. One discussion, no matter how successful, is not going to cure what's ailing in your relationship or your sex life. So plan for regular powwows and share your feelings often.

Go on a pleasure hunt. Explore your sensual side. To start, Dr. Scantling suggests identifying something that makes you feel good. It could be anything from the sight of your lover's shirts hanging in the closet to the memory of one highly romantic getaway. Re-read old love letters, listen to music, burn a scented candle and recall pleasant memories associated with the smell, or fantasize about sex with your "ideal" lover. Give yourself time to experience and savor these pleasant sensations. Make them a part of your daily experience.

Once you feel comfortable, include your partner in your sexual exploration. Dr. Seiler recommends several exercises, called sensate focus exercises, adapted from the work of noted sex researchers Masters and Johnson. One important ground rule during sensate focus exercises: Don't "go all the way." That means no intercourse and no orgasm. The point is to experience being aroused. "Intercourse and orgasm are the end of the experience," says Dr. Seiler. "We want people to learn to revel in the giving and receiving of pleasure."

This exercise will also help you avoid the "stepladder" approach to sex—where everything you do has to lead to intercourse. "In many relationships, you may want to do nothing more than hug and kiss, but you don't because you're afraid your partner will assume that you want intercourse," says Dr. Seiler.

The first exercise, called tame touch, allows you and your partner to reconnect physically in a way that won't cause anxiety. For 30 minutes, three times a week, take turns massaging each other (clothed or unclothed—whichever makes you feel more comfortable). When it's your turn to be touched, give your partner feedback. Tell him what body part you want him to massage, what feels good and what would feel even better. You can guide his hands, too. After 15 minutes, return the favor.

After you've done this exercise at least three times, move on to "Sensate Focus 1." Spend the first half-hour exploring your partner's body with your fingertips, touching anywhere you'd like except the genital area. (This exercise functions as much to help you learn what you like as what your partner likes). Your partner should focus on the sensations and give you feedback on what feels good and what doesn't. When your time is up, you and your partner should switch roles. (Your partner should also refrain from touching your breasts or genitals.)

When you've done this exercise twice without any difficulties, begin touching the breasts and genitals in your next session. Dr. Seiler advises that the first few times you do so, the toucher should be in control, exploring what he or she feels pleasure doing. The third time, the person being touched should direct the toucher, giving feedback on where and how he or she wants to be touched.

Re-order your priorities. You and your partner need to make time for one another, even if it means scheduling sex. "People will say, 'Oh, no—that's so predictable, so unspontaneous,' but the truth is that our lives are not spontaneous," says Barbach. "Our calendars are full, and if we don't pencil in sex, the time will get filled with something else."

But while you're scheduling sex, be sure to schedule time to be with each other, too. Barbach and her partner go on a "date" every Thursday night. "We hire a babysitter, get dressed up and go do something—anything," she says. "It's become an essential part of our lives, and if we don't do it for a while, we feel it."

Even more important, when you are together, be there for each other. "Remember that, for women especially, sex isn't something that happens between 8:00 and 11:30 in the bedroom between your legs," says Dr. Scantling. "It can happen all day long in your mind, if you're open to it."

Do the little things. Barbach advises her clients to send each other love notes and poems. Behringer's husband writes her a note every morning on the paper cup in which he puts her vitamins. "I can't wait to get downstairs to read it," she says.

If your relationship is mired in conflict, you may need to set up something more structured. Each of you can make a list of what you would like the other person to do. It can be anything that makes you feel good, from giving you a hug first thing in the morning to doing the dinner dishes. Make a list of 12 caring things and do 4 of them each day, even if you don't feel particularly caring. Keep a record of everything your partner has done for you and look it over each week.

Cruise to fantasy island. In her research, Dr. Scantling found that women who enjoyed imagery and fantasy reported much higher sexual enjoyment and arousal. "I'm not talking about the schoolgirl and the teacher or the pirate and the princess," says Dr. Scantling. "That's too restrictive a definition. Imagery and fantasy can be anything from a fleeting thought about someone's eyes to a lengthy daydream about a pleasant experience." Fantasies of people other than your partner—both real and imagined—are natural and normal, too, she adds.

WHEN IT'S NOT ALL IN YOUR HEAD

If your passion's in the pits, the cause might be physical—and medically treatable. See your doctor if you suspect that one of the following conditions might be responsible for your lagging libido.

Menopause. Some women report lack of interest in sex during and after menopause. The culprit, surprisingly, may be testosterone, which also diminishes along with estrogen. Many experts believe it is testosterone—a male hormone women produce in small amounts—that actually fuels libido. Some studies have shown that when a woman is given small doses of testosterone along with her estrogen replacement, her sexual desire returns.

Painful intercourse. This often occurs during menopause because low estrogen levels lead to a thinning of the vaginal lining and a decrease in vaginal lubrication. Both of these conditions can be reversed with hormone-replacement therapy or remedied by the use of artificial lubricants, such as K-Y Jelly or Replens.

But there are a number of other causes of painful intercourse, according to Mark Walters, M.D., head of the Section of General Gynecology at the Cleveland Clinic. These include endometriosis, which occurs when tissue from the lining of the uterus attaches itself to other organs in the lower abdomen; vulvar vestibulitis, a little-understood but painful condition affecting the vulva; interstitial cystitis, an inflammation of the bladder that can be aggravated by intercourse; and vaginismus, an involuntary contraction of the vaginal muscle.

All of these conditions can be treated—although for the lesser-understood conditions, such as vestibulitis and interstitial cystitis, you may need to shop for a doctor

Use marital aids. If you've tried some of the suggestions here without success, your best bet may be to seek the help of a marriage counselor or a certified sex therapist. Then, once you're handling your most critical problems, many therapists recommend watching erotic movies or reading books on sex. When McManus and her husband finally settled the chore

until you find a physician familiar with them.

Vaginal prolapse and urinary incontinence. This condition is more likely to have social consequences than physical ones, says Dr. Walters. "If a woman is leaking urine all the time, she's bound to be embarrassed about it," he says. For mild cases, Kegel exercises, which strengthen the pubococcygeal muscles (those that suspend the bladder, vagina and anal area) can be helpful. Ask your physician to explain how they're done. In more severe cases of uterine prolapse—in which the sagging abdominal muscles allow the uterus to protrude into the vagina—your doctor may need to perform an operation to correct the condition.

Breast-feeding. When a woman is breast-feeding, her body produces a hormone called prolactin, which stimulates the manufacture of milk. "At the same time, estrogen in her body is being suppressed, which can lead to vaginal dryness," says Charles Faiman, M.D., chairman of the Department of Endocrinology at the Cleveland Clinic. And the combination makes sex drive—and, often, ovulation—disappear. "That's because God designed the lactating woman to be a milk factory, not a receptacle for another pregnancy," says Dr. Faiman. An underactive thyroid, a pituitary tumor and certain drugs also may cause prolactin levels to shoot up. But see your doctor; vaginal dryness can be treated easily.

Medication. Some medications, including some that treat high blood pressure, anti-ulcer drugs, oral contraceptives and mood-altering medicines, can cause sexual dysfunction. Ask your doctor if any of your medications could be causing this side effect.

wars—with the help of a marriage counselor—they bought a large, illustrated coffeetable book on sex. "The photographs are beautiful and a real turn-on," she says. "Sometimes I look at them by myself, when I'm feeling particularly disinterested. Sometimes Mark and I look at them together, using the book kind of like a menu. You know: 'Mmmm . . . why don't we try that?' It's a lot of fun."

Your local bookstore, no matter how staid, probably has half a dozen books on sexual technique—a good many of which are illustrated. If you're too embarrassed to buy one, you can get your thrills by mail—in plain brown wrappers—from a number of good sources. For example, The Xandria Collection, P.O. Box 31039, San Francisco, CA 94131, will send you a catalog of "adult products" including books and videos for $4, which will be applied to your first purchase.

—*Denise M. Foley and Eileen P. Nechas*

DATING YOUR HUSBAND

YOU PROMISED TO LOVE, HONOR AND CHERISH. BUT ARE YOU HAVING ANY FUN?

It's a sad stereotype: Whenever you see a couple talking intimately over dinner—two heads eagerly bending in toward each other—you assume they're dating; if they're eating silently, eyes focused on the fettuccine, you assume they're married. As Connie, a 36-year-old fitness instructor, points out, "My husband and I both try to make our evenings out exciting, but we've been together for a long time. The love is there double, but I guess the old spark is missing—everything he says I've heard 12 times before. Still—I'm not knocking it: Going out is still fun."

On the face of it, there are plenty of good reasons why a date with your husband or partner would feel different from the dating in your precommitment days. At this point, you're hardly strangers to each other, and so much of the process of discovery and self-revelation that made dating fun in the old days may no longer be realistic to expect. Perhaps also, between your respective jobs and raising the children, evenings out tend to become little else but business meetings.

Says Joanne, a 37-year-old stockbroker, "The experts tell you to pick a relaxed time to discuss problems, so I wait for a pleasant atmosphere to tell him the stuff he needs to know—our son has failed three tests in a row, our daughter has no friends—but it doesn't work. He pulls in his head like a turtle. So much for dating your husband."

But wait. Perhaps some of us have the wrong idea about dating once our marriage vows are made. "Couples seem to marry," says Avodah K. Offit, M.D., a psychiatrist and sex therapist who is clinical assistant professor of psychiatry at Cornell University Medical College and author of the book *Virtual Love*, "because they laughed and had fun together when they dated. Then, they promptly forget how to do it." Or, they become so embroiled in the day-to-day tasks of running households or families that they forget to make sheer fun and play with their mates a priority.

Not every couple has this problem, of course. The 1993 *New Woman* Relationship Survey conducted by the Roper Organization found that 53 percent of married American women go out on dates with their husbands—and presumably, not all these outings turned out to be forlorn, else why would they continue to date?

Still, let's acknowledge that enjoying an evening of intimacy and laughter with your husband may be more of a rarity than we would like to believe. It's possible, too, that all those married women in the survey who do not go out on dates and would like to (more than half of them) have had little experience in the joys of married dating. What, then, can we do about this? An informal survey of some happy couples, who through sheer grace or hard-learned effort seem to carry off their dates with joy to spare, yielded some helpful tips.

Plan your dates. "Married couples, like lovers in the most intense stage of infatuation, might profit by planning their affairs, by carefully arranging their amatory meetings," says Dr. Offit. It's true. Smart married couples prepare for "play dates" just as they did when they were single: Their evenings out often turn into erotic trysts, true lovers' rendezvous. Dating can serve as sexual foreplay, says Dr. Offit, and that includes slow dancing, candles, flowers, firelight, mirrored disco balls and flashing neon—whatever your pleasure.

For these couples, many wonderful things do happen spontaneously, but make no mistake: They tend to happen within a prearranged structure.

However, too many other married couples hang around waiting for sudden moods of dizzying, spontaneous passion to strike after the barbecue delivery man has left, the telemarketers have stopped calling and the children have been put to bed. Dizzying, spontaneous passion is swell—but it rarely happens, even on a first date. True passion thrives on planned play. "The whole structure of unmarried dating usually relies on a series of prearranged rituals," says Shari Lusskin, M.D., a specialist in behavioral psychiatry at the New York University School of Medicine in New York City. "One person asks the other out. Time and place are purposefully arranged. Before the date, each deliberately prepares for the other. We primp and preen. He may even shave again. Certainly, he'll reapply his can't-fail after-shave lotion; she may also put on fresh clothing and makeup."

When you date your husband and you anticipate your time with him by the same preparation rituals you used when you were a dating single, it heightens sensation and the feeling of romance, says Dr. Lusskin. "This kind of preparation is never spontaneous: It's planned and deliberate. And, it's very wonderful."

Collect interesting tidbits of information to share. Good conversation is the essence of a good date, but too often married couples let their discussions center on additions to their houses, the new insurance bills, the babies' impossible sleeping schedules. When we first date, we thought hard about conversation that would be provocative and interesting. After marriage, there's nothing to stop us from doing the same thing, choosing material for conversation—gossip, stories, news items—that takes us beyond our little spheres.

"I read the newspaper just before leaving the office to find something to discuss that we've never before batted about," says Dori, a 34-year-old attorney, married 13 years and still planning conversational agendas for nights out. "All it takes is one or two original ideas, a funny story—anything that makes our connection new and challenging. One thing leads to another, and we're off and running."

And, adds her husband, Lou, 36, also an attorney, "It kind of makes each date feel like the first, in some ways. We think it does honor our relationship—this saving up of interesting subjects to talk about when we meet. I've learned to consciously store away ideas—I even jot them down so that I won't forget to tell Dori. And, we save the gritty, boring stuff that needs to be hashed out for calm moments at home."

Explore memories together. Nothing builds intimacy like shared memories of the good times you've had together—but also of the way you each were before you even knew the other. For example, many people use dates with mates as opportunities to find out about each other's youth. Just watch his eyes light with pleasure as he describes how it was when he was young and green. You ask: Who was your hero when you were growing up? Did you ever run away from home? What was your fondest dream when you were 15? Describe your childhood love. What scared you when you were a teenager?

Watch how couples become newly tuned in to each other when they take the time to find out remarkable things about who the other really is—10, even 30 years after wedding vows.

"We were in a restaurant the other night," says 31-year-old Susan, a jewelry designer married for three years, "and I asked my husband to tell me something he'd never told me before. He laughed it off and said I already knew everything and I shouldn't be silly, but I persisted. And, do you know—he finally came up with the story of an essay he'd written for his 11th grade English teacher that was so revealing of his heart, so exciting for me to hear about—well, you can't imagine what a great evening we had. I, of course, had to come up with something I'd never told him before, and the upshot was we never made it to the movies that night, that's how engrossed we were in sharing our secret pasts in a new way."

Express appreciation. Words are the currency of a relationship: You have to say how you feel—and if your partner has made you happy, you have to find the words to acknowledge it. Passion is born from the other's appreciation of you.

"We need to take time," says psychologist Lonnie Barbach, Ph.D., "to express loving thoughts and feelings, to tell your partner how good he looks, how much you appreciate the errand he ran for you or the meal he cooked, to let him know how funny or bright or competent you find him."

Or, how sexy you find him. A magical thing happens when you're out on a date, in a romantic place, dressed up—and you tell your mate he's the sexiest thing that ever walked the Earth and how lucky you feel to be with him. He becomes the sexiest thing that ever walked the Earth. Even if you've exaggerated the tiniest bit, saying it makes it happen.

If your partner knows you appreciate him and look at him with "enchanted eyes," a date becomes a wondrous interlude.

Note: Many of us find it hard to deliver those words of appreciation when we have not been in the habit of giving this gift. Do it anyway. Soon, the words come more easily.

Plan surprises. The element of surprise has an extraordinary effect on a husband you intend to date. Send flowers to him at the office on a characterless day. Appear unexpectedly, as Marianne, a 41-year-old teacher, did one snowy evening.

"I bought tickets to a show I knew he wanted to see. For later, I reserved a banquet table at a new, romantic restaurant. Feeding someone you're in love with is a wily sort of seduction—and if you don't have to do the cooking, it's also restorative as hell," says Marianne, married 17 years. "I pre-ordered our dinner—down to the hot fudge sundaes; no carrot juice or tofu on this night, even though we're both usually so careful. I topped it all off with a foggy boat ride on the Staten Island ferry—we cruised there and turned around and cruised right back," says Marianne. "The best, the funniest, the most romantic night. We were laughing like a couple of kids." Best of all, recalls her husband, Dan, 44, she paid for everything.

Tour guide Elaine, 53, planned an afternoon date with her companion of five years. "I called his secretary in advance to make sure his schedule was light, then I just appeared at his office at lunchtime and kidnapped him. He grumped at first, but then he loved it. The whole day that followed gave us a sense of the forbidden. Here's this average afternoon, we should be at work, but there we were, shopping, seeing an art exhibit, having a luxurious glass of champagne while the sun was still out. I think everything seemed more fun because we're not used to seeing each other on a workday."

No surprise there, actually. When you date your husband, says Dr. Lusskin, "it's not so much spending time as stealing time with him. That kind of illicit excitement is a turn-on."

Do unusual things together. Remember how in your single days you would be game for doing just about anything with a new date—bowling, going to a dog show, a flea market, an outdoor concert on a misty evening? Somehow, after marriage, you remember you're a terrible bowler, you don't have a dog, you don't have the time to flea-market browse and an outdoor concert when it looks like rain—are you crazy?

"After we were married for three or four years," says 38-year-old Lois, an advertising executive, "we both noticed that we'd lost 'explore mode.' All our dates were standard, civilized fare: nice but rarely hysterical fun."

She and her husband concertedly set out to change things. Once every month or so, each takes turns arranging a date. The rule is that the other has to go along with the plans—even if they don't sound so terrific.

"Well," grins Lois, "it's been incredible. In the last few months, we've taken a balloon ride, seen a belly dancer, eaten I don't know how much at a country fair, gone to a ball game (I hate ball games on television, but it's something entirely different to be there!). Sometimes we go alone, sometimes we schlepp friends. Do you know how much fun we've had?

"Look," she continues, "it's easier just to go to a movie and dinner. Often, we have to push ourselves to be creative. Sometimes we're broke, sometimes we're cranky, sometimes getting a babysitter is a problem. But, most of the time we make a tremendous effort to stick to the plan. And these different dates, I think, save our lives."

Above all, listen well. "Your one and only job, while listening," says psychologist Bernie Zilbergeld, Ph.D., author of *The New Male Sexuality*, "is to understand the other's experience, feelings, attitude or point of view."

This is a sage comment. While listening, your point of view is not immediately relevant. You can express it after a while, says

Dr. Zilbergeld, but only after you've understood what the other is saying.

"When she expresses an opinion, time stops," smiles Burt, a 42-year-old stockbroker. "I focus in, I hear her through. I used to have a habit of letting my eyes wander over to the other side of the room when someone was talking, but when that was brought to my attention, I stopped; I hate it when someone does it to me."

"You know what I love about him?" asks Nance, his wife, also 42, "I love that he doesn't tear apart my opinions, even when he disagrees with me. He doesn't have that what-do-you-know attitude. He listens to me with energy."

You can do this, says Harville Hendrix, Ph.D., founder and director of the Institute for Relationship Therapy in New York City, by "mirroring" what your husband says. Paraphrase or re-phrase his statements—then ask him if what you heard was what he actually meant: "You feel as though you're not doing what you were always meant to do. Your work seems empty. You're thinking about a new career—is that what you're saying?"

That's what he said. And, he's grateful you heard—and didn't even panic.

Enjoy. Certainly, all couples who have been together for some time have their share of sore points and trouble spots. And if, while out on a date, a couple can find a way to talk caringly and openly about their problems, that's wonderful. But never re-gard as a superficial event a date that's devoted to pure enjoy-ment, a date that leaves out all the serious rocky stuff. Sharing good times together creates a solid foundation from which you can later launch into creative problem solving.

Cuddle. One more thing: Don't forget necking. Remember necking on a date? We used to find an infinite variety of places to park and explore each other. That smeared lipstick, those contortionistic positions, those unfulfilled groans. Heaven.

Go back to necking with your husband on a date one night. Grab him for a long, wet kiss before you get out of the car. There is nothing more erotic.

The moral of this story? Even if you've never before dated your husband (or wife), check it out. The nicest part is that you can neck, pet and maybe even go all the way on your first date—and he probably won't even lose respect for you.

—*Sherry Suib Cohen*

THE SEX OFFENDERS

SOME MEDICINES DEPRESS THE SEX DRIVE. ARE YOU TAKING THEM?

D ear Dr. Reinisch: Recently I lost the urge to have sex with my husband, and my orgasms have become faint." This letter from a 44-year-old woman was published by syndicated columnist June M. Reinisch, Ph.D., director of the Kinsey Institute for Research in Sex, Gender and Reproduction at Indiana University in Bloomington. The woman wrote that she'd been taking Xanax for anxiety and panic attacks and wondered if the drug might have something to do with her loss of libido.

"Dear Reader," Dr. Reinisch wrote in reply, "one possible side effect of Xanax is a loss of sexual desire. Another is inhibited orgasm."

SIDE EFFECTS, SEX EFFECTS

Unfortunately, the sexual side effects that afflict some users of widely used drugs are rarely publicized. Xanax is merely the tip of the iceberg. "So many commonly prescribed drugs may cause sexual impairment that I've coined a term for them," says Theresa Crenshaw, M.D., a San Diego sexual-medicine specialist. "I call them 'sex offenders.'"

Unfortunately, Dr. Crenshaw says, many doctors prescribe sex-offending drugs without mentioning their possible sex-debilitating side effects.

"Most people have no idea that a loss of libido, vaginal lubrication, orgasm or erection might be related to a drug they're taking," Dr. Reinisch explains. "Many doctors don't know either. And it can take months—sometimes up to a year—for sexual side effects to develop. The longer it takes, the less likely consumers—and their doctors—are to make the connection."

Even worse, Dr. Reinisch says that doctors familiar with drugs' sexual side effects often don't discuss the possibilities with patients: "Many doctors believe that if they mention sexual side effects, that information alone will cause enough anxiety to produce sexual impairment. My own experience suggests the opposite. When I tell a patient that a drug might have sexual side effects, I also explain that it might not. Sexual responses to drugs are very individual. Then, if the drug causes no sexual impairment, there's no harm done. But if it does, at least the person was warned and spared the confusion and self-doubt of the woman who wrote me that letter."

Although different people have different sexual reactions to drugs, in general, medications that depress the central nervous system tend to reduce both sexual desire and responsiveness—lubrication and orgasm in women, erection and ejaculation in men. Other medications might suppress desire but not ability or vice versa. For most women loss of libido (rather than of lubrication and orgasm) is the primary sex-offending effect. Are there potential sex offenders in your medicine cabinet? Below are some of the medications notorious for causing sexual side effects.

Caution: Never discontinue taking a prescription medication or switch to another without first consulting your physician.

Tranquilizers, sedatives and sleeping pills. There's a good reason why Xanax, Valium, Ativan, Equanil, Compazine, Librium, Dalmane, Nembutal, Placidyl, Halcion and dozens of other sleeping pills and mood-altering drugs are called downers. They often send women's sexual interest and responsiveness right down the drain.

They can affect men similarly, but they present a bigger problem for women because, as Dr. Crenshaw explains, women receive "80 percent of the prescriptions for these drugs. All these medications are central nervous system depressants. While taking them, women often lose their desire and their ability to lubricate and climax. When men take them, many have trouble having erections or ejaculating."

Alternatives to these sex offenders include stress-management techniques, such as psychotherapy, meditation, a support group, volunteer work and regular, moderate exercise (but for those with insomnia, not within four hours of bedtime).

Birth control pills. By making contraception easy and reliable, the Pill has helped millions of women enjoy sex more. But birth control pills may also have the opposite effect. Some women taking the Pill experience a loss of sexual desire and/or vaginal lubrication. Why? Because women's libido and responsiveness are affected by the levels of sex hormones in their blood, and the Pill changes those levels.

Antidepressants. Here's a classic story: A woman in her twenties was in a relationship that ended badly. She has always felt insecure, and the breakup makes her feel even worse. She becomes seriously depressed and consults her doctor, who prescribes an antidepressant. However, neither her doctor nor her pharmacist tells her it might suppress her libido. The drug lifts her spirits, and eventually she meets another man. But as they become intimate, she finds she's just not interested in sex. The man feels rejected, and another relationship ends badly, which sends her back to her doctor for a refill of her antidepressant prescription.

"Most antidepressants are prescribed for women, many of them young women who have little sexual experience and self-confidence," Dr. Crenshaw explains. "If they lose interest in sex, it never occurs to them that drug might be the cause. They blame themselves and decide they must be sexually abnormal— which they're already primed to believe because they're depressed. Some young women are on antidepressants for years. Even when they finally stop taking them, the drugs can leave them with sexual self-esteem problems."

Alternatives to antidepressant medications include the stress-management approaches discussed above.

Medications for migraine headaches. About 70 percent of the nation's 17 million migraine suffers are women under age 40. Frequent migraine suffers often take daily medication to prevent attacks. The drug usually prescribed is propranolol (such as Inderal). But few propranolol users know that this drug can also suppress sexual desire. You could go from, "Not tonight, dear, I have a headache," to "No headache tonight, dear, but no interest either."

"Recently," Dr. Crenshaw explains, "I spoke with a man who got divorced after five years of marriage, in part because his wife lost her libido shortly after their wedding. It turned out that she had migraines and had taken Inderal for most of their marriage. The man had no idea that the drug might have contributed to her loss of sexual desire."

There are other ways to deal with migraines beside propranolol. You might try keeping a migraine diary detailing everything about your lifestyle (including diet) preceding attacks. With a diary, many people can identify "migraine triggers" and adjust their lives to minimize attacks. Stress-management therapies, biofeedback and acupuncture often help, too. The ergot drugs may also be used to treat migraines. They include Cafergot, Ergostat and other similar prescription medications.

Appetite suppressants. In a nation where "thin is in" and losing weight is practically a religion for millions of women, many turn to prescription appetite suppressants. Some of these drugs, Pondimin in particular, can suppress desire for sex as well as food. Most weight-management experts counsel against appetite suppressants. If you are currently taking one, think about asking your physician for a referral to a weight-loss program that doesn't include drugs, one based on a low-fat diet, exercise, psychotherapy and group support.

Blood pressure drugs. Medication to treat high blood pressure (hypertension) is usually prescribed for men over the age of 40. These drugs—which include propranolol (also used to treat migraines)—do what they're suppose to do but many cause other problems, like hampering a man's ability to have an erection.

If you're involved with a man over 40 and the two of you are having sexual problems, find out if he takes blood pressure medication. If your partner has difficulty having or maintaining an erection, switching to a different blood pressure medication could help.

High blood pressure medications are also used to treat hypertension in women, which usually occurs after menopause. Such medications can also lead to sexual problems in females—a lessening of desire and/or difficulty in reaching orgasm.

Ulcer drugs. About 10 percent of Americans develop ulcers at some point in their lives. This painful abdominal condition can strike at any age and is not necessarily associated with stress.

Traditionally, most ulcers occurred in men, but since the 1950s more and more women have been developing the disease—especially women who smoke. Today about half of ulcer sufferers are women.

For much of the 1980s, the ulcer drug Tagamet was one of the nation's most widely prescribed medications. And it's still quite popular, but few people who use it are told it can also be a major sex offender. "Tagamet can suppress libido in both men and women," Dr. Crenshaw says. "It also may cause erection loss. A newer ulcer medication, Zantac, is equally effective but causes fewer sex side effects—though it, too, may cause sexual impairment in some cases."

Additionally, recent research suggests that many ulcers result from bacterial infection and can be cured with antibiotics.

OTHER CULPRITS

Other prescription medications with possible sex-impairing effects include: steroids (such as Prednisone) prescribed for allergic and inflammatory disorders; antipsychotic drugs (such as Thorazine, Haldol, Mellaril); lithium, used to treat manic depression (Bipolar disorder); anticonvulsants used by epileptics; and many drugs used to treat cancer, angina, fluid retention and fungal infections. A good list can be found in Dr. Reinisch's book *The Kinsey Institute's New Report on Sex.*

Dr. Crenshaw says you should consider all drugs to be sex offenders until you're specifically reassured otherwise. "Whenever you or your partner gets a prescription, ask your doctor if it has any sexual side effects. If the physician doesn't know, ask him or her to look it up. Then, just to be sure, ask your pharmacist as well. If the drug is a possible sex offender, ask if another drug or nondrug approach that doesn't cause sexual side effects can be substituted. Usually, there are alternatives."

OVER-THE-COUNTER SEX OFFENDERS

The label on the popular allergy medicine Benadryl doesn't warn that it may dry up libido along with a runny nose, but it should. Benadryl's active ingredient, the antihistamine diphenhydramine, has such potent sedative effects that it's also the active ingredient in most over-the-counter sleep preparations: Sominex, Nytol, Sleep-Eze and Unisom. Many other antihistamines and decongestants can have similar effects.

"Just because a drug is available without a prescription doesn't mean it's sexually safe," Dr. Crenshaw warns. "Here's a good rule of thumb: If the label says 'May cause drowsiness,' the drug may depress sexual interest and ability."

Alternatives to the sedative antihistamines are the new nonsedating antihistamines (such as Seldane and Hismanal) available by prescription.

SEX PROBLEMS IN A BOTTLE

Alcohol is so widely consumed that people hardly think of it as a drug. But this powerful substance is probably the nation's leading sex offender. "At low doses—that first beer, mixed drink or glass of wine—alcohol relaxes inhibitions," explains E. Don Nelson, a professor of clinical pharmacology at the University of Cincinnati College of Medicine.

"You're more likely to make—or accept—sexual invitations. But after a few drinks, alcohol becomes a central nervous system depressant, which impairs men's and women's ability to function sexually."

Sometimes it's medically necessary to take a drug that impairs sexuality. "Xanax is a very effective treatment for disabling panic attacks," Dr. Crenshaw says, "and a fully informed consumer might choose to sacrifice his or her sexuality for a while to treat a serious panic problem. But in many cases, other drugs without sexual side effects can be substituted. Or nondrug approaches can be used."

The tragedy of the sex offenders is that so few doctors and pharmacists mention the possibility of sexual side effects. If your libido or orgasms aren't what they used to be, or if your partner has lost his sexual interest or developed a sexual problem, sex-offending drugs just might be the reason. And if you're at all concerned about any drug's possible sexual side effects, call your doctor or pharmacist and ask.

—*Michael Castleman*

FIVE THINGS YOU SHOULD NEVER DO IN BED

**THE SECRET TO A SATISFYING—AND SIZZLING—
LOVELIFE IS TO KNOW WHAT NOT TO DO
BEHIND THE BEDROOM DOOR.
SO WHAT'S A TURN-ON AND WHAT'S TABOO?
HERE'S THE SCOOP FROM A TOP SEX THERAPIST.**

You love him but wish he'd be a little more tender when he kisses you.

For the past few weeks you haven't been interested in sex, but you do it anyway.

While in bed with your husband, you imagine two handsome strangers making passionate love to you—and you're afraid your fantasy is too "naughty."

For women today, dilemmas like these are common. In fact, half of all relationships suffer from some kind of sexual distress, from disinterest to outright dysfunction. Yet, many times, the problems can be averted if a woman takes control of her thinking and her behavior. Here, based on the author's two decades of experience in advising thousands of men and women, are suggestions for what you shouldn't do in bed—and what you should.

WHAT YOU SHOULDN'T DO

Don't criticize. Carl and Susan had been married only six months when Susan came in for sex therapy. Although they were both the same age, 28, Susan was more sexually experienced than Carl. She initially found his naïveté charming, but over time she became increasingly annoyed, until she finally blurted out, "Don't kiss me like that" and "Don't pinch my nipples so hard." Carl huffed, "If that's how you feel, I won't kiss you or touch you at all."

Sexual criticism is damaging to the ego, particularly for men—who worry about everything from size to performance to endurance—and the slightest insult can escalate into the deepest injury. Like Carl, men often interpret any criticism to mean they're not good lovers, and they become defensive or withdrawn.

To prevent this problem, men must stop measuring their self-esteem by their sexual performance. But women must also be sensitive to their partners' feelings by pointing out what they do right instead of criticizing what they do wrong. Make him feel "safe" first by starting the conversation with "I love you dearly, and I want to tell you what I'd like to make things even better." Then describe clearly—in a loving tone—what you want him to do.

Don't panic over fluctuations in your sex life. Both of you are bound to have shifts in your sexual moods and responses; therefore, there will be times when you feel more or less out of sync. This is perfectly normal.

The most common worry couples have is incompatible sex drives. For the first four years of their marriage, Jennifer, 32, and Luke, 34, made love every morning, and occasionally again at night. But after their daughter was born, Jennifer refused sex more and more frequently. Luke felt rejected and resentful, and Jennifer wondered what was wrong with her.

Jennifer and Luke were relieved to learn that the sex drive changes over time, especially at identifiable stages—just before or after marriage, when couples become parents, at mid-life, when the children move out, at menopause and at retirement.

The ups and downs of arousal are affected by many factors. Some, over which you have no control, include hormone balances (notably estrogen, progesterone and testosterone) and brain chemistry (research suggests the master controls for sex are in the brain). Alcohol and some medications also interfere. Your sex drive can also decrease because of stress, fatigue, illness, job or family troubles or depression.

As in Jennifer's case, attitudes also affect desire. Once she became a parent, she felt it was no longer appropriate for her and Luke to be the wanton lovers they had been before. But when she allowed herself to be both lover and mother, Jennifer was able to renew her passion with Luke.

Most unsettling to men are changes in performance. Occasional erection or ejaculation problems can be a common occurrence due to stress, distraction or performance anxiety. Worrying only makes it worse. The solution: Switch anxious thoughts to pleasurable ones, or, as in the case of decreased desire, confront the real problem—stress, anger or whatever. Give yourself time to get in the mood. Many couples need a transition time in bed during which they can talk about their feelings or the events of the day before they make love.

Don't blame. Women are famous for sexual self-blame. When anything goes wrong in bed, they quickly assume it is their fault for not being attractive, skilled or sexy enough. Ironically, in many situations, he's the one who has a problem and either allows her to take responsibility, or deliberately makes her think it's her fault to protect his own ego.

Many women are sexually codependent—so desperate for their partners' approval and so eager to protect their feelings that they sacrifice self-esteem and truth. These women must stop blaming themselves and covering up for their dysfunctional partners. And sometimes, women who constantly fault themselves for problems in their sexual relationships have been sexually abused as children. In such cases, therapy can help heal the emotional wounds.

But at times, women, too, find it easier to blame a partner. Stephanie, 34, had never had an orgasm. She figured that her husband, Michael, didn't know how to please her. She began to consider having an affair.

In therapy sessions, Stephanie learned that no man *makes* a woman have an orgasm—she does it herself (with his help, of course) by learning about her body and what turns her on.

Don't confess all your secrets. The best lovemaking requires full openness of emotional and spiritual expression. But there are some disclosures that you should consider carefully before blurting out.

Patty and Bill were high-school sweethearts who drifted apart, then met again years later and got married. One evening at an art-gallery opening, Bill ran into an old girlfriend—a former model. Patty imagined a spark in Bill's eye, and for days she obsessed about it. One night, when Bill went to kiss her,

Patty blurted out, "You're thinking about her every night, aren't you?" Bill's denial and refusal to talk about it only made Patty more jealous, and she questioned him persistently. She also described to him in detail how her own looks paled in comparison to his ex-girlfriend's.

Such self-degradation and pressing a man about his past only undermines your confidence and highlights your insecurities to the point where *he* may start questioning your attractiveness. Instead of asking him about a past love or wallowing in your fears that he wants to leave you for her, immediately focus on something that enhances the connection between the two of you.

Recounting your own sexual history to your partner can be equally dangerous. Telling him about a past lover will only make him jealous or insecure about his own sexual prowess. Many men still enjoy the thought that they are the one and only.

Certainly, singles should know their potential partners' sexual histories, for health reasons, and relationship track record so they can assess their capacity for commitment. And for all couples, sharing fears can help release and dispel them. But be smart about sharing. Some pillow talk is best left unsaid.

Don't do anything in bed that makes you feel uncomfortable. Many women say their partners want to engage in certain sexual acts, and while they don't like the idea, they feel they should do it. They rationalize giving in because they want to make him "happy" (to which they might ask themselves "What about his making *me* happy?") or because "he's so cute" (to which they might imagine making a decision without seeing his face). Remember, you are always entitled to say no.

Nancy, 36, a divorced mother of two, was happily dating—and hoping to marry—John, a 40-year-old executive in the advertising agency where she worked. Then John suddenly decided he wanted to introduce another woman into their lovemaking. When Nancy protested, John said, "If you won't do it, I'll find someone else who will." Desperate not to lose him, Nancy gave in, but found the experience confusing and distressing. Next time, she stood her ground, and John announced that he wanted a break so he could see other women.

A woman risks becoming a victim when she gives in to sex despite her discomfort or objections. Assertiveness and sexual self-confidence are crucial. In therapy, Nancy imagined confronting John with her anger and being the rejecter instead of the rejectee, saying, "If that's how little you value me and our relationship, then it's over."

Of course, some sexual behaviors are completely unacceptable—anything involving children or pain. The latter includes the pain (called dyspareunia) that many women ignore during intercourse. Many women tell their gynecologists that they experience pain during sex. Many women report feeling stomach cramps during intercourse or having sex even if they're not sufficiently aroused, not wanting to upset their partner. Never dismiss pain as unimportant; it's a signal to stop what you're doing. The freedom to say no in bed means that you respect yourself—and your partner respects you, too—which is an important foundation for a loving sexual relationship.

WHAT YOU SHOULD DO

Show and tell him what turns you on. It's amazing that nearly 20 years after the supposed sexual revolution, women still hesitate to tell their partners what they like. Usually, they're too embarrassed, having grown up in a family that believed "nice" girls didn't do those kinds of things. But no thought or action is wrong when shared between two people who love each other. In fact, the consequences of keeping silent can be disastrous, with both partners ending up frustrated, angry or even unfaithful.

Though many women believe that a man should automatically know what turns his wife on—and that if he doesn't know, he must not love her—nothing could be further from the truth. In fact, most men welcome feedback from their partners. Tell him "Yes, I like that" or "slower would be perfect." Put your hand over his and show him how you want to be touched. Finally, don't be afraid to touch yourself in front of him—men find this very arousing.

Be free and expressive. Boredom in bed can happen as early as two years into a relationship. Fortunately, continued excitement is possible.

In therapy, couples sometimes receive "homework." They're

told to set aside two nights a week with at least one uninterrupted hour to try the following:

- Change the routine. Make love in a different place, in a different way, at a different time. For instance, if you're usually amorous before going to sleep, make love in the morning instead.
- Find new "hot spots." Once couples learn what turns them on, they tend to stick to what works. But any part of the body can be a source of pleasure.
- Spice things up. Some people prefer no-frills sex, but aids, such as massage oils, creams and sex toys, can light new sparks.
- Watch erotic films together. Some women are understandably turned off by crude action or derogatory treatment of women in pornographic movies. But watching tasteful erotic videos that portray women in a respectful way can be a good way to get in the mood and try new turn-ons.
- Indulge in fantasies. Occasionally, imagining you're making love with a different partner or in a different place allows you to behave in a new, erotic way. Or try "shared storytelling"—weaving a sexual fantasy together by taking turns adding to the story. Think of the best lovemaking you ever experienced or imagined, and tell him about it as if it's happening now. Then stop and let him add his own details.

Appreciate the difference between men and women. In just 5 minutes a man can reach an excitement level that it takes a woman about 15 minutes to achieve. Not only that, men have been taught to focus on quantity and quickness in sex, while women value quality and a slower buildup to passion. Obviously, such differences can cause major problems in the bedroom.

The solution: Men have to learn to slow down their sexual responses to allow the woman to become aroused. For their part, women can get in the mood beforehand by, for example, reading a sexy novel.

Couples also need to give and receive while making love. Women especially need to learn to be takers—to let their husbands give them pleasure. Husbands and wives in sex therapy do give-and-take homework: They take turns pleasuring each other using a timer so they're not always worrying that they are taking too long.

Go back to basics. Being together over time builds trust and security. But often men and women begin to take each other for granted. Fall in love with each other all over again.

- Practice pleasure touching. Explore each other's body by stroking or caressing and focusing on the sensations.
- Relive your most loving evening together. One couple was inspired by repeating the moonlit stroll they took the night he proposed. Another redecorated the bedroom to remind them of the Greek island they visited on their honeymoon.
- Pretend you're new lovers. Forget your past and court each other again. Go on a date—dress up, flirt, hang on each other's every word.
- Focus on tenderness and affection. In the middle of love-making, say gently, "I need a moment to calm down a bit; let's lie quietly and hold each other." You'll be surprised at how he welcomes the suggestion.

—*Judy Kuriansky, Ph.D.*

PART THREE

PERSONAL
SAFETY

DON'T BE SCARED—
BE PREPARED

LEAVE YOURSELF OPEN TO BECOMING A CRIME VICTIM, AND SOONER OR LATER YOU'LL BE ONE. HERE ARE 30 WAYS TO STAY SAFE IN A WORLD THAT ISN'T.

Health. We tend to think of it in terms of avoiding major illnesses, such as heart disease and cancer. But guess what? More women are robbed of their health by violent crimes every year than die of heart disease and cancer combined. More than 100,000 women are raped each year, and more than 4,500 are murdered. Tens of thousands more are "lucky": They're only shot, stabbed, kidnapped, mugged or robbed.

And it's not just in poor neighborhoods and inner-city ghettos that this stuff is happening: Research shows that violent crime can happen anywhere and to anyone—black or white, rich or poor. Leave yourself open to becoming a crime victim, and sooner or later you probably will be one. In many ways, it's up to you.

Crimes are often perpetrated against women because so many of us leave ourselves vulnerable, the experts say. Most criminals are opportunists: They aim first at the easiest targets. And by failing to take care—whether we're walking the streets, driving our cars or simply relaxing at home—we make the potentially fatal assumption that it can't possibly happen to us. That's when it usually does.

We take measures to avoid other health problems; it's time we did something to prevent violent crime from stealing away our health—and our lives. Here are 30 ways you can do just that.

Sincere thanks goes to two top crime-stopping experts for their help in putting together these tips: Cheryl Franks, the crime prevention coordinator for the Rochester Police Department in New York, and J J Bittenbinder, a detective with the Chicago Police Department whose special presentation, "Street

Smarts: How to Avoid Being a Victim," has aired on national television.

SAFETY AFOOT

It's a jungle out there on the streets, so you need to be as cunning as a lion to dodge potential dangers. Here's how.

1. *Don't be fooled by appearances.* Not every criminal is an ill-shaven, wild-eyed weirdo: Mass murderer Ted Bundy and the infamous Hillside Strangler, Kenneth Bianchi, had been described as "teddy bears," Franks and Bittenbinder point out. So don't assume that just because someone is attractive or charming, he's incapable of mugging you—or worse. Treat a stranger on the street as just that—a stranger, and a potentially lethal one.

2. *Use the buddy system.* There's strength in numbers, so walk with a friend if you must be out on the street at night. This doubles your muscle power if push comes to shove, and it will discourage confrontation in the first place.

3. *Vary your routes.* Criminals often plan their assaults based on patterns they observe, so try not to create any. For example, if you walk the same way to and from the bus stop, try a new route. Taking a few "long-cuts" is well worth the extra time if it keeps a potential attacker from fitting you into his schedule. Also, avoid walking near bushes or alleys where an assailant might hide, and stay in the middle of the sidewalk or as close to the street as possible.

4. *Phone ahead.* If you must walk somewhere alone, call a buddy and tell her where you're going, the route you'll be taking and the time you'll be calling her when you arrive. This way, your friend will be on the alert if you don't call on time. It takes just seconds to call—and it could save your life.

5. *Dress for speed.* No high heels or tight skirts allowed. Carry the impractical stuff in a tote bag if your destination requires that you wear it, but wear slacks and running shoes to get there. Criminals normally aren't the fittest folks around, so your chances of outrunning an assailant are good—if you're dressed appropriately.

6. *Don't parade your purse.* It's what most street-creeps look for first, so make yours as inconspicuous as possible. Shoulder bags

are better than hand-held purses because they're less snatchable (especially if you wear them across your body), but better yet is a fanny pack, which straps around your waist and can be hidden under your coat or shirt.

7. *Guard your jewels.* Even dime-store junk can make you a more attractive target for a snatcher—he doesn't know it's fake. Carry your jewelry in your shoulder bag or pocket, and don't put it on until you get where you're going. When you accessorize, remember that the less bedecked you appear, the less attention you'll attract and the safer you'll be.

8. *Exude an attitude.* "It's not how tough you are, but rather how tough you look," says Bittenbinder. Franks agrees. "Most attackers will tell you they chose a victim because she looked vulnerable," she says. "Women who look down when they walk, seem shy and introverted or don't take note of their surroundings are the ones who are singled out." Better to look confident—even a little overconfident. Walk with a strong and steady gait, hold your head high and look all around you to show you're aware of what's going on.

9. *Make a spectacle of yourself.* What if you do notice someone watching you—or worse, following you? Don't be afraid to make a scene, says Bittenbinder. Walk into the middle of the street if you have to. The attention you attract will only help your situation. Better to be a traffic nuisance than a mugging victim.

10. *Bear arms.* This doesn't mean "carry heat": Besides putting you at odds with the law in many states, a gun can be turned against you too easily. Better to carry Mace or pepper spray, which Bittenbinder says can stop even the most maniacal of attackers dead in their tracks. Pepper spray is his preference "because it puts them down faster than Mace," he says. He also recommends using one that contains dye—it's much easier to apprehend an attacker who has been branded. Other protective devices include: car keys (but only when held properly—one key positioned between your thumb and index finger); a battery-operated alarm device, which sends out a sirenlike wail; and what could be a woman's best friend on the street, a loyal dog.

11. *Sacrifice your possessions, not your life.* Whether it's your purse, your jewelry or even your car that a criminal wants, just say yes—then get out of there as fast as you can. "Possessions you

can replace—your life you can't," says Franks. Another reason to fork over quickly is to avoid escalating demands. Many assailants first want money, then your watch and jewelry—and before you know it, you're being shoved into a car. Avoid this potentially fatal progression simply by complying with a criminal's first demand and then hightailing it. You're not being cowardly—just smart, Franks says.

12. *If he wants cash, deliver it as "air mail."* One especially effective technique for allowing a mugger his cake but not you, too, is to carry a small amount of cash. Bittenbinder recommends a five wrapped around a few ones, held by a money clip to give it some weight. Chuck it if you're confronted with a demand for money. Your assailant will head for the cash—while you sprint in the opposite direction.

13. *Never get into an assailant's car.* Scream, kick, yell "Fire!" (People respond to this more readily than to the traditional "Help!")—do what you have to, but don't comply. "If you get into an assailant's car, you're probably in for a one-way trip," says Bittenbinder. If an assailant wants to rob you, he'll usually do it when he first accosts you. Once he's got you in his car, however, he's essentially forecasting something far worse—rape, perhaps even murder. That's one reason so many prostitutes end up the victims of brutal assaults, says Bittenbinder: They routinely get into strangers' cars as part of their business.

14. *Consider training for the worst.* Some self-defense courses are directly confrontational, such as karate and judo, while others are less so, such as assertiveness courses in which you learn to avoid confrontations by appearing to be tough in the first place. Either type can provide the extra measure of protection that keeps you from falling victim to random violence.

SAFETY ON THE ROADS

If the streets are a jungle, the highways can be even worse—especially if your car happens to break down in remote or hostile territory. Suddenly, you're a sitting duck for any lecherous lunatic who happens to pass by. But you can greatly reduce your risks on the road by following this advice.

15. *Keep your car in good shape.* It's safest not to break down at all,

so the first order of highway-safety business is to maintain your car properly. Have it checked regularly to make sure that the electrical system, battery and cooling system are in good working order and that you have four good tires plus a spare—that you can change! Carry flares, a flashlight and a tool kit, and take a routine car-maintenance course, if possible. The more you can help yourself in the event of a breakdown, the less "help" you'll need.

16. *Carry a "Call the Police" sign.* You can make one yourself or purchase one at a variety store; some police departments and community organizations even offer them for free. However you obtain it, be sure to carry it in your car. Placed inside your car's rear window, the sign will alert passing motorists to notify police of your difficulty.

17. *Always lock up.* Keep your doors locked even as you're driving and especially when you stop. An assailant could hop into your car in less time than it takes to roll down your window and retrieve your mail.

18. *Lock up if you break down.* Sorry, but even if someone who appears to be Mr. Goodwrench himself offers assistance, keep your doors locked. Allow him to notify the police or a reputable towing service, but nothing more.

19. *Never agree to pull over.* No matter how authoritative another driver may appear—unless, of course, he's unmistakably a policeman at the wheel of a police car—never agree to pull over. Put on your flashers instead and do whatever you can to drive to a safe place.

20. *Never leave your keys in the ignition.* Lock your car and take the keys with you—even if you're just running into the drugstore for a pack of gum. Many car thieves watch for just such quick stops.

21. *Never leave children in a car.* If you think that a car is safer when it's full of kids, you're wrong. Leave your child in the car—even for a moment—and you may find yourself returning to no more than a ransom note.

SAFETY AT HOME

Your home is your castle, but is it safe? Keeping doors and windows locked is obvious; take the following measures to make it—and you—more secure.

22. *Consult a security specialist.* Many police departments have crime-prevention experts who will check the security of your home and suggest safety measures based on their evaluation and on the types of break-ins common to your area. If your local law enforcement agency doesn't offer such a service, call a company that installs security systems and ask for an estimate.

23. *Install a peekaboo.* Also known as door viewers, these devices allow you to see who's at the door before you open it. If you don't like what you see, don't open the door—and call the police if the undesirable does not vamoose.

24. *Say you mean business—with dead bolts.* Not many standard door locks are designed to resist the efforts of break-in artists, so dead bolts are a must. Call a local security company or locksmith about installing deadbolts—today.

25. *Let the police take the risks.* If you discover that someone has broken into your home and may still be there, don't take chances. "Get to a neighbor's house and call the police," Franks says. "We'll come and check out the place for you."

26. *Call, but don't hang up.* If you get trapped in the house while an intruder is still present, get to your phone (if you can), call the police and give them all the information they ask for. If the intruder prevents you from completing your call, don't hang up. The open line will allow authorities to trace your address and come to your aid.

27. *Don't be afraid to get out of there.* Better to let an intruder trash your house than terrorize you, Franks says. If you can make an exit, don't feel you're being a coward for doing so. And get in touch with the police as soon as possible.

28. *Hide if you have to.* If you're not able to leave, hide, Franks says, and phone the police as soon as the intruder leaves. If this doesn't work and he discovers you, do anything you can to escape. Break a window and yell "Fire!" Bittenbinder suggests. You have to get help into the house if you can't get out of the house, and this will sometimes do the trick.

WHEN IT'S A MATTER OF RAPE

There are no hard-and-fast rules for preventing rape because no two situations are the same, the experts agree. In most cases, rape is committed out of anger rather than sexual desire, so to resist could result in fatal consequences. That being the case, our experts offer these general guidelines.

29. *Do what you must to stay alive.* Don't fight your attacker. Your first concern should be your life, Franks and Bittenbinder agree. And a nonconfrontational response from you may even prompt an attacker to back off. Rape is an act of violence; the less you resist, the less satisfaction your assailant might feel.

30. *Don't be silenced by shame.* The real tragedy of rape is that shame often stops women from reporting an assault—and allows a rapist to continue terrorizing women. Be brave and retaliate fully by doing everything you can to see that your attacker pays for his crime. "If you are raped, the most important thing you can do—for yourself and for other women—is to report it as soon as possible," Franks says.

First, get to a safe place—even if it means pounding on a stranger's door. Then go to a hospital and call the police or your local rape crisis center. And don't shower prior to being examined; you could destroy evidence vital for your assailant's conviction as well as his capture. Remember: By doing everything you can to see that your attacker is apprehended, you'll not only vindicate yourself but help to protect countless other women as well.

—*Harriet A. Washington*

GET STREET-SMART

DON'T BE A VICTIM. CHECK OUT THIS GUIDE TO PERSONAL SAFETY AND CRIME PREVENTION.

The media have driven home the message that we can no longer feel safe on our streets. It's become commonplace to find cans of self-defense spray at the checkout counter of the local convenience store. And we've heard newscasters caution us to look under our cars at the mall parking lot before climbing in. There's a whiff of fear in the air that wasn't quite so noticeable before.

But don't let all the hoopla scare you. We're not helpless. Just as we practice prevention to safeguard our health, we can take measures to protect ourselves from violent crime. And these measures work.

Meet Chicago Detective J J Bittenbinder, a 23-year veteran of the Chicago police force and a top expert in crime prevention. He has come to our rescue. Bittenbinder, 51, often dresses in dapper three-piece suits with a gold watch fob. His handlebar mustache frames a megawatt smile as he jokes about his police exploits. But when the talk turns to violent crimes and criminals, he quickly turns stern. With his bearlike build, booming voice and in-your-face, no-nonsense manner, he cuts an imposing figure. And he wants to teach the public how to look as tough as he does. Traveling across the country, he teaches community groups, corporate employees and television audiences the elements of personal safety.

How can women prevent violent crimes from starting and empower themselves in dangerous situations?

To begin with, says Bittenbinder, it takes no special intelligence to commit a crime. He likens the criminal to a lion who hangs around the watering hole waiting for prey. The lion can sit and wait, looking over the other animals to see who looks vulnerable. Like the lion, a criminal has the element of surprise in his favor. You can even up your odds of avoiding attack by looking invulnerable and having a plan, he says.

Here are a few situations and scenarios you may find yourself in—and ways to better your chances of coming out a winner in every one of them.

ON THE STREETS

The streets become a lot less threatening if you carry yourself with confidence and take a few simple precautions. Body language says a lot. Most women avoid eye contact with men on the street as a defense against unwanted advances. But looking down at your feet or the sidewalk in front of you sends a signal that you're meek. Bittenbinder urges you to hold your chin up confidently and look over the man's head or off to one side. If you feel you must avert your eyes to watch where you're walking, wear dark sunglasses to conceal the direction of your gaze. Wear your glasses on a chain so they can't be knocked away from you easily. Bittenbinder prefers a chain to a cord, in case an attacker attempts to choke you. A chain breaks faster than a cord, he explains.

A criminal doesn't need a high IQ to know that a fanny pack is harder to rip off than a loosely held purse. But when you must carry a purse, wear it under your coat or sweater. Even wearing it slung diagonally across your chest with the flap turned toward your body is better than carrying a handbag or wearing a purse that hangs loosely off your shoulder and flaps behind you.

Just as animals display their defensive weapons by baring their teeth or unsheathing their claws, so people should display their weapons. Bittenbinder prefers the sprays that contain pepper (labeled OC for oleoresin capsicum) or sprays that are a combination of pepper and tear gas. (Both products are available from gun shops and hardware stores.) Some brands contain ultraviolet or red dye that the police can detect on an assailant's clothing. You can buy a lipstick-size can to hold in your hand when you walk on the street. Just holding the can may deter potential attackers.

If you use one of these sprays, it can incapacitate an assailant for as long as 20 minutes. Check with your local police department to determine if there are restrictions regarding the use of such sprays.

Say you're strolling along with a can of pepper spray, and someone accosts you anyway. How can you tell whether the guy who's asking you for directions or panhandling for change is going to hurt you? Bittenbinder replies bluntly, "You can't. The most common things we hear from the victims are, 'It happened so fast' and 'He was dressed so nicely.' " Trust your sixth sense to give you clues about your accoster's intentions. If you feel the hairs raise along the back of your neck, don't stick around to be polite, says Bittenbinder.

"When a stranger does ask for directions, don't let him get too close," he says. "That allows him to distract you while he makes a grab for you or your purse. If the stranger persists, look him in the eye and say in a loud, commanding voice, 'I said no. Leave me alone!' and keep walking."

You can cross the street diagonally and look over your shoulder directly at whoever's following you to let him know you're on red alert. Or walk down the center of the street, where streetlights cast the most light and you're more likely to be seen. You can also mingle with a group. If this stranger continues to follow you, you needn't let the level of harassment escalate any further. Break out that pepper spray.

Of course, if a mugger is armed or seems to be, you're better off giving him what he wants—at first. Bittenbinder suggests carrying a five-dollar bill wrapped around a couple of ones in a hefty money clip. If a mugger demands your money, toss the money clip away from you and run the other way.

Next, attract attention. Yell "Fire!" as you run. Fire poses more of a public threat and is more likely to invite involvement than a cry for help. Bittenbinder advocates personal-attack alarms as well. They can be clipped on a belt, purse or key chain and come with pins that you pull like a grenade to set off a piercing alarm. Whistles are less effective, he cautions, because they sound only as long as you blow, and if you have to run, your wind may not be strong enough to broadcast a loud set of tweets. (Alarms also are available at gun shops and hardware stores.)

Bittenbinder also recommends keeping strangers off guard by introducing an element of the unknown. Walking a dog puts you at an advantage for just that reason. Since a potential attacker doesn't know how the animal may react, he'd just as soon steer clear.

ON BUSES, TRAINS AND TAXIS

If you must wait at a lonely bus stop, use the element of surprise to fortify your tough-guy pose. Have something to say to a potential harasser. Bittenbinder gives the example of the woman who noticed a man approach her from behind as she waited for a bus. "Just as he drew up to her, she turned quickly around, looked him in the eye and said, 'Don't I know your mother?' He wasn't sure. All he could say was, 'Uh,' and walk away," says Bittenbinder.

Carry pocket change so you don't have to pull out your

wallet to pay your fare. The safest place to sit on a bus is up front, near the driver, or on a train, near the conductor. On a train or subway, pick a well-lit car with a lot of people.

Don't let a cab ride become an abduction. As you enter a taxi, note the cab company and the cabby's license number and let him know, in a subtle, nonthreatening way, that you've got his number. "You might say, 'Number 1220, that's my old address,'" Bittenbinder says, "or 'that sounds like a lucky number. I think I'll play that in tomorrow's lottery.'"

AT THE BANK OR CASH MACHINE

You don't need a police detective to tell you that banks make a prime hangout for muggers. Bittenbinder reminds us that bank slips are often color coded: one color for checking, one for savings and so on. Worse, slips are often located at the bank's entrance where they're visible to anyone who hangs around. Bittenbinder urges you to go to the back of the bank to choose a transaction slip and fill it out. You're less likely to be observed there. You could even take a supply home with you and have them already filled out by the time you get to the bank.

Be alert to the possibility of being accosted outside the bank. "I've seen cases where a thief takes an ice pick to a tire, follows the car till the tire goes flat, then kindly offers his assistance to change it," says Bittenbinder.

Avoid outdoor cash machines, Bittenbinder says. A thief can use binoculars or simply loiter nearby and read the numbers you key in as you conduct your transaction. Use cash machines where a guard is stationed or where a thief can't find enough privacy to corner you. Best of all are the drive-through cash machines.

ON THE ROAD

You're most vulnerable to attack when you're loading groceries into your car or strapping a child into a safety seat, says Bittenbinder. He suggests tipping a stock boy to carry your groceries and getting into the car quickly. Lock up before you strap a child in.

Bittenbinder advises women to buy cellular phones for safety. He suggests stashing your purse out of sight when driving. The best place to put one is under your knees, but you can also put it under the car seat or in the trunk. If there's no visible purse, you're less likely to be targeted by a smash-and-grab artist.

If you think you're being followed, pull into a convenience store or a gas station—anyplace where you can ask someone to call the police. If you see a police car, signal it by blinking your lights or honking your horn. Car disabled? "Use the windshield sunshade," says Bittenbinder. "Write 'Help! Call police' on the back of it and mount it in your rear window. Keep your car locked and stay inside it. Chances are a passerby will summon help."

Don't leave your car to exchange insurance information in the event of a fender bender. Keep the doors locked and roll down your window only a fraction of an inch. You don't have to hand over your identification card to a stranger; hold it up to the window and have the other party do the same. As Bittenbinder notes, "Only your voice has to pass through the window."

If someone threatens you and tries to get you out of your car, start the car, put it in gear and drive away. If your assailant is standing in front of the car, Bittenbinder recommends that you start slowly enough to give him a chance to get out of the way. Then go! Drive to the nearest police station or public place with a phone and plenty of people around.

WORST-CASE SCENARIOS

Suppose you've tried all these tips for looking your toughest, but somehow you're overpowered by a man who gets too close. And he has hold of your arm. Bittenbinder assures you that the jig is not yet up.

"Of course, your best option is always to flee. If someone has grabbed you by the coat, slip out of the coat, run away and start yelling. That goes for whatever clothing you're wearing, even your blouse. I don't care whose name is on the label, what it's made of or who gave it to you. No piece of clothing is worth being raped or murdered for.

"Women have far less upper-body strength than men. So if you can't get away, drop down on your butt and start kicking with piston thrusts, one leg at a time, while you holler. Your attacker will have to reach down to stop you, and that will set him off balance." Aim for the soft spots: Kick the guy in the groin, knees or ankles.

One of Bittenbinder's strongest warnings is: Never *ever* get into your attacker's car. Once you're in that car, your chances of survival drop dramatically.

Even if the guy is armed, the odds are in your favor if you run away, Bittenbinder says. Letting an armed man force you into a car only raises the likelihood that you'll face consequences worse than a gunshot wound, no matter what assurances the criminal gives you.

Assume that your assailant is lying. Don't listen; just run. This advice also goes anytime an attacker tries to take you to a "secondary crime scene"—someplace out of public view like a dark alley, a deserted street, the woods or a vacant lot. Don't ever let him take you there.

—Jan Bresnick

HOW TO FOIL PURSE SNATCHERS

MUGGERS, PICKPOCKETS AND THIEVES. THEY'RE IN EVERY CITY, ON EVERY STREET. THOUGH IT SEEMS WE DON'T OUTNUMBER THE SCOUNDRELS, WE CAN OUTWIT THEM.

It can happen to anyone at almost anytime: during dinner at a restaurant, waiting for a bus at the airport, sitting in a movie theater. And, unless you stop carrying a purse, there is no foolproof method for avoiding being ripped off. However, there are some steps you can take to help prevent a theft or to make the experience less painful and costly.

DAILY PRECAUTIONS

Take only the credit cards you intend to use that day. Also, carry cash, credit cards, your driver's license and keys in separate locations (purse, wallet, pockets), so even if someone grabs your wallet, for example, damage will be minimized.

Don't carry your entire checkbook. If it's ripped off, it will be difficult to remember what checks you have written and you also risk losing money to a check-writing thief. Carry one check with you instead of the whole book.

Don't write your personal identification number for your bank card anywhere. Memorize it. Many people foolishly list the number on the card itself or in their address book under automated teller machine or ATM.

Don't send the thief home. Never list your address or phone number on your key chain.

Get insurance. Check to see if your homeowner's insurance policy covers personal theft (away from home) and to what extent.

Register all your credit cards with a protection service. Try services, such as Safecard Services, 1-800-HOT-LINE, or Credit Card Service Bureau, 1-800-336-0220. For fees starting at $12, these services will report stolen cards and request new ones for you. Although by law you are liable for only the first $50 of unauthorized charges, that sum can quickly multiply if you have several credit cards.

Keep records. If you don't use a registry, keep two lists (at home and office) of your credit card account numbers, along with their emergency telephone numbers.

Don't carry social security cards unless absolutely necessary. They're annoying to replace and a clever thief could try to use your social security number as proof of identity to apply for credit or a job.

Use caution at ATMs. Don't use an isolated automatic teller machine with no other customers in sight.

Don't make it easy. Keep your wallet or cash in a zippered compartment in your purse. And buy a purse with a secure closing. Never put your purse on the bottom of a dressing room floor unless the room is totally enclosed. Likewise, never—even for a second—leave a dressing room with your purse inside. Be careful of purse hooks in ladies' rooms and dressing rooms. A thief can stick a hand over the door, grab the strap and be gone in seconds. And keep your purse locked in a drawer at work.

Be alert when traveling. You are three times more likely to be victimized while on the road. Beware of people who "accidentally" bump into you. The stranger who comes to your rescue may be a pickpocket.

WHAT TO DO IF YOU GET RIPPED OFF

Immediately call to cancel your credit cards. Watch out for charges made by the thief that appear on future statements. You must write the company within 60 days of receiving your bill to get your account credited.

To replace long-distance telephone credit cards, call your telephone company's toll-free number. You are generally not liable for calls made on your credit card by a thief.

Call the police. Reporting the theft to the police may seem like an exercise in futility, but do it anyway: You'll need a copy of the police report to file an insurance claim or deduct losses on your tax return.

If the thief gets your checkbook, close the entire account. If only one check has been stolen, arrange for a stop payment.

If the thief gets your keys and address, ask the police to escort you home. If this isn't possible, ask a locksmith to meet you outside your home as soon as possible. You might also call a neighbor and ask him to "guard" your home until you get there.

Request a new ATM card. Even if your code is not written anywhere, thieves have been known to figure it out since many people use their birthdates or a simple sequence (like 4, 3, 2, 1) as their codes. You are responsible for $50 of fraudulent use of your ATM card if you report the loss within two days; your liability can be as much as $500 if you do not report the lost ATM card until after the first two days.

Keep receipts for airline tickets. Airline tickets are difficult and troublesome to replace when stolen. Generally, you have to pay a $50 processing fee to replace the ticket (provided you have some proof of purchase), but if you have no receipt, you'll have to buy a brand new full-fare ticket. What does a thief do with your stolen ticket? He exchanges it for one on another airline or for cash, providing you paid cash for the ticket. If stolen tickets are not used within 90 days, the airline will generally re-fund your money.

You don't have to starve. If you are stranded and need emergency cash, you can get money in minutes. Have someone wire you money to either the nearest American Express or Western Union office.

—Debra Wishik Englander

THE STRIKING REALITIES OF SELF-DEFENSE

PROTECTING YOURSELF IS MORE THAN KICKING AND PUNCHING, AS MANY WOMEN HAVE LEARNED—THE HARD WAY.

All their lives, women are socialized to be submissive and passive. So it should come as no surprise that when they're at-tacked, as more than half of all women in this country are, most have no way of protecting themselves. Many turn to self-defense lessons—but find themselves worse off than before. That's because most self-defense courses don't teach women what they need to know.

Self-defense courses are usually taught by martial-arts experts. Unfortunately, most of them are not experts in rape defense. Women's self-defense requires knowledge about rape itself, an understanding of the socialization process of women, intensive assertiveness training and constant mental awareness—as well as proficiency in physical fighting techniques specifically geared to women.

FIRST: KNOWLEDGE

Women's self-defense should be taught by someone who has researched rape and relevant women's issues. It's important, for example, that your instructor know why sexual assault is such a common crime, why it is so underreported and what a woman should do if she gets raped or has been raped in the past.

If your teacher doesn't conduct frequent discussions on sexual assault throughout the course, if he does not distribute statistics and information about rape, rape myths, men who rape and legalities, find yourself another instructor. Self-defense is not all kicking and punching; it also involves a great deal of knowledge and awareness.

THEN: TRAINING

Assertiveness training is mandatory. Again, because of the way women have learned to cope with the world, many do not have the confidence it takes to stand up to an adversary. It's not enough simply to inform women of this fact. A course must teach you how to overcome any ingrained tendency to be too "nice" or submissive. Instructors should even help you practice looking confident and walking with long, athletic strides, head held high, expression alert and assured. Rapists will look elsewhere for a victim if you do not fit the type they are looking for.

GETTING LOUD

Rapists don't like noise. A victim has a good chance of escaping if she's screaming, hollering "Fire!" and so on. Many women who have escaped attackers have done so because they have struggled and made enough noise to scare them off. However, women often find it nearly impossible to make a lot of noise without first going through training. After a lifetime of being taught to be polite and quiet, they freeze and "choke" when they're attacked. Be aware that some instructors prefer their students to be silent, but women's self-defense requires the release of anger and fear that comes with shouting.

If an instructor tells you that women and men use the same techniques, find another course. You should be learning a variety of techniques chosen with women in mind—not a series of moves that were developed hundreds of years ago by men and *for* men. There's nothing sexist in saying that men tend to be physically stronger than women. They simply have greater muscle mass and are, as a rule, larger and heavier. Women need self-defense techniques that work for their smaller size and different types of strength. For example, complicated wrist locks are not the best techniques for women, but learning to fight with their strong legs is essential. Obviously, the more weapons you have, the better.

Another big difference between men and women is that women usually can't train as strenuously as men—at first. Requiring 25 push-ups from a female novice student is ridiculous if she doesn't do push-ups regularly. Yet many instructors will ask precisely that to start with. Again, these instructors have not researched women's special needs and disregard the fact that women have less upper-body strength than men. Twenty-five push-ups on the fist day might be tiring for a man: For a woman, it can damage muscles in the arms, chest and upper and lower back. Your instructor should help you get in shape gradually and safely.

GROUND FIGHTING

Women are usually raped while lying down. Amazingly, most instructors overlook this and teach their students almost all techniques from a standing position. As a result, even women with extensive martial-arts training get raped because they don't know what to do when they're knocked to the ground. You can, however, actually fight effectively from a lying-down position: Using your legs, you can kick your assailant's knees or head as he tries to pin you. Make sure your instructor teaches ground fighting and provides plenty of realistic practice.

Self-defense training should also include falling. Falling skills are important, both for walking on icy sidewalks and for getting pushed down by an attacker. Once safely on the ground, you can then use your ground-fighting techniques to fend off your attacker and your shouting skills to summon help or frighten him away. The most important thing to remember is not to land on your spine or let your head hit the ground. Also, try not to land on your shoulder or break your fall with your hands. Check with potential instructors to see if they have appropriate mats for practice.

In many schools, you'll be taught techniques that you can barely manage in class, a nonthreatening environment. In a real attack, however, your assailant will probably be shouting abusively and often shoving and slapping you repeatedly. Practice sessions should be as realistic as possible with the "attacker" using enough force to knock you off balance both verbally and physically. If you can't handle the abuse in a classroom, then you cannot be expected to deal with it during an actual attack. You should be given the opportunity to practice taking control and overcoming normal fright with the help of a supportive, experienced instructor.

THINKING AHEAD

To be fully prepared for an attack, you must constantly be aware of potential dangers. Think about your habits. Do you park in well-lit areas away from bushes? Do you check under your car as well as inside it before you reach the door? Are your keys in your hand or in that black hole you call your purse? Do you ask about men you date to see if they have a history of "using" or abusing women? Do you trust your instincts and run immediately for help if something feels "wrong?" Your instructor should encourage you to always listen to your instincts and find ways to improve your awareness. Most situations can be avoided if you are alert to the dangers around you.

Only 20 to 40 percent of all rapes are committed by strangers. This means that there is a good chance the victim is familiar with, and may trust, her assailant. After all, it's not easy for a woman, who has been encouraged all her life to be nice, to strike someone she knows.

In addition, many rapes, especially date or acquaintance rapes, involve not physical violence but, rather, psychological coercion, such as trickery, threats, guilt and so on. Add the fear of retaliation and you can see why most acquaintance rapes never reach the police station. Unfortunately, few martial-arts or self-defense instructors take these factors into account. Proper and thorough assertiveness training should help you prepare for these kinds of assaults.

Make sure you do your research when considering taking a

self-defense course. Ask questions and do not be fooled by glib words. Most instructors will try to reassure you so that you take their class. A good test might be whether the teacher is familiar with current rape statistics or if he insists on the students making lots of noise. Ask if the instructor has "trained muggers" who will attack you as realistically as possible. Find out everything you can about the class you intend to take, and don't hesitate to choose another if something about the one you attend feels wrong. Always trust your instincts.

—*Susan J. Grill*

PART FOUR

LOOKING
GOOD

FIVE BEAUTY RESOLUTIONS WORTH KEEPING

DO YOU WANT TO LOOK YOUNGER FOR THE REST OF YOUR LIFE? THEN HERE ARE SOME IMPORTANT RULES YOU CAN FOLLOW TO CREATE A MORE BEAUTIFUL YOU.

One of the reasons New Year resolutions bite the dust so often is that either they're not realistic—a surefire reason to lose interest and motivation—or they don't offer enough of a payback. So we asked five of the top beauty experts in the country what are the very top, realistic resolutions a woman can make to most enhance her looks. Here are their responses—resolutions you can follow the year round.

1. **Give extra care to special areas.** "Resolve to pamper the most vulnerable areas of your body—the eyes and neck," says Lia Schorr, owner of the Lia Schorr Skin Care Salon in New York City. The skin around your eyes is the most delicate on your body, and it's active all through the day— blinking, winking, scrunching and generally making wrinkles. "Your eye area in particular is tired at the end of the day," says Schorr. "Everyone looks older when they're tired and great when they're not. When we have a good night's sleep, we look like we've come from vacation because our eyes look rested.

"One of the first things to do at the end of the day is to refresh your eye area with a cool compress. I recommend, in summer, some ice in a washcloth, or in winter, some cool tap water on a washcloth or splashed on the face. To help eliminate the redness of irritated eyes, fill a clean bathroom sink with cool water, open your eyes and soak your whole face.

"To benefit the skin around your eyes, give yourself an eye-moisturizer treatment. For your basic eye moisturizer, use a gel during the day and a cream at night."

The neck is another area with very thin skin. "There is a

simple neck exercise I particularly like for fighting gravity," says Schorr. "Sit up and smile, opening your mouth wide. This exercises the neck and mouth. Do this a good 30 times."

A final bit of pampering advice: Give your eye and neck areas a real treat with a moisturizing mask whenever you think about it. Make sure you go to sleep with no makeup on. And when you do your cleansing, be gentle.

2. Get hair you can live with. "Resolve to have a good haircut you can manage on a daily basis and resolve to keep your hair trimmed so it is constantly manageable and healthy," says Kenneth Battelle, master stylist at Kenneth's Salon in New York City.

There are two basic elements you should consider when deciding how you want to wear your hair. One is to choose a style that can be kept up with your hair's characteristics. The second is to realistically evaluate how much time you're willing to devote to daily hairstyling.

A hairstyle that's carefree for someone with thick, naturally curly hair might not be carefree for someone whose hair is fine and straight—and vice versa. Your stylist can help you choose a style that works for you—but you have to be honest with yourself about how much work you want to put into your hairstyle every morning.

Even the most perfect cut grows out and doesn't behave the same way after a few weeks. A trim of just a half inch can renew the style and keep your hair manageable.

3. Accentuate the positive. For a resolution that can improve your total image, we went to the prestigious Ford modeling agency in New York City, where enhancing women's beauty has been developed to an art form. We were a little surprised at the response. "My gut reaction to that question is, 'Learn to love yourself,' " says Mary Theresa Zazzera, director of special markets for Ford.

Zazzera's voice bubbles with enthusiasm and energy as she explains, "We spend too much time dwelling on the negatives in our lives or our appearance. We all have something special—beautiful, if you will—about us. The trick is to take the time to discover yours and then nurture it."

4. Shield yourself from sun damage. "Resolve to wear sunscreen every time you go out. It's the single most important commitment you can make for your skin's appearance and for its health," says *Prevention* advisor Nicholas J. Lowe, M.D., clinical professor of dermatology at University of California, Los Angeles, UCLA School of Medicine.

We'd like to assume you're already doing this, but just in case you're not, make it your number-one beauty priority. It's much harder to correct sun damage than to avoid it.

If it's been a question of forgetting to do it, buy a moisturizer with the sunscreen already in the formula, and don't forget to apply it half an hour before you go out.

5. Make posture a priority. Resolve to assess and improve your posture. "Posture is extremely important, in terms of both appearance and self-confidence," says Rebecca Gorrell, fitness director of Canyon Ranch Spa in the Berkshires in Western Massachusetts. "If you have good posture and proper alignment, your body language says to others that you are a confident person."

Poor posture can cause people to label you as lacking in energy or self-esteem. If, however, you carry yourself with your head up, shoulders relaxed, chest lifted and open, people view you in a more positive way.

Poor posture also makes you look just plain older. "If you saw Marcel Marceau, the famous mime, portray an aged person, you know that he does it just by changing his posture. He bends his knees, collapses the chest area and rounds his shoulders," Gorrell says. You can create the opposite impression of youth and vigor by improving your posture.

"To help my clients remember to check their posture, I ask them each to choose a cue that triggers their memory—something that happens maybe three or four times a day," says Gorrell. "It could be the phone ringing or the baby crying, but use that as a cue to assess your posture before you react to the stimulus.

"One simple exercise to stretch your chest and counteract the slump you get sitting at a desk: Clasp your hands behind your back or behind the back of your chair, lift your chest and pull your shoulder blades together."

—*Pamela Boyer*

THE NEW
SKIN PRESCRIPTION

**ALPHA HYDROXY ACIDS ARE BEING TOUTED AS
TODAY'S SECRET TO ETERNAL YOUTH.
HERE'S HOW TO TELL WHETHER THEY ACTUALLY
HELP STOP THE RAVAGES OF AGING—OR
WHETHER THEY'RE ALL HYPE.**

Marketing mavens are having a field day. They're hailing alpha hydroxy acids (AHAs) as a veritable beauty miracle in a bottle, enticing consumers with promises of wrinkle removal and even age reversal. Who could ask for a better sell—or a more appealing product?

They might sound more like a furniture stripper than a skin enhancer, but AHAs are nontoxic and all-natural. Made from sugar cane (glycolic acid), oranges and grapefruits (citric acid), apples (malic acid), milk (lactic acid) and grapes (tartaric acid), AHAs applied regularly to the skin alone or with moisturizers are said to enhance your skin's appearance by uncovering new cells and freeing the skin of imperfections such as scars, sunspots, fine wrinkles and even moles. Do they sell? Yes. Do they work? That depends on what you expect them to do. So it's important that you know the risks of AHA use—and have a realistic sense of its rewards—before you race to the mall to stock your medicine chest. Here's the real scoop.

AT FACE VALUE

While the hype surrounding AHAs is fairly new, dermatologists have been using these so-called age erasers in very strong concentrations for more than 20 years. The average over-the-counter product enhanced with AHAs is 2 to 8 percent fruit acid, but skin-care professionals have long used AHAs in concentrations of 50 to 70 percent as skin-peeling agents for treating acne, sun-damaged skin and precancerous lesions. Slightly milder concentrations of 30 to 50 percent acid are used to treat eczema, psoriasis and other skin disorders.

What is it about AHAs that performs such cosmetic wizardry? Experts say it's their unique molecular structure, which enables AHAs to break down old skin cells, allowing new cells to emerge. "The acids prevent dead skin cells from holding together," says Howard Murad, M.D., assistant clinical professor of dermatology at the UCLA Medical Center and director of Murad Skin Research Laboratories. "And when you get rid of old skin cells, you smooth the skin's surface and improve its appearance."

When you're in your twenties, dry, flaky cells slough from your skin's surface about every 28 days, a process speedy enough to keep your skin looking vibrant and healthy. But factors such as aging and sun damage leech moisture from the skin and cause cell renewal to occur less frequently—every 35 to 40 days, which is a tad too slow. As a result, by the time you reach your thirties or forties, wrinkles and dry, flaky skin seem unavoidable.

Enter AHAs. They speed up the process of skin renewal. After using AHAs daily for several weeks, your skin should feel smoother and appear more evenly toned—regardless of your age. Your pores may appear smaller and you may see an improvement in clarity, meaning your skin texture will seem more consistent. And this is just the beginning.

After six to eight months, some fine wrinkles may disappear, and sun spots and freckles may fade, says Karen Landau, M.D., a New York City dermatologist. In addition, some experts contend, AHAs may help regenerate collagen, the ingredient in the skin that helps it retain its elasticity and prevents it from sagging.

Others say AHAs mixed with certain vitamins may fend off free radicals—destructive chemicals that damage cells and may contribute to signs of aging. Free radicals form as a result of oxidative damage to the body from exposure to sunlight and air pollutants. Vitamins A, C and E are antioxidants—substances that control the damage caused by free radicals. And AHAs contain citric acid, which, in turn, contains vitamin C. "We know that vitamin C is helpful when taken internally," says Dr. Murad. "But we're learning that it's helpful when applied topically, too. It acts as a free-radical scavenger and may help to regenerate the skin's surface."

A BEAUTY BONANZA?

The claims are gargantuan—but what about the benefits? Many dermatologists warn that they're limited. As Dr. Murad points out, "AHAs aren't a face-lift in a jar."

"They can't do anything for big lines, such as wrinkles on the forehead or around the mouth," says Kevin Welch, M.D., assistant professor of dermatology at the University of Arizona Health Sciences Center in Tucson. "And they won't reverse sun damage if you're not using a sunscreen as well."

In addition, as competition heats up among manufacturers of AHAs, doctors warn that some companies are adding unnecessary ingredients to their products for marketing purposes or to pump up their prices. "Manufacturers have begun to make a bouquet out of AHAs, adding everything they can think of—a little collagen, some elastin, a dash of herb juice, something from China or Switzerland and an antioxidant," says Albert Kligman, M.D., professor of dermatology at the University of Pennsylvania in Philadelphia and an expert on skin and aging who is renowned for his discovery of Retin-A. "The whole thing reminds me of the early 1900s, when people were selling snake oil."

But AHAs appear to have the potential to be more dangerous than snake oil. Because they're sold as cosmetics (as opposed to drugs), AHA products are virtually unregulated—that is, there are very few restrictions on the types and amounts of ingredients that can be used in them, and manufacturers aren't required to prove to the Food and Drug Administration (FDA) that their products are safe. Consequently, more and more companies are raising the level of fruit acids in their products to 10, 15, even 20 percent, says Dr. Kligman. "These levels could damage the skin if used without a doctor's supervision," he warns. "In fact, not every skin type is well-suited to AHA use—sensitive skin, in particular, may suffer adverse effects."

And the FDA has taken note. It recently began a two-pronged investigation to determine whether over-the-counter AHAs are being dispensed safely (in other words, whether they should have to meet the FDA's stringent drug requirements) and to define the effects of long-term use of mild and potent concentrations of AHAs. The FDA expects to reveal its findings and recommendations regarding AHAs later this year.

What does all this mean for you? "We still don't know whether long-term use of AHAs will result in scarring because you're taking off layers of the skin that were meant to be there," says John Bailey, Ph.D., director of Cosmetics and Colors for the FDA. "So until the FDA can get a handle on this, you should simply approach AHAs with more caution than you would most other cosmetics that have a longer history of safe use."

Despite the fact that some questions about AHAs remain unanswered, however, most experts seem to think there's no immediate cause for alarm—simply carefulness. Dr. Landau offers the following guidelines for using AHAs wisely.

Ask your dermatologist about using AHAs before you plunk down your money. If you have very sensitive skin, she may suggest that you avoid AHAs altogether.

Choose a product that contains a relatively low level of AHAs (2 to 5 percent) to start with. If you don't develop an adverse reaction (such as burning, stinging or peeling) after a few weeks of use, you can assume it is safe to move up to a higher percentage.

Do a patch test. Before you slather on the goods, apply a small amount to your arm or just under your chin. A mild tingling sensation is normal; redness, stinging and burning aren't. Discontinue use and see a dermatologist if you experience the latter.

Apply AHAs only every other day for the first two weeks of use. If you have no adverse reaction, you can apply AHAs daily, or twice daily at most.

Avoid facial scrubs, alcohol-based astringents and coarse washcloths. They can irritate AHA-treated skin. Use mild soap to cleanse your skin instead.

Use a sunscreen daily. Newly exfoliated skin (skin that has had its dead skin cells removed) is very susceptible to sunburn. Protect it accordingly.

Apply a moisturizer daily if the AHA-enhanced product you choose doesn't contain a moisturizer. Most products will indicate the contents on the package.

—*Maureen Connolly*

TOUGH LOVE FOR YOUR SKIN

COMPLEXION BLAHS GOT YOU DOWN? BUFF YOUR WAY TO A BABY-SOFT, MORE YOUTHFUL LOOK.

If a fresher complexion sounds appealing, exfoliation (removing dead skin cells) may be just the thing for you. When used properly, it's a terrific, freshening beauty treatment. Unfortunately, on the wrong complexion or in the wrong hands, it can be a disaster. Here are the basics.

EXFOLIATION EXPLAINED

As your skin matures, the turnover of epidermal (upper layer) cells slows down. Because the dead skin cells cling together to the surface instead of being pushed off, your complexion may appear dull and pallid, with a rough texture.

"Basically, by exfoliating properly, you can increase the epidermal-cell turnover and therefore make your skin look smoother again, and pinker, and generally improve its appearance," says Diana Bihova, M.D., clinical assistant professor of dermatology at New York University Medical Center in New York City. Exfoliating not only removes the dead cells that make your complexion look ashen and uneven, it also helps stimulate the production of young epidermal cells.

The first of the two types of exfoliants are the mechanical ones—those that work by abrading the skin. Washcloths, sea sponges, exfoliation sponges (such as Buf-Pufs), loofahs, pumice stones, cleansing grains and scrubs fall into this category. But not all tools for mechanical exfoliation are created equal. "The principle behind a face cloth and a loofah is the same. What can be very different is the degree of exfoliation," says Dr. Bihova. "This we control not only by what we use but also by how we use it."

In the other broad category are the nonmechanical exfoliants, which run the gamut from cosmetic masks that work only on the skin surface cells to Retin-A and chemical exfoliants (such as the alpha hydroxy acids). Depending on the concentration used and the amount of time on the skin, these can penetrate to the living tissue. Chemical exfoliants should be used only under a dermatologist's supervision.

Both mechanical exfoliating tools and masks can be used effectively at home if you have the right type of skin and follow directions carefully.

THE MECHANICAL WAY

Mechanical exfoliants work by stimulating the skin. This can be rough—in fact, too rough if you have very sensitive skin. "People whose skin is extremely sensitive or people who are prone to broken blood vessels would harm themselves more than they would benefit," says Dr. Bihova. "These people usually tend to have fair, thin skin. If you touch that skin, it reddens. To give you an example of what can happen, a woman came to me with hemorrhages on both cheeks. They were a result of rubbing too hard and too long with a washcloth. This is normally a gentle exfoliation tool. But the best things in life can become the worst if you use them excessively." The moral here is, if it hurts, stop.

People with acne should probably not use mechanical exfoliants, either. If you have whiteheads or closed comedones (blemishes that are below the surface), they have no way out when you apply pressure or stimulate those areas by rubbing them. As a result, they can rupture inside the skin, leading to more inflammatory acne.

Exfoliation works best for people with healthy, normal or dry complexions. It can also be great for people who have dull, sun-damaged skin or skin with a tendency to form blackheads. Even thin skin can benefit from the milder exfoliants, as long as there are no broken blood vessels.

If you've had acne but are now acne-free, mild exfoliating can help keep the pores unclogged and actually help keep your complexion healthy.

"It's a very delicate line between exfoliating and seeing the benefit, and exfoliating and harming yourself," says Dr. Bihova.

NONMECHANICAL PLOYS

Among the nonmechanical exfoliants, masks never work deeper than the dead, superficial layer of your skin, and chemical peels can vary in strength according to the chemical used and its concentration. Chemical peels should be used only under a qualified doctor's supervision.

Today, light chemical peels are a "hot" treatment at many facial salons. These treatments, however, can be far stronger than store-bought treatments. Because of this, the Food and Drug Administration is currently looking at them to determine whether these peels should be done only in a doctor's office.

Masks are cosmetic products and are made in different formulas, including clay and botanicals, that provide a suitable mask for every skin type.

EXFOLIATING BASICS

Let your skin be your guide. "Generally, you can't exfoliate the same way all year round," says Dr. Bihova. "The skin changes depending on the season, the temperature and so forth, and you must change your routine to meet your skin's needs. In the summer, for instance, skin has more moisture, while in the wintertime your skin is drier, and you won't want to use your exfoliant of choice as often."

Restrain yourself. "The main problems that I have seen have occurred in women whose attitude was that, 'if a little is good, a lot will be even better.' This is definitely not the case with exfoliants," says Dr. Bihova. Generally speaking, the mildest exfoliants are the sea sponge, the face cloth and cosmetic masks labeled for dry or sensitive skin.

A complexion brush along with some moisturizer can work well to exfoliate if you use the brush gently in circular movements. (Please, don't use occlusive or heavy moisturizers—they'll clog your pores.)

For normal to thick skin, sea sponges or exfoliation sponges (especially the mildest ones) can be used effectively to exfoliate. Treat yourself no more than three times a week and in the winter once a week, for two to three minutes.

BODY EXFOLIATION

Body exfoliation is acceptable for everyone. Just avoid rubbing any area where you have inflammatory acne. Backs, shoulders and chests, as well as your face, can be affected by blemishes, and the result of rubbing would be the same.

"Exfoliation is especially great for knees and elbows, because when you then apply your moisturizer right away, you've created an ideal situation for the moisturizer to penetrate," says Dr. Bihova.

Self-tanners also give a much more even coverage when applied to exfoliated skin. If you shave your legs, you don't have to worry about exfoliating them. The razor does it for you.

—*Pamela Boyer*

HOW TO CHOOSE THE PERFECT MOISTURIZER

HERE'S EXPERT ADVICE ON PICKING THE IDEAL PRODUCT FOR PERFECT SKIN.

Confronted by scores of bottles, jars and tubes of moisturizers that range in price from a few bucks to $75, what's a quality-conscious consumer to do?

"In our years of experience, women have a very strong and accurate feeling for what type of skin they have," says Sven Thormahlen, Ph.D., cosmetic chemist and director of product development at Beiersdorf, an international skin-care company. Where women need help is in understanding what individual moisturizers will deliver and how. And that help is at hand.

FINDING AN EDUCATED SALESPERSON

Many stores and companies send their sales staffs to dermatology seminars and lectures about skin care. A salesperson's advice is especially valuable at drugstores or chain stores where she's received training in several different lines rather than just one specific cosmetics company that pays her a commission.

How knowledgeable is your salesperson? To find out, be prepared to ask questions based on your knowledge of your own skin. The best salesperson will ask for more information, such as why you think your skin is sensitive or what your past experience with cosmetics has been.

If the salesperson is not answering your questions directly, ask the head of the department to help you. If there's no one more experienced, try a different store.

PREVENTING PROBLEMS

The right moisturizer does more than prevent dryness. It also does its work without causing you to break out. Many people who've had a problem before immediately assume that the product was too rich. "Texture may be the culprit, but you could also have skin that is sensitive to specific cosmetic chemicals," says Dr. Thormahlen. "Total prediction of safety is impossible, unless you know which ingredient or chemical caused the problem in the first place." Think back to the product that made you break out. Did it contain a sunscreen? A fragrance? Was it a thicker or a lighter product? Whatever your problem was, your salesperson can recommend a product that offers the same benefits without the drawbacks.

If you've had a problem with other moisturizers, test a moisturizer first—before buying. To test a moisturizer, apply it to an area—like your throat—that you won't be washing off right away. Walk around for a while. How does your skin feel? Do you like the fragrance? Have you experienced any itching? If there's something you don't like about it, don't buy it no matter how highly recommended it is.

There's one final point to remember when choosing a product. Moisturizers don't come with a "use by" date. While these products are quite heat-stable, they can lose effectiveness if stored for too long. Shopping somewhere that has a good turnover helps ensure moisturizers' freshness. At most department and chain stores, the cosmetics company automatically changes the stock. But this may not be the case at off-price or deep-discount stores that don't buy directly from the manufacturer.

GETTING WHAT YOU PAY FOR

You can spend from $5 to $75 on a moisturizer. But what are you getting for that extra $70? "One thing you can get is more expensive raw materials," says Gary Grove, Ph.D., skin physiologist and vice president of research and development at the Skin Study Center in Philadelphia. "The manufacturer has more room to play in the $75 moisturizer." The question should be: Are those expensive ingredients actually doing anything special?

Unfortunately, there are no easy answers. In some cases, there isn't much difference. In other cases, there are differences. "Some of the newer moisturizers cost more, and they do perform better, particularly in terms of lasting effect," says Dr. Grove. "There are now better humectants—ingredients that help the water stay with the skin longer and keep it soft and supple—and some of those humectants are expensive. Two specific examples are hyaluronic acid and ceramides, which are excellent moisturizing ingredients but add significantly to the price. And then there are the outrageous prices of products, the performance of which are not justified by any objective research. A lot of that price is due to packaging and advertising."

When shopping for moisturizers, you may want to look for similar ingredients and try the lower-priced product first.

Looking at the flip side of the question, can a product that costs just a fraction of another possibly do as good a job? For many people the answer is yes. "The lower-priced products are fine for many people. They simply use more basic ingredients," says Dr. Thormahlen. "The humectant glycerin, for instance, is a highly effective ingredient and not overly expensive. In the cost-effectiveness ratio, it's hard to beat.

"In our products, there is a lanolin alcohol that is a good emollient (an ingredient that moisturizes by acting as a barrier to trap the skin's moisture) blend that mimics the skin's own lipids. Petrolatum is another reasonably priced high-performance emollient, although a lot of women don't really find it cosmetically acceptable because of its consistency," says Dr. Thormahlen.

—*Pamela Boyer*

THE REAL SECRETS OF YOUNGER-LOOKING SKIN

TOP DERMATOLOGISTS AND AESTHETICIANS SHARE THEIR BEST ANTI-AGING ADVICE.

There's no use mourning the skin you had when you were 20. Instead, use our experts' knowledge to help your skin regain the attributes of youth—or at least look as though it had.

Nix the rubbing. There are a number of things that women do to their skin that makes it look older. "A prime example is that a lot of women rub their skin when cleansing—perhaps because they want to get that last trace of makeup off," says Ronald Sherman, M.D., senior clinical instructor in dermatology at Mount Sinai Medical Center in New York City. "But such roughness can be aging and plain damaging to your complexion, eventually aggravating a crepelike look of the skin. You should always blot—not rub—your facial skin dry."

A particular danger area for too-harsh treatment is around the eyes and eyelids. "With the colder weather especially, we see an increase in cases of red, irritated lids," says Dr. Sherman. The right way to clean this area is to "just take a damp cotton ball, put a gentle, emollient cleanser on it—the cleanser doesn't even have to be specific for the eyes. Then very gently swoosh it off and blot."

Go easy on astringents. Another "skin ager" is the overuse of astringents. "First of all, only women with oily skin should use an astringent," says Dr. Sherman. "It is not a good way to help normal skin exfoliate. If you do use it, don't take your cotton pad and go over your face until the cotton pad is clean. That's overdoing it—it just irritates the skin and removes the protective layer that helps to keep the water in the skin. If you remove that, you end up with dry, irritated skin. Just go over it lightly."

Exfoliate. Of all the things a dermatologist can do to help keep your skin looking young, one of the most effective and least invasive is the glycolic acid treatment, which results in a microscopic peeling of the skin. This works quite well to improve the whole texture of the skin, to even out skin discoloration and to make the skin look fresher. This type of peel also helps minimize some of the fine lines.

Glycolic acid is a member of the alpha-hydroxy or fruit-acid family. "A glycolic-acid peel is usually done in a series of four peels at weekly to monthly intervals. After that, you need a treatment only once every several months," says Nicholas J. Lowe, M.D., clinical professor of dermatology at University of California, Los Angeles, UCLA School of Medicine.

"Because this is such a controlled peel, it works for all skin types. In fact, it's such a light peel you can go out to dinner the same evening you have a treatment," says Dr. Sherman.

Color yourself youthful. As you age, your complexion pales, so adding color to your face makes it appear younger. Using blush adds color and can also give a youthful uplift to your face—it all depends on where you actually apply it.

"The blush is darker than your foundation or skin tone; therefore, it has a shading effect," says Leonard Engelman, a well-known Hollywood makeup artist and president of TaUT Cosmetics and Skin Care. "If we go to the concept of highlight and shadow, a highlight reflects light and brings things forward. A shadow absorbs light and sets things back. Too often, women put the blush on the apple of the cheek or the cheekbone, which really flattens the face, taking away some of the contour. What we want to do is emphasize the cheekbones.

"What I recommend is putting the majority of your blush directly beneath the cheekbone," says Engelman. "And a little bit up in the temple area. This highlights the cheekbones in an upward movement. With age, everything starts to be pulled down by gravity, so the last thing we ever want to do is use a downward movement on the face. By emphasizing the cheeks in an upward movement, we're giving an upward lift to the face.

"Cream blushes are much better for a person with large pores—something else that frequently accompanies aging. With a dry, soft blush, you end up rimming the pores with color as the brush skims over them. With a cream, you're covering the sides as well. The same holds true of wrinkles and any other complexion irregularities. Powders just hit the top and outline the higher points."

Use a concealer. Age (and sun exposure) can darken skin discolorations, which may be remedied by a concealer, one of our favorite look-your-best tools. There are specific attributes that the best concealers share. "A concealer shouldn't be oily because then it pools in any facial lines you may have," says Leonard. "Also, it shouldn't be heavy, or you exchange discoloration for cracks and a crepelike appearance. It shouldn't be dry, either, so that you're pulling on the skin when you apply it. It should have a great deal of pigment so that it can go on very thin and still cover your own skin tone."

Concealers should do just that—even out your skin tone and conceal discolorations. Choose the shade closest to your own. Using a shade much lighter than your skin is a leftover beauty habit from 30 years ago. Establish a regimen. "One of the main things you want to keep is the appearance of elasticity that's a hallmark of youthful skin," says Leonard. "That can come, to a certain degree, from good eating habits (avoiding putting on excess weight, watching your alcohol consumption), exercise and, of course, not smoking. But a big part of your strategy should be a consistent skin-care regimen.

"I've seen for myself that an appropriate regimen—cleansing, toning and moisturizing—can diminish lines and puffiness and make a huge difference. In general, women seem to understand the importance of a moisturizer. But cleansing is as important as any other part of your regimen, especially in today's environment. Getting your skin clean without stripping it is an integral part of a skin-care system to keep your skin looking young. If your current program takes so long that you sometimes skip it, find a system that's going to work into your time schedule."

Be sun smart. The most important age accelerator that we can control is exposure to the sun's damaging UVA and UVB rays. "The biggest step to younger-looking skin is to control how much time you spend in the sun and to protect yourself with sunscreen while you're outside," says Dr. Sherman. "If your skin is dry, you can use a moisturizing sunscreen. If your skin is oily, you want a sunscreen in an alcohol base. Also, going on the better-safe-than-sorry theory, it's wise to reapply a sunscreen frequently if you're on the beach or active enough to work up a sweat."

The sun also promotes wrinkles in another way. If you're outside on a bright day, chances are you'll be squinting. This repeated action eventually can cause crow's-feet, which can rob your eyes of a youthful appearance. "Wear sunglasses to prevent wrinkles in the delicate eye area," says Dr. Sherman, "and don't forget to apply your sunscreen to that area, too."

—*Pamela Boyer*

DERMATOLOGIST, PEEL THYSELF

WHAT A DERMATOLOGIST PUTS ON HER SKIN IS MORE THAN A FASHION STATEMENT— IT'S A PRESCRIPTION.

Perfect skin, as much a genetic curiosity as a reed-slim body or a talent for quantum mechanics, is that enviable state of grace that prevails despite a supermodel's bad habits or an anchorwoman's jet lag. But between the preternaturally fresh-faced and the rest of us are some 2,000 women for whom great-looking skin is as vital to their careers as the medical degrees that hang on their walls: dermatologists.

It's tough to find a cardiologist who would admit to a smoking habit or a complete aversion to exercise. Similarly, we expect a dermatologist's skin to reflect her expertise. Our expectations rise when the doctor is a woman: While a male dermatologist with genuinely awful skin might lose business, in many ways a woman dermatologist's face is her fortune. "You are the standard," says Carla Herriford, M.D., co-director of the Institute for Aesthetic and Cosmetic Dermatology in Los Angeles. "My patients marvel at how great my skin looks, but if it didn't, they wouldn't be in my office."

Still, being a female dermatologist has its advantages—particularly in a world where women receive endless media messages urging them to try something new.

"Experimenting is not always a good idea," says Ellen Gendler, M.D., an associate professor of dermatology at New York University in New York City. She solves the problem for her patients by trying everything herself. "I give my patients lists of products I think are good—suncreens, foundations, everything," she says. "I spend thousands of dollars a year trying products. It's an edge I enjoy over my male colleagues—I can actually sample the stuff."

The information is there for the asking at NYU's new Center for Skin Health and Appearance, where Dr. Gendler is the director. "We look for sun damage, counsel patients on products (we don't sell any) and alternatives like plastic surgery and cosmetic dentistry," she explains. "It's sort of one-stop shopping for the skin."

Assuming that these women weren't all born with perfect complexions, we polled dermatology's top female names for a look at the skin-care routines of women who have seen—and in most instances, tried—it all.

THE IMPORTANCE OF CLEANSING

Cetaphil, fragrance-free Dove, Basis and other noncomedogenic cleansers are the hands-down favorites of the dermatologists interviewed here. (Noncomedogenic cleansers help discourage blackheads.) Dr. Gendler swears by Oil of Olay's Foaming Face Wash; Dr. Herriford cleanses with Neutrogena.

Even those dermatologists who have their own skin-care lines keep cleanser formulas simple and mild. "You don't want to remove too much oil," says Adrianna Scheibner, M.D., a laser dermatology specialist in Beverly Hills. "Oily skin will rebound and produce even more oil if you strip too much away." Dr. Scheibner doesn't even wash her face in the morning: "It's not dirty—why bother it? I splash on some water and that's it." People of color should be especially wary of too much scrubbing, Dr. Herriford points out. "I'll occasionally use a gentle Buf-Puf, but only if I have no blemishes," she says. "Abrading blemishes can discolor black skin."

SUNSCREEN IS BASIC

Predictably, every dermatologist laces her skin-care routine with suncreen. "I was like any other teenager—I had my bottle of baby oil. But my first dermatology rotation was my last day in the sun," says Deborah Sarnoff, M.D., assistant clinical professor at New York University's Ronald O. Perelman Department of Dermatology.

She offers a more personal example to her patients: "Compare the underside of your breast with the skin on your face. That's sun damage." Her colleagues agree unanimously; most of them got out of the sun long before the actual clinical evidence was in.

Dr. Gendler notes that smoking can also ravage skin: "The first thing I noticed when I started my practice was how old and awful the smokers' skin looked."

Though these doctors are typically indoors most of the day, a morning slathering of SPF 15 (sun protection factor) is the norm. "I'm neurotic about the sun," Dr. Gendler says. "You don't use a condom 'every once in while'; you don't get 'only one' sunburn." Black skin isn't exempt, says Dr. Herriford; "With sunblock, people of color can practically halt the aging process. We'll look young forever!" Rainy days are no excuse either, says Patricia Wexler, M.D., a dermatologist who is on the teaching staff of New York's Beth Israel Medical Center and a fair-skinned redhead. "I make a daily ritual of it."

For sports and days spent outdoors, most dermatologists up the ante. SPFs go higher, and hats and long sleeves come out. "I wear hats—with big 18-inch brims—most of the time. I've incorporated them into my sense of style," says Wilma Bergfeld, M.D., head of clinical research at the Cleveland Clinic Foundation and former president of the American Academy of Dermatology. D'Anne Kleinsmith, M.D., a dermatologist with the Beaumont Hospital in Royal Oaks, Michigan, notes that most people don't put on enough suncreen to get the SPF prescribed on the label. "If I'm golfing, I put on a higher SPF, in a waterproof formula, just to be sure," she says. Karen E. Burke, M.D., Ph.D., attending physician at Cabrini Medical Center in New York City, also increases SPF for sunny days, but never above a 30; she says preservatives in super-strength sunscreens can irritate the skin.

THE LOWDOWN ON MOISTURIZER

Since oil, not dryness, troubles skin most, many dermatologists don't use lots of moisturizer—unless it's a combination product that offers other benefits, like fragrance, sunscreen or antioxidants. Dr. Wexler uses Donna Karan's lightly scented Cashmere Body Lotion after a shower, and Dr. Kleinsmith likes SPF 15 lotions from Neutrogena, Purpose and Oil of Olay. Dr. Bergfeld applies moisturizer only around her eyes and mouth; Dr. Scheibner mixes hers with a 5 percent lactic acid solution to speed up exfoliation.

THEY PASS THE ACID TEST

The media's current darling, alpha hydroxy acids have been around much longer than their recent celebrity would indicate; dermatologists have been using them for years. Many doctors incorporate an acid in concentrations of 8 and 10 percent into their nighttime routine.

A skeptic until just this year, Dr. Sarnoff accompanied her husband, a plastic surgeon, to a seminar given by BioMedic (a company that distributes alpha hydroxy products for in-office lunch-hour "mini-peels" as well as for at-home use by patients). "I took the products home and loved them," she says. "Glycolic acids can get rid of little keratoses that are beginning to develop and make the skin more uniform in color and texture. I see it as preventive maintenance." (Keratoses are age spots.)

Because alpha hydroxy products on the market vary widely, Dr. Scheibner has developed her own, a 5 percent lactic acid cream. "It's the vehicle you put it in. I have six humectants and lots of antioxidants—every ingredient in there does something—and it's all nonoily." Year-round, Dr. Wexler rubs a prescription alpha hydroxy acid lotion, Lac-Hydrin 12 percent, on her feet after she comes out of the shower. "It keeps them from getting cracked."

OPINIONS ON MAKEUP VARY

Dermatologists differ strenuously on the subject of color cosmetics in general and foundation in particular. Some, like Dr. Bergfeld, love makeup.

"I started out very fresh and wholesome, but now I'm glamorous," she says. "If you can't have youth, have glamour." For her, glamour consists of concealer, eyeliner, lip liner, lipstick and—for special occasions—foundation.

Foundation is fine with Dr. Herriford, as long as it's oil-free. "Finding the proper color is a real challenge for people of color," she notes. "I have my own formula, but I also like Prescriptives because they'll custom blend it for you."

Dr. Scheibner believes that foundation and powder soak up moisture, producing an oily rebound, so she uses them sparingly.

Surprisingly, the beauty secret of several doctors is a flesh-tone antibacterial medication, Sulfacet-R, sold by prescription and worn in place of foundation. "I'll use a thin coat of Sulfacet if I need it," says Dr. Sarnoff. "A heavily made-up face turns patients off—and causes skin problems." A dusting of Elizabeth Arden's powder blush and the models' favorite, Maybelline Great Lash mascara, finishes the clear-face look.

Dr. Burke uses Sulfacet, too. "When you're over 40, foundation just catches in wrinkles and makes you look older. It can also clog your pores and cause little pimples," she says. "I use powder—Noxema or Cover Girl—and dry blush, but no foundation."

Dr. Kleinsmith sees foundation as a way to up her sun protection: "I'll put on SPF 15 and a base or tinted moisturizer with a SPF of 8."

Dr. Gendler likes Clinique's new Sensitive Skin Makeup, which has a sunscreen built in. In the summer, she uses Ultima II's Sun Sexxxy Liquid Bronzer as well. "That way," she says, "I look healthy without sacrificing my skin."

BEYOND THE ROUTINE: MEDICAL TREATMENTS

Dermatologists offer their patients a number of more serious treatments, ranging from collagen and acne-cyst injections to deep acid peels that require anesthesia. Do they treat themselves? Dr. Scheibner is perhaps the most extreme example. Her intensive laser therapy purports to stimulate collagen growth, tighten the skin and remove broken capillaries—an effect Dr. Scheibner likens to a face-lift. It also involves similar recovery times.

"For two weeks, you look ghastly," says Dr. Scheibner. "Your face swells and turns the color of eggplant. You look in the mirror and think, 'What have I done to my skin?'" Dr. Scheibner should know: She's undergone the treatment herself, at the hands of a colleague.

"I had sun damage, wrinkles, blemishes—everything showed up after I hit 30," Dr. Scheibner recalls. "Now, since I've done it myself, I can prepare people for how awful they'll look and also show them my before and after pictures, to see what the lasers can do."

Light glycolic acid or trichloroacetic acid (TCA) peels—much tamer fare—are common among dermatologists. Dr. Kleinsmith underwent a series of six light peels one summer. Dr. Gendler gets a light glycolic acid peel every three months.

Dr. Sarnoff injects small cysts, "blemishes from your period or stress," with Kenalog (a cortisone-like anti-inflammatory solution) and says her friends and neighbors beg her for the quick-fix shots. "The injections get rid of blemishes faster than anything else," she says.

Dr. Burke can't take advantage of the collagen injections she uses to smooth wrinkles; "I'm allergic!" In response to recent research in dermatologial journals, however, she takes 400 international units (IU) of vitamin E a day, 100 micrograms of selenium and 25,000 IU of beta-carotene—all antioxidants known to fight free radicals that cause aging and disease.

If the pressure to have perfect skin falls heavier on a female dermatologist than on a male, there is an up side to being a woman. It's a question of empathy, Dr. Sarnoff says. "Men don't apply foundation, their lipstick doesn't bleed into lip lines," she points out. Dr. Wexler agrees: "A male dermatologist might not discuss whether a certain suncreen has a matte finish—I will. To me, it's not a foolish detail."

Then again, Dr. Herriford reports that most of the women patients in her office go to her male partner and most of the men come to her. She can't explain the strange sex divide. Still, she says, "I do think women are perceived as natural caretakers, and that lends us an edge." Given the American Academy of Dermatology's estimate of two practicing female dermatologists for every nine males (though the ratios in medical schools are now almost fifty-fifty), it's an advantage these doctors are happy to leverage.

—*Jean Godfrey-June*

PART FIVE

THIN
FOREVER

BEAT THE DEFICIENCY
THAT MAKES YOU FAT

WHY IS IT SO HARD TO STAY SLIM? MANY
OVERWEIGHT WOMEN SWEAR THEY DON'T EAT
ALL THAT MUCH. COULD IT BE THAT SOMETHING
VERY IMPORTANT IS MISSING FROM THEIR LIVES?

The biggest underlying cause of overweight is found in the title of the classic Charlie Chaplin film *Modern Times*. What these modern times have done is create a huge exercise deficiency, resulting in big-time "flabola."

Yes, despite the heralded interest in fitness walking, aerobics and all the rest, the average woman today gets much less exercise than her counterpart did a generation or two ago. Back then, people exercised just by living—living in the 1940s or 1950s or even 1960s instead of the 1990s.

Remarkably few people realize the extent of this deficiency, even when the result of it is staring at them from the snickering face of a bathroom scale. The tricky part is that the deficiency comes from lots of little things, so little they're nearly invisible. But look at this—a kind of split-screen image, with 1955 on the left side and 1995 on the right.

A SPLIT-SCREEN VIEW OF MODERN TIMES

In the morning, Mrs. 1955 walked a few blocks (one-quarter mile) to catch the bus, as Mr. 1955 used the one family car to drive to work. Once the bus dropped her off she had another quarter-mile walk to her office, which was on the second floor of a building with no elevator. Once she was at her desk, she seemed to get precious little exercise, spending the day pounding away on an old Underwood.

Now, on the other side of the screen, look at Mrs. 1995. Hers is a two-car household, so she motors 15 minutes to work, then takes the elevator to the 15th floor, where she spends her day pounding the keyboard of a computer.

The difference doesn't seem so great, does it? After all, Mrs. 1955 wasn't working in a steel mill, and she climbed only one flight of stairs to reach her desk.

Yet, the difference is about 16 pounds, assuming they're the same size with the same metabolism and eat the same amount of food. Just this part of Mrs. 1995's daily regimen will, in time, make her close to 16 pounds heavier.

That's because Mrs. 1955 burned 100 calories a day walking to and from her bus stop, and, believe it or not, about another 100 extra calories using a manual typewriter instead of an electronic keyboard. A few daily trips up and down the stairs at work (almost three minutes) burned about another 20 calories, for a total of 220 calories.

For roughly every 15 calories you stop burning on a daily basis while eating the same amount of food, you will, in time, get 1 pound heavier—for a total of 16 big ones in Mrs. 1995's case.

Meanwhile, Mr. 1995 drives 30 minutes to work, just like his dad did 40 years ago. After a brief stop at the office, he goes out on the street, where he's a salesman driving through city traffic for about three hours a day, just like his dad.

The difference? Nearly 12 pounds. How? Mr. 1995 has an automatic, but his dad drove a stick shift, actually burning an additional 140 calories a day.

But that's just the beginning. Because they're a two-job family, the modern couple eats out three nights a week, while Mr. and Mrs. 1955 ate out just once a week.

The difference? For whoever does the kitchen work, about another five pounds—the result of not preparing dinner twice a week. What's more, this modern couple has a dishwasher!

Come late evening, the 1950s couple liked to watch their new TV, though Mr. 1955 used to pop up 15 times a night to fiddle with the aerial or change the channel. His modern-day counterpart just sits there with his thumb resting on the remote control. And, while Mrs. 1955 usually did knitting while she watched the mostly boring shows on Stone Age TV, the modern woman is completely enthralled with the vivid images on her 27-inch Sony. Besides, she doesn't know how to knit.

The difference is probably about two pounds each. Plus, one more pound can probably be tacked on because, instead of scampering to the kitchen to get the phone every time it rings, the contemporaries have a cordless that's always in reach.

Come weekends, Mr. 1955 did yard work, and so does his son in 1995. But while Dad spent 1½ hours at a shot pushing a mower over the homestead, sonny boy uses a riding mower and is done in 20 minutes. At 20 mows a year, this comes out to an extra four pounds for Mr. 1995.

When the snows came in Elmira, New York—where Mr. 1955 lived—he shoveled his steps, pathway and sidewalk all by hand, about a 600-calorie job. Junior, on the other hand, lives in the Sunbelt. At 10 no-snows per year, he's just gained two more pounds.

Both like to use hand tools, though, for pruning trees, preparing firewood and doing little projects. But—you guessed it—while dear old Dad burned 390 calories brandishing a handsaw for an hour, Junior uses a power saw and does the same amount of work in five minutes. After a year of sawing and puttering (about 25 hours' worth), Mr. 1995 has three more pounds on his belly.

Back in the 1950s, the couple frequently took short walks to the grocery store, fish store, butcher shop, library, drugstore and dry cleaner. Today, most of these little shops don't exist; they have been replaced by shopping centers, supermarkets and malls. Who carries a bag of groceries two or three blocks anymore except in New York City? You can probably slap on another 6 pounds. By now, it's likely that our modern couple is a good 50 pounds (combined weight) heavier than their 1950s counterparts. Even if they eat considerably less food, they'll still be noticeably plumper. But, there's more.

Consider the modern automobile, not just with automatic transmission (accounted for previously) but also with power steering, power brakes, cruise control, power windows, power door locks, even a power aerial. Back in 1955, most cars didn't even have turn signals—you had to roll down the window and make arcane hand signals. All that, especially the power steering, is probably worth another two pounds.

Take the modern workstation, where it's unnecessary to get up and search out bulky files from cabinets and shelves. You just sit for hours in front of a computer, seeking and processing with mere taps of the fingers. You can probably add on two more pounds.

The very design of modern homes makes people fatter. Many who were raised in vertical homes now live in ranches. No more up and down the stairs ten times a day.

No more running up and down and about to open and shut windows—the automatic climate control takes care of all our temperature needs.

And appliances. Who kneads dough by hand anymore? Or stirs a thick batter by spoon? There are automated ways of doing just about everything except peeling a banana.

There are even don't-get-up-and-change-the-record-you-might-burn-a-calorie multidisc compact disc players, not to mention the lure of the TV, VCR and PC, not to mention the CD-ROM, which further keep you from moving about.

HOW TO CURE VIRTUAL IMMOBILITY

We used to hear that modern lifestyles were becoming sedentary. Well, we're way past sedentary now and into virtual immobility.

You could turn on a motion-detector alarm system in a modern household with four people in it, and it wouldn't go off until someone had to visit the bathroom.

Because we are now in the dawn of what we could call the Age of Akinesis (total lack of human movement), we are paying the price in pounds. And we don't mean British sterling.

All the normal, everyday, no-big-deal ways we used to burn calories and keep slim are gone forever. Think about that: forever.

There is no turning back the clock. If anything, the speed of change is increasing.

That's why creating an exercise program for yourself is the best, and perhaps only, way to prevail over an environment automated to the point of biological toxicity. Fat really is toxic, greasing the skids for most of the major health threats we face today. What's more, not exercising is itself toxic, now recognized as a major risk factor for heart disease.

Put those two facts together, and the motive for regenerating your physical vitality is mighty strong.

—*Mark Bricklin with Margo Trott*

TEN TOP FAT BURNERS

EVER DREAM OF A MAGIC PILL TO MELT FAT?
IT DOESN'T YET EXIST (NO SURPRISE).
BUT THERE ARE SOME SUPER STRATEGIES
TO ELICIT A FAST FAT BURN.

Determined to trim that tummy, lose those love handles and shed those stubborn saddlebags once and for all? Don't waste your time with way-out diet and exercise schemes. Instead, make every move count—by trying these methods to maximize your fat-burning potential.

Try cross-country skiing. Research has shown that exercises that vigorously work both your arms and legs are better fat burners than exercises like running or walking, which involve only your legs.

"Cross-country skiing rates highest in lab tests for burning the most calories per minute because you're using your legs, upper body and even your torso," says Wayne Westcott, Ph.D., YMCA national strength-training consultant. Stationary rowing machines and stationary bicycles with levers you push and pull with your arms as you pedal also rate high. You can up the fat-burning potential of exercises like walking or stationary stair-climbing by pumping your arms vigorously.

Use a dash of the hot stuff. A pinch of chili powder or splash of Tabasco sauce may increase your postmeal metabolic rate significantly, according to some studies. The hot stuff makes you sweat—a common sign that your body's working harder and burning more calories. You may also be less likely to gorge on a spicy meal because the flavor's so intense. So experiment with fiery ethnic cuisines, like Mexican, Thai and Indian.

Eat breakfast. Some experts say your body burns calories at a slower rate as you sleep. Breakfast, they say, is your metabolism's wake-up call, kicking it into calorie-burning mode. If you don't eat something in the morning, you may ultimately burn fewer calories. And it's more likely that, when you finally do get around to eating, you'll grab the first high-fat snack you see.

Go for time. When it comes to low to moderate exercise,

like walking or stationary cycling (which just involves your legs), the longer you do it, the more fat you burn. "In terms of permanent fat loss, the only thing that counts is the total calories you burn," Dr. Westcott says. Of course, you burn more calories per minute during intense exercise, like running, but you can compensate by applying the three-to-one rule: The number of calories you burn in three minutes of moderate exercise is equal to about the number you'd burn during one minute of intense exercise. So, roughly speaking, you need to walk 45 minutes to burn as many calories as you'd burn on a 15-minute superfast run.

Eat 'carbos' instead of fats. One preliminary study found that women on a low-fat, high-carbohydrate diet saw an increase in muscle mass after 20 weeks. What's remarkable is that they seemed to build muscle without exercise. That may have happened, in part, because it's harder for your body to turn carbohydrates into body fat than it is to turn dietary fat into body fat, researchers say. Unfortunately, our bodies store fat very easily. It takes very little energy to digest, absorb, transport and store fat—which means your body doesn't burn many calories in the process. But to process carbohydrates instead, your body burns more than twice as many calories.

And loading your diet with complex carbohydrates—from vegetables, breads, cereals, pasta and rice—means you're probably eating fewer total calories, too. One gram of carbohydrate contains about four calories, while one gram of fat has nine.

Graze. Eating small meals throughout the day—instead of your standard three squares—may be better for fat burning, according to some experts. After you eat, your body releases the hormone insulin. The larger the meal—and the higher it is in fat and sugar—the more insulin your body releases in response. "Insulin causes your body to save fat and burn carbohydrates," says registered dietitian James Kenney, Ph.D., nutrition research specialist at the Pritikin Longevity Center in Santa Monica, California. "Things that tend to pump insulin levels higher tend to promote weight gain." Insulin helps prevent your fat cells from breaking down fat and releasing it into the bloodstream, where it could be burned as fuel. And it also helps turn your fat cells into magnets for the dietary fat that's been absorbed into your bloodstream.

But smaller meals, eaten more frequently during the day, keep insulin levels lower and more stable. "If you have less insulin in your blood, you store less fat and you burn more fat," Dr. Kenney says. "And because you burn more fat, you have less of an appetite because you're using calories instead of storing calories." But grazing only prevents insulin surges if you choose the right kinds of foods. Stick to high-complex-carbohydrate, low-fat foods, like baked potatoes (with vegetable or nonfat cheese toppers), legumes, vegetables and whole-grain pretzels, bagels and breads.

Exercise after you eat. A moderate workout right after a meal gives you a fat-burning bonus, some research suggests. If you take a brisk three-mile walk on an empty stomach, you'll burn about 300 calories—plus a fraction from the afterburn effect. But if you're walking on a full stomach, you not only burn those 300-plus calories—you also burn another 15 percent of that total.

"Eating stimulates your sympathetic nervous system," says Bryant Stamford, Ph.D., exercise physiologist and director of the Health Promotion Center at the University of Louisville in Kentucky. "Exercise after eating seems to give it a double boost, so it overcompensates and burns more calories than it needs to." Postmeal workouts should be low intensity, so you don't make your muscles compete with your digestive system for blood flow.

Pump iron. Resistance-training exercises that work two or more of your major muscle groups—such as leg presses, bench presses and pull-downs—are the best ways to build muscle, which makes them excellent fat burners, too. Why? During any type of exercise, your metabolic rate—the rate at which your body burns calories—goes up. Your body then also burns calories at rest, at a much lower rate. But if you build more muscle, you can up your "resting metabolic rate" and actually burn more fat when you're not moving around. That's because well-toned muscle tissue is like New York City—it never sleeps. It's constantly burning calories, unlike sluggish, low-energy fat tissue. Increasing the size of your muscles can increase your resting metabolic rate 2 to 3 percent, researchers say. That may not sound like much, but when it comes to metabolism, a little goes a long way. Leg presses work leg and gluteal muscles, bench presses tax the muscles in the chest and the backs of the arms and pull-downs are great for building the biceps and back muscles.

For the best fat-burning results, do ten repetitions of each exercise at the heaviest weight you can comfortably lift, two to three sets, three times a week. "Slow, controlled movement is the best for building muscle and, so, for burning fat," says Dr. Westcott. Count to two when you're pushing the weight up—or pulling the weight down, in the case of pull-downs—and count to four when you're returning the weight to starting position. (If you're new to resistance training, make sure you learn proper form from a health-club strength coach or fitness instructor.)

Have a big bowl of beans. If you're not a nibbler by nature, include lots of foods high in fiber in your main meals—like legumes, barley, oatmeal, citrus fruits and apples. Eating high-fiber foods mimics the grazing effect—they're slowly digested by the body, so insulin levels tend to remain more stable.

Vary your pace. If you're pressed for time—or you want to really maximize your fitness—introduce the concept of interval training to your walking, running or cycling workout. That means alternating higher-intensity spurts with low-intensity cool-down intervals.

"Interval training means you're burning more calories per minute and you're going to maintain a higher metabolic rate throughout the exercise," Dr. Westcott says. And it's going to ignite the afterburn effect, too. That means you'll continue to burn fat at a higher rate even after you stop exercising.

"The more intense the exercise, the greater the afterburn effect," says Dr. Stamford. With moderate exercise, like walking, the afterburn bonus is minimal. But upping the intensity with interval training or engaging in other intense aerobic activities can make the afterburn linger for hours after your workout. And preliminary research suggests that resistance training might produce a slight afterburn effect, too.

Here's how interval training works. In a 30-minute workout (walking, running or cycling), first warm up for 10 minutes at a moderate pace. Then pick up the pace till you're breathing harder (but not all out of breath), for about a minute, or however long you feel comfortable. Slow down to a speed that lets you catch your breath—probably slower than your warm-up speed—for another minute. Then pick up the pace again, for another minute. Continue to alternate as long as you can, leaving time for a 5-minute cool-down. Make sure the time you allow for recovery is equal to the time you spend at higher intensity.

—*Lisa Delaney*

THE "NO-HUNGER" WEIGHT-LOSS PLAN

"HIGH-ENERGY" FOODS CAN HELP YOU REACH A HEART-HEALTHIER WEIGHT, WITHOUT GOING HUNGRY!

You probably already know the reasons you should drop those extra pounds. Healthwise, you can cut your risk of heart attack by 35 to 55 percent and substantially lower your chances of developing other diseases, like diabetes and breast cancer.

By eating high-energy foods, your cholesterol, blood pressure and blood sugar levels will tumble, dramatically improving your health and sense of well-being. Not to mention that you'll again be able to wear that little black dress that's been gathering dust in your closet or appear in shorts on the tennis court without being embarrassed.

You know why you need to lose—the big question is how. If you've tried before, you may be haunted by memories of detailed food diaries, scales and measuring spoons to apportion your daily bread. You may recall choking down bowl after bowl of undressed salad and pining for foods you could really sink your teeth into.

LOSING IS EASIER THAN EVER

Here's some good news. Successful weight loss doesn't have to be that complicated—and you don't have to live on carrot sticks and lettuce. In fact, while you may be able to lose some weight over the short term, drastically changing your diet by cutting out substantial foods and relying too heavily on low-calorie foods may actually sabotage your chances of achieving permanent weight loss.

Here's why. Food gives you energy, and your body needs a certain amount of it to get through the day. The more active you are and the more muscle you have, the more fuel you need. When you're trying to lose weight, you're aiming to create a daily calorie deficit, taking in less fuel than you burn. But if you don't fuel your body properly—if you restrict yourself to super-low-calorie, "low-octane" foods— it's like asking your Chevy to get you across town on empty. You could end up weak, lethargic and starving.

"That can stimulate your appetite and may cause you to binge," says George Blackburn, M.D., chief of the nutrition and metabolism laboratory at New England Deaconess Hospital in Boston. Desperate for energy and feeling deprived, you're likely to backslide—to gain back the weight you lost, and then some, by going back to your old eating habits.

The solution is simple. Focus on eating more—that's right, more—"high-octane" foods that are naturally low in fat and high in carbohydrates and fiber. These five kinds of foods, in particular, are:

- potatoes and sweet potatoes
- legumes, like pinto beans, kidney beans and lentils
- whole grains, like whole-grain cereals, pastas, breads and brown rice
- fruits, like apples, bananas, berries and melons
- skim milk and skim-milk products, like cottage cheese and yogurt

These foods not only give you the energy you need to power through an active life but they can also help you lose weight the "no-hunger" way, Dr. Blackburn says. Here's how. They help keep blood sugar levels stable. Dramatic swings in blood sugar from feasting and fasting can stimulate your appetite and cause you to overeat. They're hearty foods, so they keep you feeling fuller longer. They have half the calories, per bite, as fatty foods, which means you can eat twice as much and still take in fewer calories than you would if you were eating fatty foods. (But, because high-octane foods are so filling, you'd probably be over-stuffed if you tried!) They naturally drive down your fat intake.

Simply make sure that they're not prepared with too much fat or doused with rich sauces that offset their weight-loss benefits.

EAT TO LOSE

Plus, if you focus on adding good-for-you foods to your diet instead of depriving yourself of the fatty foods you've always loved, you may have an easier time sticking with your newfound way of eating. "It's not what you shouldn't eat, it's what you should eat," Dr. Blackburn says.

Here's how this strategy can translate into a 15-pound weight loss in 12 weeks. To lose 1 to 2 pounds a week (the amount experts say is best to aim for if you want weight loss to last), you need to cut about 500 calories a day. You can do that by:

- drinking one glass of skim milk instead of whole milk
- eating one bowl of oatmeal—a whole grain—instead of a croissant
- snacking on fruit—like an apple—instead of a granola bar
- having oven-fried potatoes, baked with a bit of vegetable-oil spray, instead of french fries
- having a bowl of bean-based vegetarian chili instead of chili with ground beef

That's your 500 calories, right there! (And that doesn't take into account your exercise routine, which can burn off another 200 to 300 calories a day.) Most of the calories you cut when you fill up on these high-octane foods are from fat. That's important because our bodies easily store fat calories as fat, while they burn carbohydrates (found abundantly in the five kinds of high-octane foods) more easily as fuel.

Don't worry so much about weighing and measuring how much you're eating. Simply choose these heartier foods first when you're hungry, stop when you're full. You know when you need to eat and when you've had enough. And be a little creative with your meals and snacks.

"For example, try low-sugar, whole-grain cereal in the evenings or for a serious snack," Dr. Blackburn says. That's also a way to sneak more skim milk into your diet—something that's crucial for women in preventing bone loss as they age. If you're fighting the switch from whole milk to skim, first go to 2 percent, then from 2 percent to 1 percent, then to skim.

—*Lisa Delaney*

DE-STRESS YOUR TUMMY AWAY

AND YOU THOUGHT IT HAD TO DO WITH POTATO CHIPS! THESE DAYS LEARNING TO COPE HAS BECOME A NEW STRATEGY FOR TAMING POTBELLIES.

Those pounds of stress weighing on your shoulders . . . you feel them, even though you can't actually see them. But maybe you're looking in the wrong place. It could be they've migrated south—down to your potbelly.

This unexpected suggestion comes from researchers in the Department of Psychology at Yale University. And it could help explain why some people have more trouble with their midsections than they apparently deserve.

What could well be happening, the Yale team believes, is that uncontrolled stress triggers the release of a hormone called cortisol, which in turn causes fat to be preferentially deposited around your middle.

Now, what exactly is "uncontrolled" stress? It's not the stress of doing a very challenging task and doing it well, rather it's the stress of trying your best and failing repeatedly. It's not knowing what dreadful thing is going to happen to you next, or why. Most of all, it's a feeling that you just can't measure up, be in control, be on top. The kind of stress that's purely negative.

Researchers at Yale worked with 42 overweight women, ages 18 to 42. Some carried a preponderance of their overweight around their middles, others didn't. During tests, these women were given stressful tasks like being rushed through math problems and making a speech—during which they were falsely told their performance was poor. At the very same time, their levels of cortisol were measured. Women who carried their overweight in their bellies were secreting notably more of the stress hormone while under pressure. Readings taken the next day—with no special stressors—showed no unusual elevation of cortisol.

Backing up the connection, the women with the relatively larger bellies were also found to have a poorer self-control style. In other words, it's not the stress itself but how you cope with it.

"This is the first time this chain of events has been shown in humans," says researcher Marielle Rebuffe-Scrive, Ph.D. She and colleague Judith Rodin, Ph.D., have been investigating this relationship between stress and abdominal fat for some time. Earlier work was largely based on animal experiments, one of which clearly demonstrated that lab rats subjected to stresses they can't control tend to get fat—especially in their tummies. So the new research findings are not exactly a surprise—the biological link between stress and the potbelly syndrome has already been made.

BEYOND LOOKING GOOD

It's important to mention that fat carried on the belly, as opposed to the hips and thighs, has much more than aesthetic importance. The potbelly syndrome is strongly associated with an increased risk of heart disease, stroke and diabetes.

So banishing that pot—or preventing a future outcropping— is something that's surely worth doing, even if your body's geography doesn't wound your self-image. It may mean living a longer, healthier life. The added benefit—fitting into a slinkier negligee or a sleeker two-piece bathing suit—is just fat-free icing on a low-fat cake!

Now, you may be wondering if trying to get a better grip on your stress-control handlebars can actually help shrink your equator.

"Yes, we really suspect this might help," says Dr. Rebuffe-Scrive. "No, it's not going to be the single answer to make women lose all their abdominal fat. There are many causes of abdominal fat."

But, she adds, since high levels of poorly handled stress are also risk factors for several health problems—heart disease, for instance—it's definitely smart to try improving this area.

"Try to think," she says, " 'Why am I under stress? Why is this happening?' " Understanding the source of stress is the first step to dealing with it, "which everyone must find their own way to do," says Dr. Rebuffe-Scrive.

The number-one suggestion for combating stress is regular, enjoyable exercise. Exercise is often reported by individuals to reduce stress and help them cope. Plus, walking—like any exercise— tends to burn belly flab for energy, so this is a two-way health and shape improver.

RELAXING YOUR MIND

Redford B. Williams, M.D., director of the Behavioral Medicine Research Center at Duke University Medical Center in Durham, North Carolina, suggests this simple routine to help get the *un-* out of uncontrolled stress. "There are some older studies from the early days of meditation research by a fellow named Ron Jevning, Ph.D., at California State University, Long Beach. His work showed that cortisol levels go down with transcendental meditation," says Dr. Williams.

Here are Dr. Williams's instructions for everyday meditation. "Just pay attention to your breathing. Every time you breathe in and out, you notice it. Every time you breathe out, you say a word or phrase to yourself that conjures up the mental image you're trying to achieve, like 'calm down, cool it,' for example. When your mind starts to wander and you're back thinking about whatever it is that was bugging you, just say to yourself, 'Oh, well,' and come back to paying attention to your breathing and saying the word or phrase.

"To build your meditation skills, you need to practice for about ten minutes at least once a day. Then you will be able to do it well and you will be able to call on these skills—when you're in a traffic jam, sitting there stewing, when you're angry at somebody or worried about something. This puts you in control."

In addition to controlling stress, be sure to cut back on fat in your diet, exercise regularly and avoid serious drinking. You're

bound to be healthier and, with any luck, you'll see your waistline shrink, too!

—*Mark Bricklin with Michele Toth*

THE MYTH AND PROMISE OF HERBAL WEIGHT LOSS

HERBS CAN'T MELT OR BURN FAT, BUT THEY CAN HELP ASPIRING THIN PEOPLE EVOLVE THEIR DIETS TO ONES LOWER IN FAT WITHOUT SACRIFICING TASTE AND VARIETY.

Stop in at any natural food store or herb shop and you're sure to see herbal blends whose names and packaging tout their ability to help people lose weight. Open many of the magazines that cover herbal medicine and, periodically, you're sure to see articles with headlines like "Slimming Herbs for Weight Loss."

Herbs have many remarkable medical benefits, but unfortunately for those who hope to shed a few pounds, weight loss is not one of them. Like quick-fix diets, so-called weight-loss herb blends rarely, if ever, help anyone achieve permanent weight control. But herbs can play a supporting, though indirect, role in medically responsible weight-loss programs. Herbs won't make you lose weight, but if you're committed to weight loss, they can help the process feel more bearable.

DUPED BY DIURETICS

Herbs touted for weight loss include buchu (*Barosma betulina*), celery seed, dandelion, juniper, parsley and uva-ursi (*Arctostaphylos uva-ursi*). They are all diuretics. They increase urine production, allowing the makers of herbal weight-loss formulas to claim that they help people lose "water weight." But water weight isn't the kind of weight overweight people should lose. They should lose fat.

A steady diet of diuretic herbs is no solution to weight problems. The body senses the increased water loss diuretics cause and reacts with increased thirst to replace lost fluids. If you continue to ingest diuretics, the body eventually adjusts and retains water despite them. Coffee is a diuretic in addition to being a stimulant. But no one loses weight drinking coffee because the body adjusts to its diuretic action and compensates for it.

So what do advocates of weight loss with diuretics do? They load up weight-loss blends with several diuretic herbs to produce greater fluid loss than you get with a cup or two of coffee. But it's a mistake to use powerful diuretics without medical supervision. The body may be only about 50 percent water, but the brain and muscles are 75 percent water, and the blood is 85 percent water. Over time, diuretic herb blends may cause minor dehydration, which is not life-threatening but can impair judgment and coordination. As people age, they become more sensitive to minor dehydration. So while a steady diet of diuretics is not a good idea for anyone, it's most likely to cause problems for the elderly.

When should people take diuretics? A physician may prescribe potent diuretic drugs to treat high blood pressure and a few other chronic medical conditions. Diuretic herb blends can also help you cope with premenstrual bloating. But for premenstrual syndrome women should only use them a few days a month, not steadily as they may be used for weight loss.

STUNG BY STIMULANTS

In the past few years, Chinese ephedra, or *ma huang*, has also been touted for weight loss, thanks to the decongestant chemical it contains, ephedrine. (A laboratory analog of ephedrine, psuedoephedrine, is the decongestant in many over-the-counter cold formulas, and the word, pseudoephedrine, has contributed to one popular brand name, Sudafed.)

Ephedrine is also a powerful stimulant. Like caffeine, it can wake people up in the morning, keep them up at night and cause "speediness" in large doses. Ephedrine also stimulates basal metabolic rate (BMR). BMR is the speed at which the body burns calories while at rest. Increase your BMR and you burn more calories faster. One three-month study conducted by Danish researchers in 1985 showed that, compared with overweight women taking a placebo, those taking ephedrine (20 milligrams three times a day, by mouth) lost significantly more weight.

Another two-month experiment in 1987 by Italian researchers showed that, compared with a low-calorie diet alone, overweight women lost significantly more weight if they also took ephedrine (50 milligrams three times a day, by mouth). And a 1992 study by the same Danish group from 1985 showed that a combination of ephedrine and caffeine (20 milligrams and 200 milligrams three times a day, respectively) helped a group of obese women lose slightly more weight than untreated controls. However, the weight-loss benefits accrued only among those who were clinically obese, at least 20 percent heavier than their recommended weight. Ephedrine has shown no weight-loss benefits for mildly overweight people who simply want to lose five to ten pounds.

Those who are clinically obese should not rush out and fill their cupboards with *ma huang*. In addition to boosting BMR, the ephedrine it contains can also raise blood pressure, a potentially hazardous side effect for these individuals because obesity itself often raises blood pressure—and high blood pressure is a significant risk factor for both heart attack and stroke. If you are clinically obese and wish to try *ma huang*, check with your physician first. If you're not clinically obese, don't expect to benefit from this herb.

HOW TO LOSE WEIGHT FOR GOOD

To lose weight permanently, you have to lose fat. Herbs can't melt fat or burn fat, but they can help aspiring thin people evolve their diets to ones lower in fat without sacrificing taste and variety. Here's how weight-control experts recommend shedding that extra baggage.

Eat a balanced diet. Eat a diet high in carbohydrates and fiber, one based on fresh, whole, unprocessed foods. Despite what your mother may have told you, starches are not fattening. High-carbohydrate, high-fiber foods, such as potatoes and whole-grain breads, contribute to weight control. They fill you up quickly, so they satisfy hunger without costing you many calories. It's not the baked potato that adds the pounds, it's the high-fat butter and sour cream you pile on top of it.

Here's where herbs can help. Instead of butter and sour cream on your baked potato, try nonfat yogurt with curry, rosemary, garlic, onion powder or any other herbs that strike your fancy.

Herbs can also turn fresh fruits and vegetables into exotic, tasty treats. Like whole-grain breads, they're rich in nutrients, and they fill you up without filling you out. You can eat as many fruits and vegetables as you like without fear of gaining weight. And compared with high-fat food, low-fat, high-fiber items are considerably less expensive.

Trim the fat. Eat less fat—a lot less. The typical American diet contains about 40 percent of calories from fat. Aim to cut your fat to 25 percent or less of your total daily caloric intake. (One gram of fat contains nine calories.) High-fat diets are also associated with cancer, stroke and heart disease. Culinary herbs are low in fat. Use them as liberally as you like.

Eat breakfast. Surveys show that people who are overweight tend to skip breakfast, eat a light lunch, then gorge on dinner and snacks until bedtime. One key is to start your day with a high-carbohydrate breakfast, such as cereal and fruit, then eat a light supper. Eating triggers a rise in BMR that lasts several hours, so the earlier you begin eating, the more calories you burn throughout the day. What's good for breakfast? Instead of butter or margarine on toast, try cinnamon. Instead of that instant breakfast drink, try a "smoothie" of blended banana, nonfat yogurt or skim milk, orange juice and your favorite herbs.

Try grazing. Traditional dieting advice dictates three meals and no snacks between them. But mini-meals of low-fat, high-fiber foods every two to three hours prevent the blood sugar from dropping so low you feel ravenous. Then at mealtimes, you eat less because you feel less hungry. Air-popped popcorn is a quick low-fat, high-fiber snack that lends itself to herbal innovation. Try it with curry, ground red pepper or powdered ginger. Resist the urge to add salt or melted butter.

Exercise regularly. Regular, moderate exercise is essential to both good health and permanent weight control. Even modest exercise programs can make a difference. Brisk walking for as little as 20 minutes a day can burn fat calories, rev up your BMR and dramatically decrease your risk of heart disease and stroke. Aerobic exercise is even better. It burns more calories and revs up your BMR for hours longer. One excellent form of regular, moderate exercise is gardening. Grow you own herbs.

Be patient. The herbal formulas that promise weight loss are nothing but quick fixes. Permanent weight loss is a slow process. Aim to lose one pound every other week. At two pounds a month, you'll lose 24 pounds in a year. Culinary herbs can help as you reshape your diet. Just don't get suckered by the extravagant promises of herbal weight-loss formulas.

—*Michael Castleman*

THIRTY POUNDS DOWN... NOW AND FOREVER!

HERE'S HOW TO MAKE SLIMMING LIFESTYLE CHANGES THAT REALLY LAST A LIFETIME.

Let's be brutally honest for a moment. Odds are, you've attempted some form of weight loss in the past. It could even be that you were successful. But the fact that you're reading this chapter may mean that you weren't successful for very long. Like a pack of bloodhounds hot on your trail, those unwanted pounds picked up your scent and once again have you surrounded.

So how do you lose those dogs . . . er, pounds . . . once and for all? You have to change your scent. Become a new person. Become a person who no longer leads a 30-pounds-overweight lifestyle with its 30-pounds-overweight habits. And the trick is to do it without taxing your willpower, without subjecting yourself to undue deprivation and without adding additional rules and regulations that you can't wait to be rid of.

In other words, you have to create a new lifestyle that you can follow long enough to have it become second nature . . . an old friend that hangs around for the rest of your life, guarding you against ever gaining weight again.

UNDERSTAND THE BASICS

Does the phrase "Look before you leap" ring a bell? You can't make an honest commitment to do something unless you have some idea of what is required. So let's go through the weight-loss facts of life.

The first fact of life is that you're not going to become 30 pounds lighter by Valentine's Day . . . or by Memorial Day . . . or by the Fourth of July—nor would you want to. After all, you not only want to lose the weight but you also want to lose it permanently. And most experts agree that you have the best chance of doing that if you take a gradual approach—no more than one or two pounds a week.

The second fact of life is that through some combination of the right foods and the right exercise, you need to establish a daily deficit of 500 calories to lose that weight. Most weight-loss experts favor a program in which you cut 200 calories of fat (roughly 22 grams of fat) from your daily diet and burn off 300 calories through exercise to achieve the magic number. (When it comes to diet, it's actually better to count grams of fat instead of calories.)

And the third fact of life is that the first two facts are useless unless you follow them consistently and maintain them long after the 30 pounds are gone. That means being comfortable with the changes you make and not demanding more of yourself than you are prepared to give.

THE ALL-AMERICAN FAT FEST

Fat! Fat! Fat! We're not calling you names. We're talking about your diet. The average American's diet is approximately 40 percent fat. And because fat calories are more readily converted into body fat, those kinds of calories are the first ones you want to reduce. But the question is, by how much?

Diet experts advocate a fat intake of 25 percent of total calories. If you take a look at "Your Fat Budget," below, you can see that for a woman to maintain a weight of 130 pounds, her caloric intake should be 1,600 with a fat allowance of 44 grams a day. If you are a 160-pound woman eating 2,000 calories a day (40 percent fat), you're currently consuming about 89 grams of fat. To reach a streamlined 130, you need to figure out how to be satisfied with 45 fewer grams of fat per day. But not all at once.

As mentioned before, to jump onto the pound-a-week

YOUR FAT BUDGET

Fat calories are more readily converted to body fat than calories from carbohydrates and proteins. And a high-fat diet is a risk factor for heart disease, diabetes and some cancers. Diet experts advocate a fat intake of 25 percent of total calories—that's substantially lower than the 38 to 40 percent most Americans consume. The easy way to manage your intake is to use our "fat budget." Here's how it works. Find your goal weight. In the middle column is the number of calories you should take in each day to attain that weight and in the right-hand column the number of fat grams you should consume—your fat budget. Simply count the fat grams in each serving of the foods you eat to make sure you don't blow your budget. You can easily find that figure on most packaged food products.

So, for example, if you're a woman weighing in at 140 and you'd like to get down to a lithe 130, your fat budget is 44 grams (25 percent calories from fat). That knocks a whopping 280 calories from your daily total, just from fat, assuming that you're eating about 1,700 calories a day, with 40 percent of those calories coming from fat. (Remember that each gram of fat equals 9 calories.) These figures don't take exercise into account—for every 100 calories you burn working out, you can add 3 grams of fat.

weight-loss wagon, you need to cut 500 calories a day: 200 from your daily intake and 300 through exercise. Since each gram of fat you eat is good for a whopping 9 calories, all that is really required to get the weight-loss wagon rolling is that you bid farewell to approximately 22 grams of fat per day.

After a period of time, your 22-gram fat deficit, along with exercise, can slim your body to a point where it functions so efficiently that you stop losing weight. At this point, having become used to the dietary changes you've made, you can then go ahead and cut your fat intake far enough to reach the target fat budget on the chart that corresponds to your dream maintenance weight.

Your Goal Weight (lb.)	Calorie Intake	Fat Budget (g.)
WOMEN		
110	1,300	36
120	1,400	39
130	1,600	44
140	1,700	47
150	1,800	50
160	1,900	53
170	2,000	56
180	2,200	61
MEN		
130	1,800	50
140	2,000	56
150	2,100	58
160	2,200	61
170	2,400	67
180	2,500	69
190	2,700	75
200	2,800	78

Warning: While sheer instinct may tell you to grit your teeth and cut all the fat in sight, hoping your willpower holds out, this is the last thing you should do. "Completely eliminating your problem foods may set you up for failure," says registered dietitian Judith S. Stern, Sc.D., professor of nutrition and internal medicine at the University of California, Davis. "You have to determine what those foods are and find ways to replace them if you can't control your appetite for them."

Diane Hanson, Ph.D., a lifestyle specialist at the Pritikin Longevity Center in Santa Monica, California, thinks of it as leveraging your food choices: "doable changes that make a big difference. For example, if that blue cheese dressing at lunch is dumping 16 or 24 grams of fat (equivalent to two or three tablespoons) onto your daily intake, a small packet of low-fat dressing brought from home can shave off the grams and still leave you satisfied."

The concept of food substitutes is nothing new. But what makes them so exciting now is the ever-growing selection of low-fat products that are on the market. The difference between a regular meat lasagna entrée and a low-fat one translates into a fat savings of 7 grams. And the fastest-growing selection of products are the nonfat foods, which can really shave off the grams. Just to whet your appetite consider this: a nonfat, fruit-filled breakfast pastry that saves you 15.9 grams of fat over the real thing. Suddenly, dropping your fat intake for life doesn't look like such hungry work. But whatever you drop should be dropped for good. So choose carefully or the pounds will return.

YOU CAN'T DO IT SITTING STILL

Before you lull yourself to sleep with visions of breakfast-pastry weight loss, remember this: At some point you're going to have to sweat. A study conducted by Drs. Susan Kayman, William Bruvold and Judith Stern at the University of California, Davis, found that 90 percent of the participants who kept the weight off exercised regularly.

"To my mind, exercise has been undervalued with respect to weight loss," says Dr. Hanson. "As a matter of fact, when you look at what determines the continuation of a healthy lifestyle, exercise turns out to be the biggest behavioral driver."

It helps you look good and feel even better. It gives you a sense of accomplishment and mastery over your situation. "Current research is even showing that exercise may enhance your preference for fruits and vegetables," says Dr. Hanson.

Even if you already like veggies, exercise serves another important purpose. When you lower your caloric intake, your body, with an instinct for survival, slows down its metabolic rate and conserves energy. Exercise turns up the furnace so you become more efficient at burning fat. And, to drop a pound a week, you want that furnace stoked to the tune of 300 calories burned a day.

How you accomplish that goal is a matter of what you like to do. But the good news is that even a brisk, 45-minute walk will do the trick. But the real trick is to do it every day.

MAKE THE COMMITMENT

The difference between losing weight—and losing weight for good—is commitment: a truly motivated desire not only to change but also to maintain that change. You can think of your commitment as a contract with yourself, a lifelong contract.

But as the old saying goes, "Contracts are made to be broken." And there isn't one of us who hasn't cheated on a deal with ourselves to become better, more effective or, more to the point, slimmer. In most cases, the problem isn't our willpower, but our initial commitment. It just wasn't strong enough.

Before starting your new, 30-pounds-lighter life, you need to make sure that you're revved and ready to do it. That the contract you make with yourself is so strong the Supreme Court couldn't break it, much less a tempting éclair with your name on it. Here's how to really, pardon the expression, commit yourself.

Choose the right moment. "It's not easy to begin a program during complicated periods in your life," says Kelly D. Brownell, Ph.D., professor of psychology at Yale University. "Divorce, an illness in the family, problems at work—these are all things that can sap your energy and make your environment less supportive for the changes you want to make."

Of course, some people thrive on complications. A divorce,

for example, may be just the motivating kick one person needs to make big changes as part of a whole new lifestyle. "The thing you need to consider," says Dr. Brownell, "is how you respond to complications. If stress, worry and a frantic pace erode your eating plan, making serious lifestyle changes in the midst of what's currently happening may be a mistake."

And you don't want to look just at the present. If you're due for stormy weather in the upcoming weeks and months, you may want to bide your time and embark on your new lifestyle once things calm down and the sun comes out again.

Choose the right commitment. Do you want to lose 30 pounds or do you want to lose the bad habits that made you overweight to begin with? While these two goals may seem to be heads and tails of the same coin, the side that lands up after the toss can make all the difference between 30-pounds-down forever and 30-pounds-down for an all-too-brief amount of time.

"If you find yourself fantasizing about the moment when you've lost 30 pounds and your diet is over, you're going to have problems," says Dr. Brownell. "At the point when you've finally reached that all-important number on the scale, there's a chance that your motivation to continue your healthy lifestyle may decrease, leaving you right back where you started."

So to make the commitment that will keep those pounds away forever, focus on the changes you plan to make, not on the 30 pounds. "Change your view of success," suggests Dr. Hanson. "Rather than making weight loss your goal, make lifelong health your goal. Rather than getting up each morning and heading for the scale, wake up and notice how much better you feel."

"I also find it helpful to think of overweight as a chronic condition," adds Dr. Brownell. "Just as diabetes requires constant maintenance lest it gets serious, maintaining your ideal weight requires a lifetime of healthy eating and exercising practices."

Choose the right reason. "Some people lose weight because their husbands or wives want them to," says Jerome Brandon, Ph.D., an exercise physiologist from Georgia State University in Atlanta and member of the American College of Sports Medicine. "The problem is that they make the effort to lose weight for someone else rather than because they themselves are personally motivated to do it. And eventually they will get tired of doing it."

So, do it for yourself and not for someone else.

GET PREPARED

Every great journey begins with a great deal of preparation. How far would Christopher Columbus have gotten if he'd just awakened one morning, kissed his wife and headed out to discover the New World without the proper clothes, food, transportation or navigational equipment? To put it mildly, about as far as the Lisbon bus station.

Changing your life is not much different from making a journey. In both cases the most disappointing thing that can happen is that you have to give up because of difficulties you weren't prepared for. So no matter how charged up you are to start your new life, take some time to make the following preparations.

Educate yourself. If you're going to make lifestyle changes that you expect to practice for the rest of your life, you better darn well believe in them. And the best way to believe in something is to know beyond a shadow of a doubt how it works, and, more important, why it works.

"First, when it comes to weight loss, there are scientific reasons for why it's best to eat and exercise a certain way," says Dr. Hanson. "If you understand how your body is designed to work, you'll believe in what you're doing and not be so inclined to give it up when the results are not happening as quickly as you want."

Second, by not understanding their body's own weight-loss mechanisms, people often select popular methods that doom them to failure. Then they blame themselves when they never really had a chance. "You may think that the more calories you deprive yourself of, the faster you'll lose weight, and that's initially true. But if you don't realize that the body slows down its fat-burning furnace when calories are suddenly reduced, you're ultimately in for a big disappointment," says Dr. Hanson. "The only thing that will happen over time is that you'll be hungrier, less inclined to continue your program and still not sure why you aren't maintaining the initial weight loss."

So start out right by getting the facts. Know without a doubt that what you are doing is right and will eventually provide you with the results you want regardless of how things appear to be going on a day-to-day basis.

Find substitutes for eating. "When talking to patients, I often ask them why they overeat, and why they are doing something that they know is ultimately harmful," says Dean Ornish, M.D., author of *Eat More, Weigh Less* and director of the Preventive Medicine Research Institute in Sausalito, California. "And the answer often is that it helps to get them through the day. They may feel alienated or isolated, and eating helps them deal with the pain. One patient described how food temporarily fills the void and numbs the pain."

According to Dr. Ornish, change is not brought about solely by focusing on new behaviors, such as changing your eating habits and exercising. You need to address the underlying reasons for your behaviors. Otherwise, the problem remains and will eventually sabotage all your good intentions and commitments.

If some form of mental stress is behind your eating problem, you'll need to find a nonfattening substitute. Relaxation techniques and spending more time with friends are both great alternatives that are far lower in calories than a banana split.

Remove roadblocks. Visualize the changes you want to make, then visualize all the things that could keep you from doing them. "It could be that you are unwilling to start exercising," says Dr. Brownell. "But, if you dig a little deeper, you may find that the reason for this is that you are embarrassed to be seen exercising."

If this is the case, then starting your new lifestyle by taking out a membership at the trendy new health club that everyone is going to would probably be a mistake. That membership card will get about as much use as a coupon good for five free pro-wrestling lessons.

Instead, acknowledge your fear and create an environment that guarantees privacy—maybe a stationary bike in your bedroom or an early morning walk. The same thing goes for food. If you know in your heart that you will never give up apple pie, then don't say you will and set yourself up for failure. Create a new recipe that makes apple pie less fattening.

Get support. "If you look at the factors that predict successful, permanent weight loss, social support ranks near the top of the list," says John Foreyt, Ph.D., coauthor of *Living without Dieting* and director of the Nutrition Research Clinic at Baylor College of Medicine in Houston. "I'd go so far as to say it is absolutely critical."

When starting your new lifestyle, Dr. Foreyt insists that you make a public commitment, but not for the normal reasons. "It's not that you want to force yourself into a situation you can't back down from because everyone knows about it. What you are actually doing is making an assertive appeal for people's help and understanding."

In his book, Dr. Foreyt outlines four levels of support, each with its own special purpose. "First there's your family. They're going to need to get used to your new lifestyle. It may be that certain foods have to be kept out of the house. Compromises on family time may need to be made when your exercise or other activities conflict with family plans."

The second level consists of close friends. "Everyone should have someone they can call at three in the morning when temptation rears its ugly head," says Dr. Foreyt. "Even one really good friend can make the difference in a crisis."

The third and fourth levels involve support groups and your doctor. "Support groups are the perfect place to get advice and encouragement from people experiencing the same things you are," notes Dr. Foreyt. "And your doctor gives you information and knowledgeable feedback and helps you monitor your progress."

For some people, maintaining all four levels of support is not necessary. But Dr. Foreyt still contends the need for some form of social support, even for loners. And more important, the kind of support you solicit needs to be specific.

"You don't want people giving you negative support," says Dr. Foreyt. "While someone pointing out your mistakes may work in the short run, it isn't motivating over the long haul. So you want to be very direct about asking people to say something positive about your accomplishments."

Find a monitoring system that works. "Your actual weight is the least important thing you can monitor," says

Ronette Kolotkin, Ph.D., director of behavioral programs at Duke University's Diet and Fitness Center in Durham, North Carolina, and coauthor of *The Duke University Medical Center Book of Diet and Fitness.* "Instead, I always encourage people to keep a diary not just of food and exercise, but also of any important behavioral problems they encounter, such as rapid eating in certain situations or a tendency to binge at particular times."

At the end of each week, Dr. Kolotkin suggests that you study your diary as if you were a weight-loss professional studying someone else's case history. What advice would you give the patient? In her one-year follow-up study, Dr. Kolotkin found that people who monitored food intake, exercise and motivation were more successful than those who monitored weight only.

Paying daily homage to the bathroom scale is a dicey proposition for two reasons. First, your body weight is in constant flux. Up a pound today, down two tomorrow. A momentary gain in water weight may have you on the floor in despair even if the overall picture is improving.

Second, because your new lifestyle of healthy food and exercise is constantly trimming the fat while boosting the lean, a scale may show no change in weight even though you are getting slimmer and more toned by the minute. "That's why I always encourage people to wear form-fitting clothing," says Dr. Kolotkin. "As you lose weight, or even as your body composition changes, you'll get feedback every time you need to have your clothes taken in or even downsized a bit. You'll constantly be aware of what your body is doing by the way your clothes fit."

Plan for trouble. "I always tell people that they can expect to slip," says Dr. Kolotkin. "It will happen. And the difference between moving on and just plain giving up has to do with having some strategy to deal with momentary failure."

There are two ways you don't want to react to a temporary backslide. On one hand, you don't want to be cavalier: "Oh well, I ate that box of doughnuts, but I'll worry about it tomorrow." On the other hand, you don't want to overreact: "Oh no, this is the end! How can I go on after eating my weight in doughnuts? I'm no good."

"You've got to be rational," says Dr. Kolotkin. "The first

thing to do is acknowledge exactly what happened. 'I was at a party, lost control and ate 5,000 calories.' Don't overemphasize or underemphasize what occurred. Next, put things into perspective. 'Over the last six months, I've made some great changes; I've exercised regularly, eaten right and made serious progress. Compared to what I've achieved, this one incident is hardly a catastrophe. I don't feel great about it, but it also isn't the end of the world.'"

Next comes action. A good general doesn't waste time dwelling on defeat. Instead, he immediately plots a course of action that will take him back on the road to victory. "This does not mean that you should exercise twice as long tomorrow to make up for today's mistake," says Dr. Kolotkin. "That's a lot like punishing yourself. Instead, you want to take steps to ensure that what happened does not happen again."

If you found yourself bingeing on a bag of chips lying wantonly open in the kitchen, you may want to purge your house of binge foods. If you stopped exercising for a week because of scheduling difficulties, spend some time arranging things so that it doesn't happen again. "Then get right back into your program," says Dr. Kolotkin. "Set two alarm clocks so that you can't avoid waking up and exercising. Meet a friend for lunch who will make sure you eat the right foods. Write out a meal plan."

In other words, make your lifestyle changes foolproof and inescapable for the next few days just to get yourself back on track. Dr. Kolotkin finds that for most people, it only takes three days for them to turn around a negative incident.

Learn from past mistakes. What went wrong the last time you tried to lose weight? "When I ask people that, I'll normally get an unproductive answer like 'I started eating again,'" says Dr. Kolotkin. "But you need to look at the underlying reasons. Was the diet you placed yourself on too restrictive? Did you find your meal plans were falling apart because you were often pressed for time and had to eat whatever was available?" Take some time to dig deep and honestly analyze what went wrong.

Create an environment that makes change easy. Weight loss and lifestyle change are so often looked at as matters of sheer willpower. This is the belief that you can bulldoze your way through anything by the unyielding power of your mind.

But why make things tough when you can make them easy? "I call it environmental engineering," says Dr. Hanson, "and it's really where you make changes in your environment that make it easier to succeed."

Environmental engineering is a powerful yet simple concept. If you find yourself getting hungry at 3:00 P.M. each day and the only thing available is a candy machine down the hall from your office, rather than fighting the urge to merge with a chocolate bar, why not reach into your desk and pull out the apple that you brought in for just such a moment?

As simple as the idea seems, it can be applied to all areas of your life. And more to the point, once you've determined why you've failed in the past, you can set up your new environment in a way that will help you avoid past mistakes. "When I encounter people who have a problem with after-dinner eating, I often suggest that they get a small refrigerator for beverages and keep it in the den," says Dr. Kolotkin. "That way, even if they are thirsty, there's no reason that they should enter the kitchen and be tempted by an open refrigerator."

What about exercise? The last time you tried a walking program it petered out after a week because you never seemed to have clean socks, batteries for your personal stereo or rain gear. This time, get equipped. Keep everything where you can get at it immediately. Keep an extra pair of walking shoes in your car for impromptu opportunities. Environmental engineering translates into "Make it so easy on yourself that you can't possibly fail!"

GET READY . . . TAKE ACTION

You're ready to get started, but at what pace? Do you purge all the fat from your diet, change your eating habits and throw yourself into a daily exercise program at one fell swoop? Or should you ease into a lifestyle change like you ease into a hot tub; a few food substitutions . . . get comfortable . . . exercise a couple days a week . . . get comfortable.

When making your decision, you shouldn't be thinking about how fast you want to lose weight. The real question is, which technique makes it easier to assimilate changes that you can keep for life?

"If you're looking to make permanent lifestyle changes, my feeling is that incorporating them slowly makes them easier to get used to," says Dr. Kolotkin. "It's less overwhelming. The goals seem more attainable if you go step-by-step rather than full force."

Dr. Kolotkin experienced the power of small changes first-hand in working with a woman who, at age 45, had never exercised and was so out of shape that a flight of stairs would leave her winded. When she started her program, five minutes on a stationary bike was all she could do. "But rather than dwell on the thought that five minutes was not a very big or important change, she embraced the notion of small, gradual changes and took pride in the fact that she was actually exercising at all," says Dr. Kolotkin. "And gradually, over the following months, as she got comfortable with one level of exercise, she increased it. She's now been in four walking marathons!"

Dr. Kolotkin admits that gradual change means gradual results, sometimes too gradual for some people. "It's not as exciting or motivating to make small changes, and so some people resist it, thinking that they'll never get where they want to be," she says. "But then I remind them that they tried cutting calories too quickly in the past and found the diet too restrictive to continue. Although they did lose some weight fast, in the end they went back to their old habits and gained it back."

But, if you like big, exciting changes, you have an ally in Dr. Ornish. According to him, comprehensive changes can make people feel so much better so quickly that rather than being overwhelmed by the changes, they are instead strongly motivated to continue.

So which is right for you? Part of the answer lies with your doctor and your current situation. Big dietary changes may be within your capability, but if you haven't been exercising regularly, too much activity too fast could be dangerous.

The second part of the answer has to do with your own mental makeup. Do big challenges bring out the best in you, or do you find them intimidating? What's worked for you in other situations? Remember, the only right answer here is the one that's right for you.

—*Mark Golin with Linda Rao*

PART SIX

THE NUTRITION/HEALTH
CONNECTION

A NUTRITIONAL SURVIVAL GUIDE FOR WOMEN

YOU WANT TO EAT RIGHT. THERE'S A LOT OF ADVICE OUT THERE, SOME OF IT CONTRADICTORY. WHAT'S A HEALTHY WOMAN TO DO?

Eating right may appear to be a Herculean challenge—especially for a woman, whose nutritional needs change dramatically as she moves through various stages of her life. But you can master the task. In fact, you must—if you want to remain healthy and active into your eighties. Here's why.

Your body endures a great deal as you age. It submits to physical changes, such as pregnancy and menopause, and rises to lifestyle challenges, such as a hectic job and the demands of motherhood. But your body requires something in return—proper sustenance. And it exacts a steep toll if you don't deliver.

Inadequate intake of key nutrients not only compromises your immediate health by lowering your body's defenses against infection, but it also increases your risk of developing serious illnesses later in life. Debilitating diseases such as cancer, heart disease and osteoporosis are all directly related to diet. But as menacing as they sound, you can dramatically decrease your odds of having to tackle them simply by eating right. Our nutrition survival guide will tell you how. Arranged according to life stages—the younger years, the baby years, the mommy years and the golden years—each section addresses a woman's nutritional requirements at particular times in her life.

THE YOUNGER YEARS

Sidestepping snack machines and 7-Elevens can be quite a wrangle for young working women. Between fast-paced workdays and out-of-town travel, many women in their twenties have little time to prepare food—much less to eat three balanced meals a day.

During your early twenties, your bones continue to grow and

accumulate calcium—they're boning up, so to speak, for the future. And if you don't take in enough calcium (80 percent of women ages 19 to 24 don't), your bones will remain underdeveloped and your risk for osteoporosis (a disease in which bones become brittle and prone to breaking) will increase greatly.

The key to getting your Recommended Dietary Allowance (RDA) of 800 to 1,200 milligrams of calcium (and 5 micrograms of vitamin D, which promotes calcium absorption) is thinking in threes. Simply eat three servings each day of low-fat dairy products (which have the added benefit of being low-fat sources of protein and riboflavin, a B vitamin that active women need in mega-amounts); tofu; or greens, such as broccoli, spinach, collards, bok choy or turnip greens. If you find that your diet doesn't provide your calcium requirement, take a daily supplement of 400 to 500 milligrams.

In addition to paving the way for problems with osteoporosis later on, poor eating habits can also amplify the symptoms associated with premenstrual syndrome (PMS). Excessive sodium intake from take-out meals, frozen foods and high-fat treats can cause you to retain more water before and during menstruation than you would otherwise. And caffeine from coffee, tea and soda can augment the anxiety and mood changes often associated with PMS.

What's more, falling short on a group of vitamins and minerals known as antioxidants (vitamins C and E, beta-carotene and the mineral selenium) can leave your body susceptible to disease. Antioxidants help to stave off heart disease, cancer and cataracts as well as protect your skin from damage caused by air pollution and the sun's rays. To make sure you're eating your share of these preventive-health powerhouses, supplement your diet with several daily doses of fruit, such as oranges, cantaloupe, strawberries and papayas; yellow-orange vegetables, such as carrots, pumpkins, sweet potatoes and squash; and whole grains, such as whole-wheat bread and brown rice.

In addition to supplying adequate calcium, minimizing PMS and warding off heart disease, cancer and cataracts, establishing healthful eating habits during your twenties sets the stage for a lifetime of overall good health. Now's the time to develop a taste for low-fat fare, hone your broiling and stir-frying skills and limit your consumption of alcohol (which has been linked to breast cancer) and caffeine (which in large quantities is tied to infertility). In short, follow these quick tips for super nutrition in your twenties, and you'll be healthy into your eighties and beyond.

Savor a serving of yogurt a day. It's a great source of calcium and is more easily digested than many dairy products. Opt for refrigerated over frozen yogurt for more live and active cultures (which improve health) and less sugar.

Choose fast food wisely. Order grilled chicken sandwiches, low-fat milk shakes and salads with reduced-calorie dressings. Forgo the burger and fries.

Invest in the essential tools of low-fat living. Purchase a set of no-stick cookware and a cookbook that features low-fat recipes and healthful cooking tips.

Avoid buying snacks in bulk. Buy small or single-serving packages of chips, cookies and other high-fat snacks to guard against overindulgence.

Stock your desk with power snacks. Keep dried fruit, unsalted pretzels and small cans of low-sodium vegetable juice and fruit juice on hand for a low-fat, nutrient-packed boost at work.

Customize your takeout. Ask for MSG-free fare when you order Asian food—and skip the soy sauce while you're at it.

Graze. Eat small meals or snacks every three or four hours to maintain your energy and to guard against late-night gorging.

Eat smart when traveling. Opt for pretzels instead of peanuts while flying and go for salsa or cocktail sauce instead of the creamy, fat-laden dips that are popular at hotel salad bars.

THE BABY YEARS

Attention to nutrition is never more important than when you're thinking of having a child. Not only must the foods you select before, during and after your pregnancy meet your own nutrition needs, but they must also satisfy your baby's.

Folic acid is the key before and during the first three months of pregnancy. Also called folate, this B vitamin plays a crucial role in making new blood, muscle and skin cells, but its claim to fame is its ability to protect babies from severe neural-tube defects (damage to the part of the spinal cord that regulates the nerves).

The U.S. Public Health Service advises all women of child-bearing age to take in 400 micrograms of folic acid a day. While lentils, garbanzo beans, spinach and black beans are all good sources, it's tough to take in this much folic acid a day through diet alone. Ask your physician to recommend a good supplement.

After conception, your body's demand for vitamins and minerals skyrockets. Your need for calcium, which will build your baby's skeleton and boost your own stores in preparation for breast-feeding, jumps by 50 percent. Your iron requirement doubles to 30 milligrams. And your body's demand for folic acid, thiamin, riboflavin, niacin and vitamin C shoots up, too. Because it's tough to take in all these nutrients through food alone, ask your doctor to recommend a good prenatal multivitamin/mineral supplement, then continue to take it (and a calcium supplement) after your baby is born—especially if you're breast-feeding.

Your milk must supply your baby with all the nutrients it needs during the first four months of life. As a result, you should take in an additional 500 calories and 14 grams of protein every day (meaning: no dieting). Skimping on calories may lower the level of fat in your breast milk and retard your baby's growth, and falling behind on fluids may slow your production of milk.

The following tips will help you take in plenty of nutrients without putting on lots of pounds during the baby years.

Choose foods that are rich in nutrients but low in fat. Good choices include whole grains for B vitamins and fiber, nonfat dairy products for calcium and riboflavin, and poultry, lean meats and tuna packed in water for iron and zinc.

Look for color. Eat at least two servings daily of richly colored veggies, such as broccoli, bok choy and green and red peppers for vitamin C, folic acid and other B vitamins.

Drink oceans of water. Keep a bottle handy for frequent sips during the day.

Resist the sauce. Avoid alcoholic beverages while you're pregnant or breast-feeding.

Cut back on caffeine. Since it passes through the placenta during pregnancy and into breast milk while you're nursing, drink no more than the equivalent of two cups of coffee a day. (Soda and tea contain about half the caffeine of coffee, and chocolate contains even less.)

THE MOMMY YEARS

Super mom may be able to get the kids up, dressed and ready for school and still get to work by 9:00 A.M. without sacrificing her own breakfast. But the run-of-the-mill mortal mom often falls short of her nutritional needs. She may grab a hot dog or two here, a few spoonfuls of macaroni and cheese there, dining on kiddie favorites because she feels she has no time to do otherwise—and she compromises her health in the process.

Eating with little tykes often treats you to excess fat, but it cheats you of vitamin C, the B vitamins, iron, zinc and fiber. The results? A weakened immune system, ineffective at fending off the slew of cold and flu viruses your crew or kids exposes you to, and a sluggish digestive tract, which, in addition to causing chronic constipation, can increase your risk for colon cancer later on in life.

Use the following tips to keep your body fueled and your spirits up during these chaotic years.

Stock your fridge with fresh fruit and veggies. They're tasty, fat-free and packed with vitamins, minerals and fiber. Nibble on them when your children are chowing down on pizza and french fries. Who knows? Maybe they'll join you.

Snack on cereal. Most are fortified with vitamins and minerals and many are fat-free. Try Wheat Chex and low-fat granola.

Sit down for a meal. Even if it's only for ten minutes, you'll feel as though you've eaten and had a mini-break.

Encourage your children to eat healthful foods. This way, the family can eat well together.

Shun the fat. Buy low-fat or nonfat cheeses, dips, chips, crackers and the like—and feed them to your children, too.

THE GOLDEN YEARS

The older you get, the more important an "eat right for a longer, healthier life" philosophy becomes.

Age-related changes in your body such as menopause (which increases your risk for osteoporosis), slowed metabolism and declining intestinal function demand that you follow a low-fat, high-fiber diet that is rich in disease-fighting antioxidants. Otherwise, you risk poor daily performance and chronic illness, such as heart disease, breast cancer, osteoporosis, high cholesterol and intestinal problems, such as hemorrhoids and inflammation of the colon, later on. Unfortunately, this dietary goal is tough to meet because while calorie needs decline with age, the propensity to gain weight increases.

What's a health-minded woman to do? Choose foods that pack lots of nutrients into small packages (fruits and vegetables are best bets), take a calcium supplement of 500 to 1,000 milligrams daily to help slow bone-mineral loss, and use the following tips to help you maintain a healthful diet and a disease-resistant body.

Get your calcium and protein without the fat. Purchase nonfat or low-fat (1 percent) dairy products such as milk, yogurt and cottage cheese.

Toss down lots of salad. Strive to eat several servings of fruits and vegetables daily for loads of fiber and antioxidants—just watch how you dress them.

Read labels. Select low-fat or nonfat packaged foods, such as crackers and frozen dinners. Strive to eat no more than 15 grams of saturated fat a day.

Exercise in order to eat more. Walk daily and start strength-training two or three days a week to help build muscle and increase calorie burning.

—*Liz Applegate, Ph.D.*

AVOCADOS: THE "FAT" FRUIT THAT FIGHTS CHOLESTEROL

YOU'RE PROBABLY CONVINCED THAT THERE'S NO SUCH THING AS GOOD FAT. HERE'S GOOD NEWS ON THE "MONORAIL" TO HEALTH.

Break the rules of good nutrition and you'll pay: Your waistline and cholesterol level may puff up, for instance, or your thinking may falter.

But what if you break the rules, and instead of paying, you receive new health dividends? Maybe then it's time to change the rules, if only a little.

Take avocados, for instance. Look in most nutrition books, and you'll read that avocados are one of the rare plant foods that is very high in fat and should be eaten with caution.

Boldly throwing all caution to the wind, Australian researchers who suspected that the oil-rich fruit is probably good for you went ahead and put a group of people on an avocado diet for three weeks. Their suspicion appeared to be correct, they reported. The people on the avocado regimen (anywhere from ½ to 1½ avocados a day) saw their cholesterol levels go down significantly, from an average of 236 to 217.

But, before going on the avocado diet, the people spent an equal amount of time on a low-fat diet. Oddly, their total cholesterol dropped more eating avocados than it did on the low-fat diet (an 8.2 percent reduction, compared with only 4.9 percent).

What's more, the avocados preserved high-density lipoprotein (HDL) levels (the good cholesterol that actually removes bad cholesterol), while HDLs went down almost 14 percent on the low-fat diet.

MONO-MANIACS TO THE RESCUE

But just why did the Australians suspect that avocados would help? The answer is one word: monounsaturates, the chief fat in avocados and the same fatty acids that are present in olive oil.

Building on earlier work suggesting that olive oil is a heart-friendly dietary component, the Aussies have now seemingly made an equal case for avocados.

Besides olive oil and avocados, the other notable sources of "mono" fats are canola (now used widely in cooking) and nuts. Nuts have also been included in the same "eat-with-caution" rule because of their high fat and calorie density. But that may change.

In one surprising study, researchers found that when people ate about 3½ ounces of almonds a day, their cholesterol levels went down 20 points, even though the nuts raised their fat intake considerably.

Researchers working with 30 people recruited at the YMCA

Cardiac Rehabilitation Unit in Palo Alto, California, added nuts (both whole and ground almonds) to the low-fat diet most of the people already ate.

A cholesterol drop came from harmful low-density lipoproteins (LDLs); protective HDL was unchanged. Although these results seemed somewhat "nutty" to physicians who believe that adding fat to the diet is never a good idea, another piece of research conducted independently adds credibility to the "nut theory."

More nut research was done at the Loma Linda University's Center for Health Research in California. Instead of giving nuts, scientists tracked over 30,000 people for up to six years, then tried to find relationships between what the people said they ate and the appearance of fatal and nonfatal cardiac events. They found a clear correlation between a high frequency of nut consumption and a low risk of winding up in a cardiac unit.

IT PAYS TO BE NUTS ABOUT NUTS

People who ate nuts more than four times a week had about half the risk of people who ate nuts less than once a week. People who ate nuts somewhere between those extremes generally had a risk that was also between the extremes.

Roughly one-third of the nuts eaten were peanuts, about another third almonds, while the rest were walnuts and others—all high in monounsaturates.

While some scientists are not yet ready to rewrite the rule book on fat consumption, some think we should at least put in some boldface footnotes about monounsaturates. Two who feel that way are Frank M. Sacks, M.D., and Walter C. Willett, M.D., both of the Harvard University School of Public Health.

Dr. Sacks says that he sees a possible problem with low-fat, high-carbohydrate diets that lower not only total cholesterol but the good HDL as well.

Better, he thinks, is to get the saturated fats out of your diet by cutting back on meat, full-fat dairy products and eggs and to replace some of the missing calories with monounsaturated fats—like those found in olive oil, canola oil and nuts.

The result, he says, will be lower cholesterol, but not lower HDLs. To him, that's a smarter equation.

Plus, says Dr. Sacks—like other like-minded physicians—a diet where monos are allowed is more palatable and versatile. The "Mediterranean diet" is cited as an example of just such a cuisine. It's replete with vegetables, beans, fruits, grains and fish, but with relatively little saturated fat. In this diet, olive oil is used extensively for cooking, salads, even as a substitute for butter. And the heart health of those who eat it—in Spain, Italy and Greece, for instance—is outstandingly good.

Prevention magazine advises cutting back on saturated fats as a primary strategy. Virtually everyone agrees they're harmful. We're talking about some American staples: hot dogs, cheeseburgers, steaks, lunch meats, sausage, pepperoni pizza, ice cream, butter, whole milk (or cream) and eggs. Do that and you not only cut back on these very harmful saturates, but probably on your total fat.

Then, add some of the known good guys—the veggies, whole grains, fruits, the nonfat and low-fat dairy team and seafood. Third, replace some of those saturated guys with the mono squad. After you take the sausage or meatballs out of your pasta, splash on some olive oil. And drizzle some on your big green salads, too.

If you make your own pizza with low-fat or even nonfat cheese, add some olive oil to the dough to give the pizza more pizzazz.

Canola oil is good for cooking and baking, anywhere you don't want the fragrance of the olive grove. For stir-frying, use peanut oil, as the Chinese do. Finally, avocados are great in salads and sandwiches—and, of course, guacamole.

—*Mark Bricklin with Margo Trott*

THE CARDIO-NUTRIENTS

VITAMINS AND MINERALS PACK AN ADDED PUNCH AGAINST HEART DISEASE. HERE'S HOW TO GET THE RIGHT STUFF.

It's becoming more and more clear through scientific research that certain vitamins and minerals, along with exercise and a healthy diet, are associated with a lower risk of heart disease.

Right now, most of the scientific evidence centers around vitamins C and E and beta-carotene—otherwise known as the antioxidants. Research supports their heart connection on two fronts. First, a number of large studies suggest that people who have a high dietary intake of C, E and beta-carotene have a lower risk of heart disease and heart attack than people whose diets aren't as nutrient-rich. Second, there's laboratory evidence that suggests these nutrients help prevent low-density lipoproteins (LDLs)—the bad stuff—from being damaged by mutated oxygen molecules known as free radicals. Free radicals, the theory goes, cause changes in LDL that make it accumulate in your arteries, forming the "fatty streaks" that are the first signs of heart disease.

Preliminary research has also linked supplemental vitamins and minerals with lower risk of heart disease. They include the B vitamins (B_6, B_{12} and folate), potassium and calcium and trace minerals, like magnesium, chromium and selenium.

SHOULD YOU TAKE SUPPLEMENTS?

Nutritional experts have long held that eating a proper diet—containing generous amounts of whole grains, fruits and vegetables—should supply adequate amounts of all the nutrients the body needs.

But sometimes, it seems, eating the healthiest diet may not be enough. Case in point: vitamin E. Not too long ago two large studies made a connection between vitamin E intake and risk of heart attacks. One of these studies involved over 87,000 female nurses. In it, the women taking at least 100 international units (IU) of vitamin E per day for two or more years had 36 percent fewer heart attacks than those who didn't supplement their diets.

Doctors say they are not yet willing to recommend vitamin E supplements until more research is conducted, but with such promising data at hand, some researchers admit that they have begun to supplement their own diets.

One thing to consider is the fact that a heart-smart diet—one that's very low in fat and cholesterol—limits foods like eggs and seed oils, such as sunflower or sesame-seed oil, which are key sources of vitamin E. Whole grains, kale and spinach—all super foods in a heart-healthy diet—are good, not great, sources of vitamin E. Consider, too, that aside from the cost, taking vitamin E supplements (up to 400 IU per day) doesn't appear to have any negative effects.

WHAT ABOUT IRON?

You may have heard about a recent study linking high levels of iron in the blood with a higher risk of heart attack. Those findings created a big stir. So, should we trash our daily iron-formula multivitamins, iron-fortified cereals and high-iron foods in the name of heart health? The bottom line is, we can't tell from a single study whether high amounts of iron compromise your heart health. Experts point out that there are some research flaws.

The take-home message has two parts, says registered dietitian Sonja Connor, research associate professor of clinical nutrition at Oregon Health Sciences University School of Medicine and expert on nutrition and heart disease. "First, if you cut back on animal sources of fat, using small amounts of vegetable oils and margarine, and eat more fruits, vegetables, grains and beans, you don't need to worry about getting too much or too little iron."

Second, "No one should take iron supplements without a demonstrated need for them," Connor says. That even goes for people at risk for low iron levels like premenopausal women, vegetarians and people with bleeding ulcers and bleeding disorders. If you are in a high-risk category, ask your doctor to perform a serum ferritin test—a special blood test that measures the amount of stored iron in your body—before you start supplementing. Some people—perhaps as many as one in 300—have a genetic disorder that makes them susceptible to iron overload, which could lead to liver damage, diabetes or heart problems. If you have a family history of this disorder, known as hemochromatosis, avoid iron supplements and seek a doctor's or dietitian's advice about your diet.

By contrast, vitamin C and beta-carotene, the two other promising antioxidants science is aggressively studying, are readily available in fruits and vegetables—the core ingredients in a heart-healthy, low-fat diet.

Despite this, a multivitamin/mineral supplement may protect against the diet fluctuations we all face. Top heart specialist Dean Ornish, M.D., director of the Preventive Medicine Research Institute in Saulsalito, California, advocates a very low fat diet to reverse heart disease. He also suggests that his patients take a daily supplement.

—Lisa Delaney

FOODS THAT KILL PAIN

THINK ASPIRIN IS ALL THAT CAN HELP YOUR HEADACHE? THINK AGAIN. NEW RESEARCH SAYS YOUR DIET CAN PREVENT PAIN.

Some days, the aches just won't quit. Nothing major, mind you—a nagging headache, a stiff back or menstrual cramps that refuse to let up. So you pop a couple of over-the-counter painkillers and resign yourself to waiting for the discomfort to subside. You've done all that you can.

Or have you? New research on the connection between diet and pain suggests that if you eat the right foods, you may be able to make yourself less susceptible to the annoying aches that are part of everyday life. Some of the studies focus on sugar and pain relief, particularly in infants and children. Others are investigating the pain-killing abilities of hot chili peppers and similar fiery condiments.

But the most substantial body of research concerns the pain-preventing properties of minerals. Instead of waiting until the pain hits to do something about it, you may be able to stop the pain before it starts by making sure your diet includes plenty of calcium, manganese and copper.

What's the connection between minerals and pain? The research is still in its infancy, so scientists aren't completely sure. But what they do know is that minerals are important ingredients in neurohormones, the brain chemicals that send signals to the body. Some neurohormones, particularly the beta-endorphins, are known to be part of the body's natural pain-control system. To make these neurohormones, the body requires minerals.

COMFORTING CALCIUM

The connection between calcium and pain was discovered when the U.S. Department of Agriculture nutrition scientist James G. Penland, M.D., was trying to figure out how to prevent osteoporosis. While conducting studies on the topic, he noticed that women who had adequate levels of calcium in their diets had less menstrual pain.

At the Human Nutrition Research lab in Grand Forks, North Dakota, Dr. Penland supervises careful, long-term studies of mineral status. Most of his research concerns major public health problems, such as osteoporosis, the brittle-bone disease caused by a lack of calcium that afflicts many American women after menopause.

Suspecting that calcium might somehow be involved in pain relief, Dr. Penland asked the ten women in his first calcium/osteoporosis study to fill out daily questionnaires, marking down the days they felt menstrual pain. Some members of the group were on a diet that provided them with about 500 or 600 milligrams of calcium a day—a figure well below the Recommended Dietary Allowance (RDA) of 800 milligrams. Others took a supplement and averaged 1,000 milligrams a day. The result: "We found strong beneficial effects of calcium on reported pain," says Dr. Penland.

Now, Dr. Penland is repeating the study on 80 women in the community. Although no results are in yet, a preliminary review of 40 of the women confirms the effects of calcium on pain. In fact, some of the women have guessed that they are taking calcium. "It's surprising the number of women who know what diet they are on, based on pain relief," says Dr. Penland. Another study revealed that manganese, a trace mineral that works with calcium, helps to make the general pain-relieving effect even stronger.

Other scientists report similar findings. At Mount Sinai Medical Center in New York City, Susan Thys Jacobs, M.D., an internist, found that calcium supplements help reduce some symptoms of premenstrual syndrome (PMS). Another study reported that women who drink milk on a regular basis also report less menstrual pain.

James Chuong, M.D., a reproductive endocrinologist and director of the PMS program at Baylor College of Medicine in Houston, studied ten women who suffered from premenstrual syndrome and ten who didn't. In the days just before their periods, the women with PMS experienced a drop in blood levels of calcium. That wasn't true of the women without PMS.

The levels of calcium in the PMS women weren't low enough to make them deficient, but the drop may have been enough to

WHAT ABOUT NIACIN?

You've probably heard that niacin's a supernutrient when it comes to having a healthy heart. And it's true—in fact, many studies have shown that it's the best choice for people who haven't had any luck lowering cholesterol with diet, exercise, smoking cessation or other lifestyle changes. It's been known to increase the level of high-density lipoproteins (HDLs)—the good stuff—by as much as 30 percent, with fewer side effects than other cholesterol-lowering drugs. But it takes megadoses of niacin to achieve these results—doses so high that it's considered a drug, not a vitamin.

Large amounts of niacin should be taken only under a doctor's supervision. Niacin may aggravate stomach ulcers, liver problems, diabetes or arthritis. Unless your cholesterol profile and risk factors put you at high risk, you probably get as much niacin as you need by following a well-balanced diet and taking your daily multivitamin/mineral supplement. If you think you need therapeutic doses of niacin, talk to your doctor.

affect the brain neurohormones that suppress PMS pain. "Our studies suggest that PMS patients have low levels of calcium before their periods, which may be associated with PMS symptoms," says Dr. Chuong. "They are consistent with Dr. Penland's results."

Dr. Chuong tells his patients that while he can't guarantee that taking a calcium supplement will help with the pain of PMS, it may—and it certainly won't do any harm. "Taking 500 to 1,000 milligrams a day is just fine," says Dr. Chuong, "and it protects the bones."

"The converging evidence is exciting," says Dr. Penland. "There's also a lot of anecdotal evidence. A lot of women told me, 'Oh yeah, my mother told me that a long time ago.'" In the '60s, he notes, Adelle Davis, the nutrition guru and best-selling author, also wrote that calcium could help with premenstrual symptoms. Says Dr. Penland, "Now we have good data."

Dairy products are the best sources of calcium. If you can't tolerate them (or their fat and cholesterol content), broccoli and green leafy vegetables are also full of calcium. One cup of kale is nearly as calcium-rich as a cup of whole milk.

COPPER CURE

Copper is another mineral that has shown promise in relieving pain. While Dr. Penland hasn't studied calcium in men (they're not part of osteoporosis studies), he has found that copper status affects general susceptibility to pain in both men and women.

Dr. Penland's studies usually last six months, and everything is monitored. When his volunteers have headaches, they have to get even an over-the-counter painkiller from the infirmary. Looking back over the records, Dr. Penland found that when study participants were on low-copper diets, they asked for more painkillers. He excluded people who were acutely sick— those who had the flu or had broken a bone. In four different studies, low copper status was associated with increased requests for painkillers.

Combining low levels of copper with high fructose intake intensified the effect. That's because fructose interferes with copper nutrition. Fructose is found in sodas and many sweetened commercial foods. Men on a low-copper, high-fructose diet requested painkillers 7.1 percent of the time. When they received sufficient copper, that number dropped to about 3 percent.

A study of women found that those on an adequate copper diet requested painkillers 11 percent of the time. But when their copper was cut in half, their painkiller requests jumped to 22 percent.

Even if you're not experiencing everyday aches and pains, it makes sense to eat more copper-rich foods. As an antioxidant mineral, copper may play some role in cancer protection—and many Americans don't get enough.

Seafood, nuts, seeds and liver are all excellent sources of copper. Multivitamin/mineral supplements may also contain copper. Although adults need between 1.5 and 3.0 milligrams a day, you can buy much more in a health food store. But don't. Too much copper can interfere with the absorption of other minerals.

SWEET RELIEF

It takes a long time to become deficient in minerals or, once deficient, to restore the body's levels to normal. But some foods can affect our pain sensitivity within minutes. Sugar may have this instant effect on pain, if recent studies of newborns and young children are any indication.

In every U.S. hospital, infants are given a heel prick to draw blood to test for phenylketonuria, and most male infants are circumcised. For safety reasons, anesthesia is not used in either case. And predictably, the babies cry. But at Cornell University in Ithaca, New York, Elliot M. Blass, Ph.D., professor of psychology and nutrition, has discovered a quick, cheap, safe and effective painkiller: a pacifier dipped in sugar water.

In one study, children undergoing the heel prick who were given a few drops of sugar water before an operation cried 50 percent less than infants given plain water. Similarly, infants undergoing circumcision cried 67 percent of the time. Give pacifiers and crying drops to 49 percent. Dip the pacifiers in sugar, and the figure falls to 31 percent.

At Montreal's McGill University, Simon Young, Ph.D., professor of psychiatry, found a similar effect in 9-, 10- and 11-year-olds. He asked them to hold either water or a sugar solution in their mouths while submerging an arm in very, very cold water until it started to hurt. The children with the sugar water in their mouths could keep their arms in the water longer.

Dr. Blass believes sugar reduces pain sensation by stimulating the body's natural pain-killing endorphins. Of course, here, too, moderation is the key. Eating your weight in brownies to get rid of a headache will probably get you a stomachache in return, but the evidence does suggest that a little something sweet can bring big relief.

POTENT PEPPERS

It's not only pleasant substances that stimulate the brain's natural painkillers. Some scientists speculate that fiery hot chili peppers may also get the body to produce more endorphins. Advocates of their theory cite one study in which a man who loved chilis was given an endorphin-blocking drug. Once the body's natural painkillers were turned off, he could no longer stand the peppers.

This makes sense if you understand how the system works. Endorphins are often synthesized in response to pain. Chili peppers may "fool" the body into thinking it's in pain. They irritate the tongue, causing a searing sensation; tears come to your eyes. Your body thinks it's being hurt (although capsaicin, the active ingredient in hot chilies, is actually benign). As a result, endorphins flood your body, and you start to feel better.

Mustard, black pepper, radishes, alcoholic drinks and even cinnamon in high concentrations may have the same effect. But some scientists are skeptical.

"It's an intriguing hypothesis, but there's no good evidence for it or against it," says Barry Green, Ph.D., a research scientist at the Monell Chemical Senses Center in Philadelphia. The endorphin system is so central to pain sensation, he notes, that when you block it, you "muck up the self-control of the pain system. It doesn't mean that the release of those opioids is what makes eating peppers pleasant."

It may just mean that if it feels good, it feels good. Says Dr. Green, "The release of endorphins is thought to be associated with any kind of pleasant experience." The very pleasure we take in eating, especially with friends and family, in a relaxed environment, may make us less susceptible to pain. It's certainly the easiest cure to take.

—*Robert Barnett*

HOW COMMON DRUGS CAN ROB YOU OF VITAMINS

BEFORE YOU TAKE THAT ANTACID OR ASPIRIN, KNOW HOW IT CAN AFFECT YOUR NUTRITION.

When you take an aspirin or antacid, you're usually trying to soothe a headache or an upset stomach. Unfortunately, you may also be preventing yourself from absorbing the nutrients in the food you eat. And while occasional medication generally doesn't pose problems, frequent use can have health consequences you never considered.

Both prescription and over-the-counter medications as well as such nontherapeutic drugs as alcohol and caffeine are capable of affecting your nutritional status in a number of ways. The most obvious consequence is that they can decrease your appetite so that you don't eat enough food in the first place. Some drug-nutrient interactions, however, are complicated and much less apparent.

Medications can bind themselves to nutrients, changing their structure so that they won't fit through your intestinal walls. Drugs can also speed up the action of your intestines, so nutrients don't remain there long enough to be absorbed. And they can tamper with the digestive juices and enzymes that are necessary for nutrient absorption. Medications such as diuretics and laxatives can increase the excretion of certain vitamins and minerals.

Older women as well as women who diet or drink heavily are at risk for these drug-induced nutrient deficiencies. So are women who have taken drugs for a long time—for anything from diabetes to birth control. Here are some common drugs and the nutritional consequences of using them.

Antacids. These are a quick remedy for heartburn because they reduce stomach acidity. But many vitamins and minerals, such as iron, folic acid, vitamins A and B_{12}, require an acidic digestive system for maximum absorption. As a result, it is best to take an antacid on an empty stomach rather than with meals or with supplements.

Many women consume calcium-carbonate-based antacids—like Tums—as a supplementary source of calcium. While calcium carbonate is good for protecting your bones, only 10 percent of the calcium in an antacid is absorbed, because the medication is taken on an empty stomach. Antacids that contain magnesium or aluminum hydroxides, such as Maalox HRF, actually inhibit calcium absorption, especially if taken three or more times a day. Antacids containing aluminum hydroxide should not be consumed with citrus fruits or juices because the citric acid increases the absorption of aluminum, which can be toxic to the nerves and bones.

High blood pressure medications. Some diuretic medications used to treat high blood pressure (hypertension) increase urinary excretion of magnesium, a mineral which is believed to protect against heart disease. To avoid problems, people taking these drugs should consume daily several servings of magnesium-rich foods, such as dark green leafy vegetables, low-fat milk, wheat germ and bananas, or take a supplement of no more than 500 milligrams of magnesium. Two hypertension medications, captopril and enalapril, may reduce zinc levels and compromise the immune system. To boost zinc, be sure to eat foods such as oysters, turkey and lima beans or take a 12 to 15 milligram supplement.

Antibiotics. These drugs are designed to destroy disease-causing bacteria. However, they also destroy bacteria that help maintain good health. The beneficial bacteria manufacture several nutrients in the large intestine, including biotin, which is essential to the metabolism of fats and protein, and vitamin K, which promotes wound healing. Long-term use of some antibiotics, such as tetracycline, may reduce or halt the manufacture of these nutrients, produce a vitamin K deficiency and deplete the small amount of vitamin C that is stored in the body.

In addition, consuming such antibiotics as tetracycline with meals or with milk reduces the absorption of both the medication and several minerals (including calcium, iron and magnesium). These deficiencies can be prevented by eating a nutrient-dense diet. Researchers at the Harvard School of Public Health found that vitamin C taken with antibiotics increased the effectiveness of the medication.

Antidepressants. The monoamine oxidase inhibitors (MAOIs) used in the treatment of depression can cause several potentially harmful effects. MAOIs allow tyramine to enter the bloodstream directly, which can lead to hypertension and headaches. People taking them should limit or avoid foods containing tyramine, such as aged cheese, sour cream, smoked meats, soy sauce, beer and red wine.

Alcohol. By irritating the digestive tract, alcohol inhibits the absorption of folic acid, protein, calcium and vitamins C, B_1, B_{12}, A, D and E. Alcohol also increases a woman's requirements for vitamins B_1 and B_6, biotin and niacin, because these nutrients aid the liver in the detoxification of alcohol.

In addition, alcohol drains the body's tissue stores of several nutrients, including vitamins A and E, selenium and calcium. Since many of these nutrients function as antioxidants, their depletion can leave the body defenseless against disease and infection. Even the best diet combined with vitamin and mineral supplements cannot completely protect the body's organs from the damage caused by alcohol abuse. Alcohol abuse commonly results in malnutrition.

Birth control pills. Long-term use can lower your levels of vitamin B_6, an essential component in the production of serotonin, which regulates mood. Women using the Pill should increase their dietary intake of such B_6-rich foods as bananas, kidney beans and chicken.

Cigarettes. Inhaling tobacco smoke removes vitamin C from the tissues and blood, increasing a smoker's Recommended Dietary Allowance from 60 milligrams to 200 milligrams. It also results in lower absorption of vitamins A and B_6 and beta-carotene. Since tobacco smoke increases free-radical damage to tissues, it is important for smokers to increase consumption of the antioxidant vitamins as well as folic acid and vitamin B_{12}.

Aspirin. Since aspirin can cause bleeding in the digestive tract, long-term use can lead to iron deficiency, anemia and reduced formation of red blood cells. In large doses, it can also block absorption of folic acid and vitamins B_{12} and C. To prevent this nutrient interaction, take aspirin in the morning and supplements at night, or vice versa: Don't take them at the same time.

Caffeine. Tannins and other compounds in coffee and tea reduce mineral absorption, especially iron, by as much as 90 percent. Extra vitamin C helps counteract the iron depletion. Since more than two cups of coffee or tea may cause calcium imbalances, women should drink coffee and tea between meals, rather than with food.

—*Elizabeth Somer, R.D.*

PART SEVEN

BODY
SHAPING

EXERCISE IN DISGUISE

DON'T SWEAT IT. WORK YOUR BODY
WITHOUT WORKING OUT—
JUST CHOOSE THESE EASY MOVES.

Anne bought a stationary bike a few years ago, anticipating many hours of wonderful cycling fitness; its handlebars now serve as her husband's tie rack. Jane had grand plans to shape up by lifting weights; her dumbbells now function as bookends. And Renee? She's still making payments on a StairMaster that her 15-year-old daughter uses more than she does.

"I just never have the time to work out," she says. "The day they invent a way to exercise that will allow me to get dinner ready, do the laundry, clean the house and watch the kids at the same time, give me a call."

Well, ring-a-ling, Renee. They have. Go ahead and ditch your fancy equipment—and your guilt, too—because new research shows that you can get fit without sweating miserably.

"Exercise doesn't have to happen in gym clothes or make you sweat to be good for you," says Jerome Brandon, Ph.D., an exercise physiologist at Georgia State University in Atlanta. "All exercise really has to do is get you off your butt."

Bryant Stamford, Ph.D., director of the Health Promotion and Wellness Center at the University of Louisville in Kentucky and coauthor of *Fitness without Exercise* agrees. "For years, scientists thought exercise had to be aerobic—of a sufficient intensity and continuous for at least 20 to 30 minutes—to produce cardiovascular benefits," he says. "But new research shows that any activity that gets you moving will produce worthwhile results—regardless of how long you do it or whether it gets your heart rate into an aerobic zone."

FIGHTING THE NATIONAL EXERCISE DEFICIT

Despite much goading from marketing executives at Nike few of us "just do it." Surveys show that fewer than 15 percent of all Americans get their recommended thrice-weekly half-hour aerobic workouts. Why? Because the idea of "no pain, no gain" runs smack into basic human nature. "Not only is it unnatural from a physiological standpoint to push ourselves to the limit with exercise," says Dr. Stamford, "but it's a huge burden psychologically. Most of us work hard enough as it is without having to torture ourselves with strenuous exercise routines."

Not that there's anything wrong with more traditional exercise, says Victoria Johnson, fitness instructor and author of a health and self-empowerment book entitled *Victoria Johnson's Attitude*. "For some, this is the best way to go," she says. "But for others, it's simply not. And it's just nice to know there are other more practical and enjoyable ways to exercise."

Getting the picture? If it gets you moving—regardless of how fast or how far—it'll burn calories. And the key to achieving good health is to move enough to burn at least 200 calories a day beyond what you would by lounging in front of the TV. Whether you hang wash on the line instead of throwing it in the dryer or take a swim with the kids instead of taking them to the movies, the activity will boost your heart health and slim your waistline.

And this is important. Sedentary people are at greater risk for heart disease, diabetes, high blood pressure, obesity, stress and even some forms of cancer than reasonably active people. Here's how you can be one of the latter.

ON THE JOB

You say you work too hard as it is? Perhaps mentally, but probably not physically. Unless your job is very physical, you most likely don't burn any more calories on the job than you would by lying on the beach. With a little imagination, however, you can squeeze some physical activity into your workday. And since this movement will help you feel more energetic and alert, it may turn out to be as good for your career as it is for your health. Here are some tips to get you started.

Take the stairs instead of the elevator. Believe it or not, stair-climbing burns more calories per minute than running. In fact, researchers at Johns Hopkins University in Baltimore figure that the average person can gain four additional seconds of life for every step climbed—something to keep in mind the next time you're waiting for the elevator. *Estimated calorie-burn:* five for every average flight of stairs climbed.

Park as far as possible from the fray. Walk the extra steps; you'll burn calories and save fuel. *Estimated calorie-burn:* 20 for every five minutes.

Do more talking face-to-face. Why tie up the telephone lines when you can walk over to a colleague's office? It's a great calorie-burner and a highly effective bridge-builder, too. *Estimated calorie-burn:* 20 for five walks of one minute each.

Walk when you need to think. It's a good way to burn calories and a great way to stimulate thought. Some studies even suggest that swinging your arms while walking boosts your concentration by improving the communication between the right and left sides of your brain. So take "long-cuts" to the restroom or do more walking than talking during coffee breaks. *Estimated calorie-burn:* 20 for one five-minute walk.

Stay vertical. By replacing an hour of sitting with an hour of standing each workday, you'll burn enough calories to lose a pound of fat in a year. *Estimated calorie-burn:* 15 for each hour spent standing rather than sitting.

Pace when appropriate. Just as standing burns more calories than sitting, pacing burns more calories than standing— about 1 calorie for every 15 steps taken. Pace when you're on the phone, waiting at the copy machine or deep in thought. *Estimated calorie-burn:* 15 for each five minutes of pacing.

HAVIN' FUN

That's right—fun! Activities you enjoy are every bit as effective at burning calories as those you don't. In many cases they're even better because you're likely to participate for longer periods of time. Here's proof positive.

Dance your way to fitness. Forget the sweatsuit—put on your best dress instead. Groovin' while you're movin' around the house can burn calories at a rate of approximately 340 an hour—about the same as riding a stationary bike!

Watch the ball, not your heart rate. It's amazing what a little competition will do to take your mind off the rigors your body is going through. Games such as softball, basketball, tennis, volleyball and even golf (if you ditch the cart and the caddy) are exceptionally good calorie-burners, and they are relaxing and lots of fun. An hour of shooting hoops, for example, can burn as many calories as a three-mile jog.

Find fitness between the sheets. Calories burned in the bedroom count as much as those burned in the gym—heavy breathing is heavy breathing, after all.

AROUND THE HOUSE

What has walls, windows and more potential for offering high-quality exercise than any fitness gizmo? Your house! The chores you do in and around it can be valuable exercise. Start thinking "a neater house for a slimmer shape," and your body—as well as your abode—will be in better condition before you know it.

Stoop to better health. While there's arguably no more odious task than scrubbing floors, the job can do wonders for your waistline. In fact, a good afternoon of "floor work" can help you scour away more body fat than cycling or weight training by burning approximately 380 calories per hour. How do you think Mr. Clean got such a great bod?

Turn on your muscles, not an appliance. Kitchen appliances are convenient, but they rob us of some valuable exercise opportunities in addition to pumping up our electric bills. So put the squeeze on your utilities company and enhance your health by using some energy of your own.

Hire your heart, not a professional. Have some indoor painting to be done? Some furniture to be refinished? Bookshelves to be built? Why spend lots of money when you can spend calories instead? Just try sanding a piece of furniture by hand and you'll get the picture pronto.

WITH THE FAMILY

Not only can your children bring more activity into your life, but you can add some much-needed activity to theirs, too. In fact, it's vital that you do—studies show that about 40 percent of today's kids display at least one major risk factor for heart disease (high blood pressure, high cholesterol or a weight problem) by the tender age of eight.

"Youth doesn't protect kids from the junk they eat or the 25 hours of TV they typically watch each week," says Dr. Brandon. "The more active you are, the more your children will be—not just now but for the rest of their lives." Here's how to peak your kids' interest in fitness—and raise your own activity level in the process.

Encourage sports. Just say yes—to softball, basketball, football, soccer, swimming, volleyball and gymnastics. It may inconvenience you to get them where they need to go, but you'll be laying the foundation for an interest in athletics that could last a lifetime. Better yet, you'll get plenty of exercise yourself by helping them to perfect their newly developed skills at home.

Push play—and play along. Kids don't need to be star athletes to be active. Show them that physical activity can be loads of fun, and they are likely to move their bodies for the rest of their lives. Besides, there's some great exercise to be had by you, too, if you join your kids in the fun. A little jump rope, hopscotch or T-ball is guaranteed to work a few muscles you may have forgotten you have.

Take walks. The family that walks together, talks together. So head for the nearest park or playground—on foot, of course—then hop on the swings, monkey bars, seesaws and slides. You'll work your body as much as you would by wrestling with some hydraulic monster at the gym, and you'll spend some quality time with the people in your life that make your efforts all worthwhile.

—*Porter Shimer*

GETTING THE MOST OUT OF YOUR MUSCLE

USE THE TRICKS OF THE BODYBUILDING TRADE TO REV UP YOUR METABOLISM AND TONE UP FAST.

Thinking of giving weight lifting a try? What's stopping you? Perhaps this one key question: "With the very limited amount of free time I have in my schedule, can I really do enough strength training to benefit my body?"

The answer is simple. Yes, you can get stronger, firmer and shapelier without spending hours in your gym shorts. As long as you hit the muscles the right way—with the right exercises, the right number of sets and the proper amount of rest—you can get great results in minutes. That's right, minutes—12 of 'em, to be exact.

LESS IN MORE (MORE OR LESS)

You have hundreds of muscles in your body. Some help you get your luggage off a rack; others help you blink an eyelid. The key in training is to narrow the field.

You want to target the biggies—the major muscle groups. But to do it in less time, you want to hit them in bunches. And to do that you need compound exercises.

A compound exercise combines movements that work out more than one muscle at the same time. A leg press, for example, hits the quadriceps (the large muscles on the front of your thighs), hamstrings (the large muscles on the back of your thighs) and buttocks as well as the calves of the lower leg. "Essentially, with a leg press or similar compound exercise, you're doing four exercises in one," says exercise physiologist and physical therapist Phil Dunphy, director of Hudson Physical Therapy in Jersey City.

By doing compound exercises like the bench press, military press and leg press, you avoid doing specific exercises that cover less territory but eat up more time. You get the same results with time to spare.

ORDER EQUALS SPEED

To keep your workout short and to the point, get yourself in order.

"By alternating upper-body exercises with lower-body ones, you don't tire as quickly and you don't need to rest as much," says Doug Semenick, certified strength and conditioning specialist and director of the wellness program at the University of

Louisville in Kentucky. If you must do upper-body exercises in a straight sequence, then alternate the pushing ones with the pulling ones.

With the bench press, for example, you push the weight up; with the lat machine pull-down (works the latissimus dorsi, a back muscle), you pull the weight toward you. Each exercise works an opposing, or antagonistic, muscle group. Do those one after the other, and tired muscles won't slow you down. And you shave minutes of rest off your workout.

If you have time to do exercises that work smaller muscles as well as those that work big muscles, start with the biggies first.

The reason for this is simple: Smaller muscles tire faster, and if you do them before the larger muscles, they'll fail on you. "If you went to do an arm-and-back exercise, but you already exercised your forearms, for example, then that smaller area of muscle may be too tired to hold the bar and keep a strong-enough grip throughout the exercise," says Semenick.

Put the small stuff that isolates the smaller muscles at or near the end of the workout. Given limited time, you get the most bang for your buck by working the larger muscles.

And if you plan on doing lower-back, neck or abdominal exercises, hold them off till the very end, too. You may bog down if you start with them.

For proof, you can try this experiment (or maybe just think about trying it). Do as many partial sit-ups as you can—safely—in two minutes. Then turn over and try a couple of push-ups. "Your belly should flop to the floor," says Semenick. Sit-ups nail your upper and lower body's stabilizer muscles, so once they're taxed, your body becomes unable to perform any other total-body exercise with any real force.

If you're in a big hurry and would rather skip abdominal exercises, you can sneak them in when you're doing other exercises. "By tensing up your abdominal muscles when you're doing a triceps push-down, for example, you're working those muscles effectively," says Dunphy. "And when you're doing pull-ups, all you really have to do is think about your abdominals, and they're getting worked." By concentrating on them as you pull up and let yourself down, your body's on automatic pilot, tensing those muscles every step of the way.

GETTING A RIGHTFUL REST

Rest is vital, but you don't need a siesta. When you're exercising a muscle, you're working through its "energy system," which is really no more than the muscle's gas tank. In the time it takes to do those crucial eight to ten repetitions, you've sapped the muscle's immediate energy source of fuel—now it needs a nap to get it back to full power. "Temporary muscle failure drains all the energy the muscle has stored in it," says Semenick. Rest for 30 seconds, and you've recovered half of it. In one minute, you've recovered roughly 75 percent. After two minutes, nearly all—or 94 percent—is recovered. "You shouldn't have to wait any more than that to get back into the next set with adequate strength and power," says Semenick.

You can rest two minutes between heavy sets of the same exercise, but you can probably shorten or eliminate the rest when you change from one exercise to a new one that works different muscles. You may have to rest only a minute or less between a leg press and a bench press, for example, since the former targets the legs, and the latter hits the chest.

TWO SETS AND YOU'RE SET

Remember that you perform exercises in sets, which are groups of repetitions done successively, with rest in between each group. The key is to do enough, but not to go overboard. But how many is enough?

When you're lifting weights, you're constantly breaking down muscle that is later rebuilt with a bonus. One powerful set hits the muscle hard. Another set repeats the process but to a lesser degree, as your muscles fatigue more. Same for a third set.

As you go on, improvements in strength and muscle mass get smaller and smaller. "The number of sets begins to mean very little," says James Graves, Ph.D., exercise physiologist from the University of Florida in Gainesville. "If you exercise to momentary fatigue or muscle exhaustion, you have used most fibers in the muscle. That's really what you want." You can do that—believe it or not—in just one or two sets.

"By trial and error, researchers and athletes have found that once you've depleted the energy from the muscle and tired it out, the extra sets aren't worth the time required to complete them," says Dr. Graves.

The law of diminishing returns starts coming into play—"unless, of course, the participant has specific goals related to muscle size and endurance," he says.

Less, therefore, may mean more. As long as you push your muscles to fatigue—where you can barely lift the weight at the last repetition—you've done the job.

HOW HARD SHOULD I PUSH MYSELF?

A question women frequently ask regards intensity. "How should the exercise feel when I'm doing it? Should I be grunting and groaning to near exhaustion, or should I pick a weight level that offers little resistance at all? How do I know where to start?"

Ideally, you should try to do sets of 8 to 10 repetitions at about 75 percent of your 1-repetition maximum (the amount of weight you can lift in one shot). That means if you can lift 100 pounds once in a given exercise, then your sets should be at around 75 pounds, to be done for 8 to 10 repetitions. Once the 10th repetition becomes easy, you move up. (Wait a workout or two before moving up, and increase the repetitions to 11 or 12 in the meantime, just to be on the safe side.)

To find the right intensity, you don't really have to find how much you do at one repetition. Instead, simply start out with a light weight and feel your way up the ladder. Once you find a resistance in which 10 repetitions are kind of tough to do, you're probably near or at that 75 percent range. Stay there until it gets easy. You can even start out at a lighter level anyway. That just gets you prepared for tougher sets down the road. The reason for exercising at this level of intensity has to do with the makeup of the muscle. Muscle is made of fibers, which respond to stress. Research and anecdotal evidence suggest that the level of intensity mentioned above is what's needed to stimulate muscle growth and strength.

Settle on one or two sets per exercise. After that—by doing three, four or more—you aren't substantially upping the load as much as you did with that increase from one to two sets.

In each set, do your repetitions in a slow, controlled fashion, concentrating on the movement. Make it last roughly six seconds—two for the phase when you're bringing the weight up (called the concentric phase) and four for the phase when you're letting the weight down (called the eccentric phase). By doing this with a reasonable weight, you tire the muscle fully.

By doing more sets with a minimum rest interval, you may be building endurance, but further improvements in muscular strength are minimal. "You get infinitely more out of doing a few slow sets than you get by doing six sets real fast and sloppy," says Dunphy.

Think about it—two sets of ten repetitions at six seconds a pop. Throw a two-minute rest between the sets and you have four minutes total for the muscle group. Not much, eh?

The same goes for abdominal exercises. Many folks feel the need to spend hours on that section of flesh, when only a handful of repetitions will do. Don't do 1,000 abs—do 20 slow, hard ones.

"Eccentric sit-ups—when you stress the movement slowly on the way down—are a perfect example of an exercise that creates full intensity with very few reps needed," says Dunphy. "You can do all the reps and sets in the world, but without the tension brought on by the eccentric phase, forget it."

Aim for a full repetition every time. When you can't do most of your full range of motion in any exercise while keeping the weight under control, it's time to quit. And remember—if you're just beginning, don't knock yourself out. Get your body used to lifting weights by using light amounts and going slow. As you get comfortable with the exercises, then you can start pushing yourself a little harder. At that point, you should exercise with a partner—someone who can monitor you (and you them) in case the weight is more than you can handle.

TWO WORKOUTS THAT WORK

Strength-training workouts can last two or three hours, and you may spend only minutes actually doing any real work. But we're out to change that. Below is a program that incorporates all the tips we've discussed. We're talking total work, no waste—hitting all the major muscle groups with enough rest time in between. And it adds up to 12 minutes flat, with 18 minutes added in for rest.

If you're aiming for a little more mass, or you just want to spice things up a bit and you have the extra time, we've added a few specific exercises to push the time commitment up to 30 or 45 minutes.

You can mix and match these workouts, too. For example, during the week, you can do the short program twice and then reserve one longer workout as "the weekender"—something to do on a Saturday or Sunday when you have more time to spare.

Or if you plan on working out just twice a week (which is the minimum prescription from the American College of Sports Medicine), you can alternate one with the other. Remember to take it slow, and check with your doctor if you have any medical conditions that may interfere with exercise.

12-MINUTE FLEX

- 2 sets of leg presses—1 minute per set, with 2 minutes rest between sets; 1 minute rest between last set and next exercise: bench press.
- 2 sets of bench presses—1 minute per set, with 2 minutes rest between sets; 2 minutes rest between bench press and next exercise: rows.
- 2 sets of rows—1 minute per set with 2 minutes rest between sets; 2 minutes rest between last row and next exercise: military press.
- 2 sets of military presses—1 minute per set with 2 minutes rest between sets; 2 minutes rest between last set and next exercise: lat pull-downs.
- 2 sets of lat machine pull-downs—1 minute per set with 2 minutes rest between sets; 1 minute rest between last set and next exercise: abdominals.
- 1 set of sit-backs—2 minutes.

Total time: 12 minutes of exercise + 18 minutes of rest = 30 minutes flat.

Bench press (a compound exercise). This builds and strengthens the chest muscles, triceps of the upper arm and upper latissimus dorsi muscles (lats) of your back. Lie on an exercise bench, with your feet flat on the floor. The bar should be in line with your chest. Hold the bar with your hands about three inches from the outside of the chest. Bring the bar down slowly. Press the bar back up. Keep your head and hips on the bench at all times.

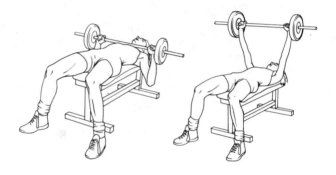

Leg extension. This focuses on the quadriceps muscles of your thighs. Sit on the exercise machine with your feet under the foot pad. Raise the weight until your legs are parallel to the floor. Return down, very slowly. Don't swing the legs up fast—do it slowly and in a controlled way.

(*continued*)

Seated pulley row (a compound exercise). This exercise helps work the lats, rhomboids (upper back), brachialis muscles (located on the upper arm), deltoids (on the shoulder), biceps and forearms as well as the trapezius (the largest muscles of  the back and neck) and erector muscles, which support the spine. Take a grip with your hands set close together. Place your feet against the restraint and sit down facing the pulley. Keep your arms straight, with your legs slightly bent. Let the weight pull your shoulders forward so your torso is inclined. Pull the handle in to touch your upper abdomen, sitting back until your torso is perpendicular to the floor. As you pull in, keep your arms close to your sides. Hold this position for a moment, then slowly reverse the process and return.

Leg press (a compound exercise). This hits your quadriceps and hamstring muscles, along with the gluteus maximus and calves. Hold the handrails. Place your feet on the pads of the machine. Press out slowly until your

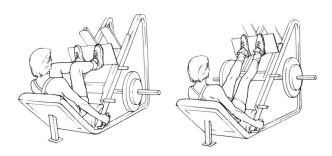

thighs are straight and your knees are locked. Now let the weights down slowly. No slamming—keep a light touch and feel the tension as you let the weights return. Keep the knees slightly out.

Military press (a compound exercise). This nails the deltoids, along with the triceps and the upper-back muscles. Rest the barbell across your trapezius muscle behind your neck. Rotate your el-bows to a position di-rectly beneath the bar. Slowly straighten your arms to press the bar directly up. Lower slowly back to the starting position. Don't bounce the weight off your chest. If a barbell is too hard on you, try doing this with sepa-rate, light dumbbells, alternating arms.

Lat machine pull-down (a compound exercise). This targets the upper back, biceps, forearm flexors and brachialis muscles. Stand facing the lat machine, reach up and take an overhand grip on the bar with your hands set three to five inches wider than your shoulders. Straighten your arms and use your weight to pull your body downward, and then wedge your knees under the re-straint. Allow the weights to pull your shoulders upward to stretch your lats. Use your upper back and arms to pull the bar down to touch be-hind your neck. Hold for a moment, then return slowly to the starting position.

(continued)

Biceps curl. The exercise below targets the biceps, but also gives some work to the brachialis muscles and forearm flexors. Hold weights, keeping elbows in place at the hip. Keep your back straight and look straight ahead. Slowly curl your fists up and forward toward your shoulders. As the weights pass the halfway point, flex your wrists as you finish the rep. Reverse the movement slowly with the same arc as you lower the weight.

Triceps push-down. This targets the triceps muscle of the arms. Stand in front of the lat machine and grasp the bar, palms down. Start with forearms and biceps touching. Press the bar down in a semicircular motion until your arms are extended. Return slowly to starting

45 MINUTES FOR EXTRA TONE

If you have the time to sink your teeth into a meatier workout, try this one on for size. Just do the same as above, but continue on with 1 minute of rest between abdominals and the next exercise: biceps curls.

- 2 sets of biceps curls—1 minute per set with 2 minutes rest between sets; 1 minute rest between last set and next exercise: leg extension.

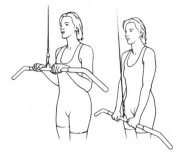

position. While you're doing this, try your best to keep your abdominal muscles tense.

Sit-back. This exercise really targets your abdominal muscles. While sitting tilted back at a 45-degree angle on a mat, with knees bent and your hands across your chest, lower yourself all the way down to a count of ten. Uncross your hands, turn onto your elbow and push yourself up again; then do another. Try a set of six for starters—add a repetition or two as they get easier.

- 2 sets of leg extensions—1 minute per set with 2 minutes rest between sets; 1 minute of rest between last set and next exercise: triceps push-down.
- 2 sets of triceps push-downs—1 minute per set with 2 minutes rest between sets.

Total Time: 30 minutes of first workout + 6 minutes of new exercises + 9 minutes of rest = 45 minutes flat.

—*Greg Gutfeld*

PEDAL POWER!

GET BACK IN THE SADDLE AND INTO GREAT SHAPE WITH YOUR STATIONARY BIKE.

Face it—riding a stationary bike in your bedroom can be about as exciting as . . . well . . . riding a stationary bike in your bedroom. Sure, when you bought it, you pictured a cozy fat-burning alternative to frigid walks in blustery winter weather. Now the bike is getting its own workout—buried under a load of laundry.

What a waste: Riding a stationary bike is a superb way to shed fat fast while building lean muscle to boot. In fact, in a recent study done at Tufts University a group of stationary cyclists—burning only 360 calories a day over 12 weeks—were able to lose a whopping 19 pounds of fat and gain 3 pounds of lean muscle (all without dieting!).

There's hope, though, for you and your machine. Following are strategies to breathe new life into your bike routine and give yourself—especially your heart—a healthy workout without being bored to tears.

PEDAL WITH HEART

One powerful way to make time pass quickly during stationary biking also gives your ticker a boost: pulse monitoring. "Use the bike's speed and resistance to change your heart rate and manipulate it to an ideal spot—then try to keep it there for 20 to 30 minutes," says Michael Schreiber, D.O., medical director of Sports Medicine Associates at the Sports Club/LA in west Los Angeles. "It becomes an interactive experience with your bike—like a vigorous form of biofeedback while also conditioning your heart and lungs."

After a brief three- to five-minute warm-up, exercise harder to get your heart rate within the target-heart-rate zone. That zone falls anywhere from 65 to 85 percent of your maximum heart rate, which is your age subtracted from 220.

To find your heart rate as you exercise, stop briefly and place the tips of your index and middle fingers (not your thumb) over your wrist. Count your pulse for ten seconds and multiply by six to get your heart rate. But do it fast—your heart rate drops quickly when you stop exercising. If the number you calculated is 65 to 85 percent of your maximum heart rate, you're doing fine.

If your heart rate is too low and you're not feeling over-stressed, kick up the pace. If it's too high, you may need to slow things down. That's where the boredom-bashing comes into play, says Dr. Schreiber. "By monitoring your heart rate and always trying to coax your heart into an ideal range, time passes faster. You're playing a game with your body." Having two variables to play with—changing the speed and turning up or down the specific levels of resistance your machine may provide—gives you different recipes to reach your ideal heart rate.

The target zone is simply a helpful guidepost. Because resting heart rate drops with improved fitness, you'll have to work harder to reach that point, which is okay—it simply means that you're in better shape. But if you don't want to bother with equations, you can do what feels comfortable. When you're pedaling away, breathing should be deep and rapid, but you should still be able to talk while you exercise. If you can no longer speak, you've gone beyond that target heart range.

PROGRAM YOURSELF FOR PEDALING

Ideally, you'd like to get onto the exercise bike five times a week at a moderate pace. "That seems to be the magic threshold for changing heart-disease risk factors like high blood pressure and cholesterol levels," says Ralph LaForge, exercise physiologist at the San Diego Cardiac Center Medical Group.

Although, if it has been a while since you've been pedaling, you need to ease yourself back into the saddle first. Begin pedaling three days a week for the first four weeks. Start out doing 12 to 15 minutes the first few times. "You might even do two spins a day—8 or 9 minutes in the morning, then repeat it in the afternoon or evening," says LaForge. "That prepares your leg muscles for doing more as you become more fit." Use the first few minutes of each workout as a warm-up, with a cooldown period at the end. You can pedal at a moderate speed, with little or no resistance, if your machine offers that option.

Over the course of three months, you can work up to 45 minutes (including warm-up and cooldown) a shot. After the first month, try four workouts per week for the next two weeks. In the remaining weeks, work up to tackling five cycling sessions a week.

If your bike offers resistance options for pedaling, pick one that allows you to go 15 comfortable minutes. "You should break a sweat and feel like you're working hard, but not so hard it feels like a struggle," says LaForge. Remember, this is an aerobic exercise, not strength training for the legs.

KEEP COOL

The biggest mistake people make with indoor exercise is lack of proper cooling. Because you aren't moving through the environment, you aren't being cooled by air. That lack of ventilation can cause most people to overheat after just 20 minutes.

"Get a three-speed fan and correlate the speed directly to how hard you're working," says LaForge. For a warm-up, try low speed; for your workout, set it at high speed.

If you can't reach the fan from where you're seated, just keep it at a constant level, targeting as much skin as possible. "Make it fresh air, too—keep the fan near a window," says LaForge. This can keep body temperature about a degree cooler, which leads to a lower heart rate. "You can actually burn more calories by staying cooler because it can prolong your workout," he says.

GET COMFORTABLE

Make sure your bike seat is adjusted properly. You know you're at a proper seat height if on the down stroke your leg is almost but not completely extended, with a slight bend in the knee, when you have the middle of your foot (not your toes) on the pedal.

If you have an uncomfortable seat, you can remedy that with a foam or sheepskin pad. While riding, you can also lift up off the seat for a few seconds now and again just to relieve pressure.

If the handlebars are adjustable, set them so you lean slightly forward—but not too much. "There's a tendency to lean too much when you get tired, and that can lead to lower-back pain," says Dr. Schreiber. Sit upright as though you're on a regular bike. Don't grip too tightly on the handlebars, either. That can numb your hands. If numbing still occurs, try some biking gloves.

USE BOREDOM BREAKERS

Riding a stationary bike requires more than motivation. It also calls for an attentive kick in the cerebellum, with mind-occupying activities that can help make indoor pedaling more bearable. Here are a few tips to keep you in the saddle and smiling—instead of laid out on the sofa groping for the remote.

Do intervals. Once you've gotten into a steady pace, kick up the speed and spin faster for a half-minute or minute. Then return to the original pace. Keep alternating speeds during the workout. It can break the monotony and burn calories to boot.

Take a stand. Get an attachable reading stand so you can peruse the morning paper or a thick paperback as you burn fat.

Use big words. Try finding big-print books and magazines so you don't have to bend forward to read, risking a backache.

Listen up. If reading on a bike makes you dizzy (like reading in a car makes you queasy), try getting the masterpieces on audiotapes. That way you can still work on your mind as you work on your body. You can program your workout by chapters or "reread" the steamy parts to work up a better sweat.

Keep moving with the movies. Rent some of your favorite videos. Or tape episodes of your favorite soaps and catch them while riding. If you want to get really creative, there are even a few videos available that provide tours through beautiful terrain or that allow you to race against other riders. Just position the bike near a television (or your stereo, for music) and pedal away.

Make it scenic. If you have a window with a nice view of a busy street, park your bike facing it and people-watch, dog-watch, bird-watch or whatever-watch. . . . If your bike is easily movable, take it outside, weather permitting.

Tune in. A personal headphone stereo can help keep the mental beat going. Keep the volume low enough, however, to hear the phone, doorbell or comments from your envious, inactive relatives.

Get a speaker phone. While sweating away, call your friends, your accountant, the Weather Channel, the Home Shopping Network or anyone who will listen to you. You'll be amazed how this makes time fly.

Pedal with a pal. If you belong to a gym, you can arrange a time to meet a friend there to ride. But if you're at home, consider sharing a bike—doing light calisthenics while your pal pedals and vice versa.

Sing! Sing! Hey—what's more fun than riding a stationary bike? How about doing it as you bellow off-key renditions of Broadway show tunes?

'Perspirate' and dictate. A hand-held Dictaphone is great for letters, random thoughts, shopping lists or awful poetry you wouldn't share with anyone.

—*Greg Gutfeld*

DE-STRESS WITH A SPECIAL KIND OF STROLL

YOU ALREADY KNOW THAT WALKING IS SUPER EXERCISE. NOW YOU CAN ADD MIND POWER TO YOUR DAILY OUTINGS TO SOOTHE YOUR SPIRIT.

We know that aerobic exercise has the power to calm jangled nerves and boost drooping moods. Research has shown that one brisk 20- to 30-minute walk can have the same calming effect as a mild tranquilizer. And we know that, over time, a regular exercise program can enhance self-esteem and reduce depression. But now there's research suggesting that even something less vigorous than a brisk walk—a comfortable stroll—can leave you feeling less anxious and more positive. By adding simple mental techniques, strollers get the same positive mental benefits that brisk walkers enjoy.

THE BODY/MIND CONNECTION

Recently, researchers from three institutions brought together their expertise to see how "cognitive," or "mindful," exercises might enhance the effect of exercise on the body and mind. The study was conducted by Ruth Stricker, owner and director of The Marsh: A Center for Balance, in Minnetonka, Minnesota, and James Rippe, M.D., director of the exercise physiology and nutrition laboratory at the University of Massachusetts Medical School in Worcester.

This research, called the Ruth Stricker/MindBody Study, investigated five groups (135 people in all) over a 16-week period. Of the three walking groups, one walked at a brisk pace, one at a low-intensity pace and one at a low-intensity pace but with an extra element.

This latter group practiced a mental technique to bring about the "relaxation response" developed by Herbert Benson, M.D., president of New England Deaconess Hospital's Mind/Body Medical Institute in Boston, in an attempt to see how the mind and body work together. This relaxation response is a physiological response characterized by decreased heart rate and blood pressure and feelings of tranquillity. The fourth group practiced mindful exercise—a Westernized application of tai chi developed by Stricker. The fifth group served as controls and were asked not to change anything about their lives.

The low-intensity walkers using the mental technique listened to a tape that explained that, while exercise and relaxation techniques seemed very different, they actually produced very similar results through the power of repetition. They were instructed in how to do a simple meditation. During their walks they were asked to pay attention to their footsteps, counting one, two, one, two. They were also instructed to visualize the numbers in their minds. If they found their thoughts drifting, they were to say "Oh, well," and come back to counting their footsteps.

The results of using this simple technique were "dramatic," according to Dr. Rippe. The low-intensity walking group that used the relaxation tape showed decreases in anxiety and had fewer negative and more positive feelings about themselves—equal to the effect that the brisk walkers gained. These effects were evident after just one exercise session and were maintained over the duration of the study. The low-intensity walkers who did not use the mental technique showed no improvements until the 14th week, but even then the improvements were not as extensive. The mindful exercise group experienced very similar results to the relaxation-response-plus-walking group—lending support to the idea that various cognitive strategies could yield similar benefits.

"For people who have difficulty with brisk walking or other moderately intense exercise, this is a very encouraging study," says Dr. Rippe. "They can be encouraged to exercise knowing that with a simple mental technique, they can get the same psychological benefits as a person who can exercise at a higher intensity."

David Brown, Ph.D., research psychologist at the Centers for Disease Control and Prevention in Atlanta, who designed the study, thinks this type of research may prove even more fruitful in the future: "In the Ruth Stricker/MindBody Study, we used healthy volunteers from the general population. They did not have any physical disabilities, nor were they abnormally anxious or depressed. It's difficult to get improved ratings on psychological tests when your subject already feels just fine. I believe a study done with a clinical population, a group of people experiencing physical limitations or mental distress, would show even greater improvement from the walking/mindful approach."

FINDING EXERCISE INSPIRATION

Many people know that exercise is beneficial. In fact, a survey showed 93 percent of adults think that exercise is good for them. Yet only 20 percent of Americans exercise regularly.

"It's certainly not that they don't have enough information," says Dr. Rippe. "But maybe it's a bit overwhelming to some people to think they have to maintain their exercise for weeks, even years, to gain those health benefits. This study shows people that they can experience almost immediate psychological benefits, that they can feel better from exercise right away, even if they can't move at a fast pace. Maybe when people are educated about exercise in this way, they'll be more inclined to give it a try and more likely to stay with it."

Deena and David Balboa, co-directors of the Walking Center of New York City, think this study confirms what they've experienced for years in working with hundreds of clients. "We teach people to tune in to their bodies when they walk," the Balboas explain. "It doesn't matter what mindfulness technique you use. If you concentrate on your body, whether it's your form, rhythm, posture or breathing, a calming takes effect as body awareness increases. Just moving in an unconscious fashion can't produce the harmony and aliveness that emerge naturally from being mindful during exercise."

—*Maggie Spilner*

YOGA: THE RIGHT MOVES

IT MAY NOT BURN CALORIES, BUT YOGA CAN MAKE YOUR BODY STRONGER, MORE FLEXIBLE AND LESS OF A TARGET FOR MODERN-DAY STRESSORS, STRAINS AND SPORTS INJURIES.

Joan Prevett, 45, a vice president at an asset-management firm in Boston, began taking yoga classes a little more than a year ago, after she became dissatisfied with her existing exercise routine. "I was running and doing aerobics, but I'd find that I was still checking my watch. Finally, I thought, this is the same thing I do all day. It isn't helping me to relax." After three or four weeks of yoga, Prevett noticed a difference. "I was more flexible, and I could deal with stress better," she says. "I had a sense of strength and balance and well-being."

Though yoga is many centuries old, only in the past half-decade or so has it slipped into the athletic mainstream of

Western culture. Demand for yoga classes at health clubs and fitness centers has soared, and the once sleepy *Yoga Journal* in Berkeley, California, has seen its circulation grow by 60 percent since 1988 to 70,000. About 75 percent of its readers are women, and the readership's average age is 46. "Women often come to yoga at 35 or so, searching for vitality as well as meaning in their lives," says Mary Dunn, 51, a senior teacher with the Iyengar Yoga Institute in New York.

BENEFITS MULTIPLY

Whatever their motives, an estimated three million to five million Americans practice it in some form, and many of them have had to overcome powerful preconceptions about yoga and its semimystical and countercultural overtones. In fact, some yoga instructors still make claims that may sound a little bizarre—insisting, for example, that their brand of yoga enables practitioners to develop psychic powers, or, more defensibly, perhaps, that it enhances sexual powers or pleasure.

The more popular forms of yoga aim to provide a variety of physical and mental benefits, from pain relief and stress management to flexibility and fitness. Many enthusiasts say yoga is spiritual, too—but the mass of yoga devotees simply want to feel better. "Yoga isn't a religion," insists Alice Christensen, president and founder of the 45-year-old American Yoga Association. "It's a practical tool for physical, mental and emotional health and well-being."

One of yoga's attractions, in contrast to running or other activities that involve strenuous or jarring repetitive motions, is that it doesn't exact a long-term physical price. In addition, yoga doesn't hurt (if it does, you're probably doing something wrong), it doesn't take much time (a few 15- to 30-minutes sessions a week may be sufficient for your purposes) and you can do it almost anywhere—at your desk, in bed, even on an airplane.

GETTING STARTED

The yoga industry doesn't offer a certification program for teachers, although such organizations as the Iyengar Yoga Institute certify teachers who meet their demanding criteria. Your best bet is to experiment with experienced instructors until you find one you like. Your health club may be one source of recommendations: you can also check the yellow pages under *yoga instruction*.

Books and videotapes for the beginning yoga student abound. The *Yoga Journal* offers the *Yoga Journal's Yoga for Beginners* and three other videotapes on yoga for strength, flexibility and relaxation. The American Yoga Association offers such books as *The American Yoga Association Beginners's Manual* and *Easy Does It* (yoga for older people).

Still, it's wise to take at least a few lessons to get started. You'll be less likely to injure yourself if you have someone around to help you adopt the right poses. And a teacher's guidance can also be useful in giving you a sense of what you are working toward in the early stages.

"At first, the postures seem intensely physical," says instructor Mary Dunn. "But you also are being trained to concentrate. You learn to feel the muscles and skin and bones moving—you consider the internal workings of your body. As time goes on, you realize the other effects of yoga. You experience the peacefulness of the union between the physical and the mental and the spiritual."

That kind of talk is easy to mock, but it gets at yoga's central appeal for women who are seeking more than a physical workout. Sarah Waite, 53, a social worker in Portland, Maine, has been practicing yoga off and on since 1973. "I used to do that Jane Fonda tape. It was always 'Feel the burn! Feel the burn!' Yoga isn't presented that way. It's quieter. It's very much an internal experience. You get to know your body, know which side is tighter than the other, for example. The class is an oasis; I look forward to it all week."

CUSTOMIZING YOUR ROUTINE

The most popular approach, known as hatha yoga, teaches students to use poses (asanas) in combination with breathing exercises and specific movements. Once you've taken a few lessons, you can begin to practice some basic asanas and breathing exercises on your own. Eventually, you'll want to make them part of a routine. "I try to do it before stressful meetings," says Prevett, "I find that I'm nicer to people after yoga."

You can tailor private workouts to correct specific problems or to pursue your own physical agenda. For example, you might adopt a program of three or four exercises that you do regularly—each one at least once a week, for 15 to 20 minutes at a time. Some exercises improve balance; others focus on better breathing or on stress reduction; still others will increase flexibility or build leg muscles. But use caution with the more advanced positions, which can do more harm than good to people with stiff joints or back problems.

Some yoga fans argue that yoga can help cure medical problems from cancer to chronic fatigue syndrome—and while they may overreach in their claims, there's an indisputable connection between yoga and physical health. "I thought yoga was mainly basic stretching," says Susan Woods, 43, a psychotherapist in Greenwich, Connecticut, and a former physical therapist. "But to my amazement I found that it also increased my stamina and endurance and muscle tone. I've also seen benefits in things like cardiac output, circulation, respiration and digestion. It sort of does all these things without your realizing it. After a while, I found that my eating habits had changed. Eventually, my shape changed, too."

HELP IN HEALING

Yoga can also prevent or help heal injuries related to sports or other physical activities. Sports that require repeated muscle contraction (like running) can lead to chronic stiffness or lack of flexibility; yoga poses and stretches can make muscles more elastic. For this reason, many physical therapists recommend yoga or yoga-derived stretching exercises for back patients or people with chronic pain.

Recently, Linda Gajevski, 37, vice president of business development at Meldrum and Fewsmith Communications, an advertising firm in Cleveland, sustained a displaced disk in her neck in an auto accident. Her doctor recommended that she participate in a biofeedback program to relieve pain from the injury. "I told him I did yoga," says Gajevski, "and he hooked me up to a computer to take some readings while I meditated. There was a measurable decline in my heart rate and my skin temperature." Gajevski was excused from the biofeedback program; in effect, she was already trained to manage her pain.

"When I first began yoga," she recalls, "I was taking medication for some pain in my legs. I started with some really simple stretching exercises, and within a few months I was practicing on my own. After a while, the pain just cleared up."

And it's hard to deny that yoga provides health benefits by relieving mental stress. "My husband, Andrew, and I agreed that the main feeling when we started was relaxation," says Woods. "Within three or four months I noticed a reduction in stress— and an increase in my ability to focus and concentrate."

What *doesn't* yoga do? Most styles won't burn lots of calories—so you shouldn't necessarily cut out your trips to the gym or your time on the track. But yoga will make you feel better and stronger when you get there. "The most important thing is to do a little bit as often as possible," says Gajevski.

Adds Christensen, "Yoga isn't something you make your primary thing. You can use different parts of it as tools to make the rest of your life better."

—Clint Willis

(

PART EIGHT

YOUR MENTAL
AND EMOTIONAL HEALTH

YOUR STRESS-
REDUCTION RDA

HERE'S A FIVE-POINT STRESS REDUCTION PLAN THAT CAN BOOST YOUR EMOTIONAL AND PHYSICAL HEALTH.

It's pretty common knowledge that exercising and eating a healthy diet are essential to heart health. Less well known are the techniques that reduce stress and get rid of the killer emotions that contribute significantly to illness.

"Increasing scientific evidence demonstrates that isolation and suppression of feelings—among the major causes of stress—are linked to illness, whereas intimacy and social support can be healing," says Dean Ornish, M.D., architect of the well-known revolutionary lifestyle program to reverse heart disease and author of *Eat More, Weigh Less*. That intimacy, he says, includes not only relationships with others but also being more in touch with yourself.

It's hard to take time out for yourself, especially when deadlines hit, chores pile up and your "To do list" is two feet long. But this stress-reduction plan helps you make yourself a priority. When you take care of yourself, then you can help others. It rewards you not only for practicing traditional stress-management techniques, like relaxation exercises, journal writing and yoga, but it also recognizes that you can find refuge from stress in everyday activities—a heart-to-heart with a good friend, a walk in the park, a total-body stretch.

GIVE YOURSELF THE GIFT OF PEACE

Here's how it works. At the end of this chapter are suggestions for stress-reducing activities, listed according to the number of points you'll earn for doing them. The more intentional the activity is, the more points you earn. One point is awarded for more everyday activities that may result in short-term stress reduction—like having a lighthearted dinner with friends or watching your favorite TV sitcom. You earn two points for activities you go out of your way to fit into your day, such as a

THE TEN-SECOND TOTAL-BODY STRETCH

"This is a great exercise because it lengthens the spine and stretches the chest, shoulders and hamstring muscles in the backs of the legs—and you can do it just about anywhere," says Jean Couch, author of *The Runner's Yoga Book*. Here's how you do it: Stand in front of your refrigerator (or any other ledge of that height). Inhale and stretch your arms overhead.

Bring them down in front of you until your wrists rest on the ledge. Then walk your feet back until you are bent at the hips, your legs directly under your hips. Let your feet point gently outward and bend your knees slightly. As you exhale, extend your fingers, lift your buttock bones and let your spine lengthen. Your back will be slightly bowed. (Think of how a dog looks when he's just gotten up from his nap.) Deepen the stretch with each exhalation for five or six breaths. Release by walking toward the ledge and lowering your arms.

---

massage or a nature walk. Activities specifically intended to reduce stress, like yoga or meditation, earn you three points.

Your goal is to accumulate a minimum of five points a day. That means, for example, that you can fulfill your daily "tranquillity quota" by doing a ten-second total-body stretch when you get up in the morning, during your afternoon coffee break and before you go to bed at night for one point (see "The Ten-Second Total-Body Stretch"); walking at lunch for two more points; spending some quality time with your kids when you get home from work (one point); and reading a chapter of that bestseller by your bed (one point).

Now, stress relief is often an individual thing. A rousing step-aerobics class, for example, may help you work out frustration and leave you ready to conquer the world. Or, it might make you feel more out of control, if you're constantly tripping over your own feet or struggling to keep up. Make sure the stress busters you choose leave you with a sense of rejuvenation or relaxation. If they don't, pick others from the list—or come up with some of your own.

One Point
- Socialize with friends.
- Read a book or a magazine.
- Engage in a favorite hobby—cooking, painting, sewing, gardening, for example.
- Watch a favorite movie or television show.
- Do three total-body stretches.
- Do five one-minute meditations.
- Play with your kids (or your dog).
- Take a five-minute "time-out."
- Listen to music.
- Take a catnap.

Two Points
- Take a long, warm bath.
- Have a massage.
- Play a team sport.
- Sit in silence for ten minutes or more.
- Do volunteer work.
- Take a 30-minute walk (or do 30 minutes of any exercise).
- Have a heart-to-heart with a friend.

Three Points
- Take a yoga class.
- Meditate or pray for 15 minutes or more.
- Attend a meeting of an organized support group.
- Write about your feelings in a journal.

—Lisa Delaney

SHELTER YOUR HEALTH FROM EMOTIONAL STRESS

HERE'S HOW TO KEEP YOUR IMMUNITY HIGH IN THE MIDST OF LIFE'S LOWS.

A 52-year-old salesman, never "out sick" a day in his career, comes down with one flulike infection after another when new management threatens layoffs.

A 36-year-old mother discovers she has breast cancer less than a year after her baby is critically injured in a car accident.

Maybe these are coincidences. But when you hear of cases like these, you can't help but wonder whether severe or ongoing emotional stress can sap your health, perhaps by impairing the body's immune function. In fact, an amazing discovery directly links emotions with the chemistry of the immune system. Meanwhile, other researchers are in the process of piecing together important clues to certain stress-coping skills that may help immunize the body against emotional assaults.

THE NEW MEDICAL FRONTIER

Scientists on the cutting edge of mind/body research liken the current skepticism among many physicians to that of nineteenth-century physicians when Louis Pasteur first introduced his germ theory. At that time, no one believed that microscopic enemies could invade your body and make you sick. It took decades before hand washing became common presurgical practice.

Candace Pert, Ph.D., a visiting professor at the Center for Molecular and Behavioral Neuroscience at Rutgers University firmly believes that the emotional landscape represents today's newest frontier in health maintenance. Over the past two decades, she and her colleagues have blazed new territory— studying the biochemistry of emotions. What they've found is that emotions are not just in your head.

"Our research shows that emotions are intimately connected with the entire physiology of the body," she says. "The chemical processes that mediate emotion occur not only within our brains, but also at many sites throughout the body—in fact, on the very surfaces of every single cell."

ANATOMY OF EMOTION

Early in her career, Dr. Pert discovered a way to measure chemical receptors on cell surfaces in the brain. These little vibrating molecules are like keyholes to which certain chemicals hold the key. At this time, Dr. Pert was studying opiate receptors in the brain, which act as keyholes for opiate drugs like morphine and heroin. "The chemical binding of an opiate to its receptor is what creates the emotion of euphoria," Dr. Pert explains.

Soon after, it was discovered that the body makes its own opiates internally (called endorphins). Released during events such as childbirth and traumatic injury, endorphins serve as natural painkillers.

It wasn't long before a host of other receptors besides opiates were found in the brain, along with the natural chemicals, called neuropeptides, that fit them. Not all neuropeptides are associated with emotions as strong as euphoria. "Some are more subtle," explains Dr. Pert.

These discoveries broke new ground. But what really shocked the scientific community was when researchers found endorphins in the immune system and began to find opiate and other receptors distributed in parts of the body outside of the brain.

THE IMMUNE CONNECTION

Comprised of lymph nodes, thymus gland, spleen, bone marrow and immune cells, the immune system is the body's means of defense against infectious disease and cancer. For many years, it was believed that this elaborate defense system operated independently of any other body system. When opiate receptors were found on immune cells in the spleen and thymus, however, it became clear that the immune system must be connected to the nervous system, involving the brain in the control of the disease-fighting process. "Why else would opiate receptors, which everyone knew could be found in the brain and had something to do with emotions, be on immune cells?" asks Dr. Pert.

Here was a mind/body connection that challenged the long-cherished notion that the immune system was independent of the nervous system. To Dr. Pert, the implication was crystal clear: Your mental and emotional states must directly impact the functioning of your immune systems, and in turn, your ability to fight disease.

THE STRESS FACTOR

Researchers today agree that the brain and the immune system do indeed "talk" to one another, but exactly how—and which specific states of mind and mood affect health—is a mystery just beginning to unravel.

Studies suggest that bursts of short-term stress or even undesirable emotion may bolster some aspects of immune function. When emotionally arousing situations become chronic and are experienced as inescapable, however, the immune system may falter and health problems may arise.

When researchers from the University of California-Los Angeles recently examined the relationship between stressful life events and the development of colorectal cancer in more than 1,000 men, they found that those with a history of severe work-related problems were five times more likely to get colorectal cancer than men who didn't. Other major stresses, such as changing residence, suffering the death of a spouse, getting divorced or being unemployed for longer than six months, also increased risk, but not as much. (The researchers were careful to screen out the influence of other factors like diet and exercise.)

"A serious occupational problem is one of the worst life events that can occur because it's a more chronic stressor," explains lead researcher Joseph Courtney, Ph.D., UCLA epidemiologist. "A lot of times, people have to stay in jobs, keeping a smiling face whether they're happy or not."

Dr. Courtney explains that the colon, in particular, is sensitive to stress. "A lot of people appreciate the fact that if they're under stress, certain bowel habits may be negatively affected," he says. "It's one of the organs that translates mental stress into physiological dysfunction."

Dr. Pert concurs. "The same neuropeptides that are found in your brain and are associated with various emotional states also innervate every sphincter of your digestive system," she says. "When you see that, you are forced to come to the conclusion that the digestive tract is more than just a passive pipe."

Dr. Courtney's study did not measure changes in immune function, but evidence from both human and animal studies shows that stress has the potential to depress immunity, which may be one of the reasons why some people under stress are more susceptible to illness.

One of the best studies to show that chronic stress leads to depressed immune function involved 69 people who had been caring for spouses with Alzheimer's for an average of five years. In comparison with a similar group of non-caregiving adults, the caregivers showed decreases in three measures of cellular immunity. They were also ill for more days with respiratory tract infections.

What's more, the caregivers who felt the most distressed by the dementia-related behavior of their spouses and who reported lower levels of social support suffered the greatest decline in immunity. "It's not stress that really causes the problem, it's inappropriate responses to stress that put us at risk of depressed immunity and possible disease," says Nicholas Hall, Ph.D., director of the psychoimmunology division at the University of South Florida Psychiatry Center in Tampa.

THE CONTROL FACTOR

In particular, if stress precipitates feelings of helplessness and powerlessness, increased susceptibility to sickness may result, researchers tell us.

Dr. Hall cites laboratory animal studies in which rats who have no control over intermittent electrical shocks develop tumors faster than those who have access to a turn-off switch.

In contrast, studies suggest that instilling people with a sense of personal control appears to have a profoundly positive impact on health. In a benchmark study conducted by Yale researchers, nursing-home residents who were encouraged to make decisions for themselves and given something outside themselves to take care of—in this case, plants—became more active, more alert, happier and healthier than a similar group for whom the nursing staff did everything. In just a few weeks, the group with no control grew more debilitated, and a year and a half later, they were less likely to be alive.

That so simple a measure had any effect at all on the patient's health suggests how important increased control is, the researchers conclude.

"Different behaviors give different people a sense of control, but the important issue isn't whether you meditate or use imagery or do yoga," says George Solomon, M.D., professor of psychiatry at UCLA and a leader in mind/body research. "The critical variable is doing something to take active control of your own health process—the opposite of helplessness and fatalism."

Coping actively in the face of stress can buffer its ill effects in two basic ways. First, it can help by directly reducing the release of stress hormones, such as cortisol and adrenaline, which suppress immune function. Second, it can give a person more energy to invest in healthy behavior, such as eating better, exercising and getting plenty of sleep—all of which are habits that can affect immunity and are likely to suffer during hard times.

"If a person has an inner sense of control—a sense that her own behaviors and attitudes play a role in her health—she's more likely to do things that help her be healthy and less likely to allow the stressor to get her down," explains Dr. Solomon.

THE POWER OF EXPRESSION

Unfortunately, it's in the midst of emotional turmoil that you're most likely to feel robbed of motivation, unable to take charge. One of the big problems with any kind of emotional trauma is that it affects every aspect of your being: who you are, financial issues, relationships with loved ones. "The tendency when overwhelmed is to ruminate, obsessing on just one or two concerns and losing sight of the big picture," explains James Pennebaker, Ph.D., professor of psychology at Southern Methodist University in Dallas, and author of *Opening Up: The Healing Power of Confiding in Others.*

"We literally get stuck, bogged down by the weight of a single emotion like anger, sadness or whatever it is we're troubled by," he notes.

One of the most effective ways to pull yourself out of the mire and regain a sense of control, however formidable it may seem at first, is to explore the full spectrum of your tumultuous thoughts and emotions.

In a series of studies Dr. Pennebaker conducted over the years, people were asked to write about extremely traumatic events or about relatively trivial topics for 15 to 20 minutes a day for three to five consecutive days. The series found that those who disclose traumatic experiences have fewer doctor visits during the months following. Immune function is also enhanced by such disclosure, noted in blood tests by the multiplication of certain white blood cells in response to invading organisms.

"When people write or extensively talk with somebody else, it allows them to put the different dimensions of their experience into a meaningful framework," says Dr. Pennebaker. "Once we do that, it's easier to move on and get past those events."

GET SUPPORT, GAIN CONTROL

Feeling support through the turbulent process is critical. Social support is considered one of the most powerful buffers against the ravages of stress. In fact, studies show that social isolation is as much a risk factor for mortality as smoking or high cholesterol.

The mere presence of others, however, doesn't necessarily reflect support. The quality and depth of interaction needs to be of a truly supportive nature. Yet many are reticent to discuss troublesome emotions with friends and family.

"There are all sorts of reasons why people actively avoid talking about their feelings," says Dr. Pennebaker. "We found in our own research with men who've been laid off that they don't like to bring it up around their spouses because they're afraid to worry their spouses."

"Handling your pain head on, dealing with the strong emotion and feeling supported while you do it are crucial during any kind of major life stress," says David Spiegel, M.D., psychiatrist and author of *Living beyond Limits: New Hope and Help for Facing Life-Threatening Illness.* In the book, Dr. Spiegel describes in detail his landmark study of women with advanced breast cancer, some who attended a weekly support group for one year after diagnosis and some who didn't.

Dr. Spiegel originally designed the study with the intent only of improving the women's psychological well-being. But much to his amazement, he found that the women who met in the support group lived an average of 18 months longer than those who did not. "Studies like mine indicate that psychosocial variables, such as social support and how one manages stress, have an impact on survival," he says.

When Dr. Spiegel first organized the support group for the

advanced-stage breast cancer patients in his study, he was afraid that talking about their illnesses might make the women feel worse. Ironically, it did just the opposite.

"What we did in our support group was help the women look their problems right in the eye and see what was scaring them," he says. "That helped them decide the parts of their circumstances they couldn't control and focus on the parts they could.

"Facing and sharing difficulties puts people in a more active stance in relationship to even very serious problems," he explains. "They say, 'I may not live forever, this illness may shorten my life, but I'm going to take hold of how I spend the life I have.'"

One dramatic study from UCLA suggests that not facing up may have dire consequences. Of 68 people with melanoma, those who minimized the importance and threat of cancer to their well-being at the onset of illness were the ones most vulnerable to recurrence and death from the disease years later.

"Where there appears to be a lack of concern about the disease and its possible effects, there is little motivation to improve coping skills and take the measures necessary to prevent further illness," says lead researcher Fawzy I. Fawzy, M.D., in explanation of his study.

The people in Dr. Fawzy's study who were most likely to be disease-free and healthy five to six years later were those who had been randomly assigned to attend a six-week educational program shortly after diagnosis. In the meetings, participants received information about melanoma, learned coping skills and stress-management techniques and developed camaraderie by sharing their concerns and feelings. Facing up cut the death rate by more than half; six years later, only 3 of the 34 in the educational program had died, compared with 10 deaths out of 34 patients under regular care.

"The support group helps you face directly things that are terribly threatening and gives a place where you can express strong feelings and feel supported," says Dr. Spiegel.

"People need to know that no matter how bad they feel, talking with someone can make them feel better," he says. "The group is a place you can go to feel better about feeling bad."

—*Sharon Stocker*

CONQUER
CHRONIC WORRY

POWERFUL STRATEGIES FOR STOPPING THE FRETTING THAT'S RUINING YOUR LIFE.

Asked the secret of longevity, comedian George Burns once put it this way: "My attitude is, if something is beyond your control—if you can't do anything about it—there's no point worrying about it. And if you can do something about it, then there's still nothing to worry about."

For most of us, unfortunately, the comedian's easygoing attitude isn't so easy to adopt. "We're a society that seems to worry a lot," says Denise Person, Ph.D., worry researcher at Pennsylvania State University. "If you watch the news, we go from crisis to crisis—one isn't even over before the next one starts."

Most of us don't have to look as far as a national crisis for something to worry about. Surveys show that the most common sources of worry for Americans are family and relationships ("What if she leaves me?"), job or school ("What if I fail?"), health ("What if I get sick?") and finances ("What if my check bounces?"). And then there's a miscellaneous category that includes everything from the environment to world peace.

While most people worry about 5 percent of the time, for some people, worrying becomes a way of life. Chronic worriers report that an average of 50 percent of each day is spent worrying, and some report as much as 100 percent, says psychologist Jennifer L. Abel, Ph.D., associate director of the Stress and Anxiety Disorders Institute at Pennsylvania State University.

Worrying drains energies and can be a burden to family and friends. It can also cause physical problems. Researchers have identified a characteristic group of symptoms common among worriers: restlessness and feeling edgy, easy fatigability, concentration difficulties, irritability, muscle tension and aches and restless sleep.

HOW TO STOP WORRYING

The good news is that worry has received a great deal of attention from psychologists. They have begun to develop a multifaceted approach to treating it—combining relaxation, behavioral changes and cognitive (thought) therapy to reduce unnecessary worry levels. Here are some of the effective techniques they recommend.

Learn to be a problem solver. Worrying may reflect a form of ineffective problem solving, says Timothy A. Brown, Psy.D., associate director of the Center for Stress and Anxiety Disorders at the State University of New York in Albany. "Examination of a typical chain of thoughts reported by worriers often reveals that the worrier is jumping from topic to topic without reaching a solution to any particular element."

Barry Lubetkin, Ph.D., director of the Institute for Behavior Therapy in New York City, concurs. "Probably the single best thing people who worry too much can do is learn to be good problem solvers," he says. "The better you are at solving problems, the less of a worrier you will be. You need to learn to dispassionately and objectively confront a problem."

Dr. Lubetkin uses this exercise to help people determine if they're good problem solvers. "Draw a little picture on a piece of paper, cut it into six or seven jigsaw pieces, mix it up and try to put it together. While you're doing this, become aware of your thoughts. The people who aren't good problem solvers are telling themselves, 'I can't do this, I'm not good at puzzles.' We want them to think like nonworriers, who are telling themselves, 'The straight edge goes on the outside' and 'With time I'll get there.'"

If you're not a good problem solver, you can learn the skills. That's one of the goals of therapy. At the Albany anxiety clinic, therapists do what's called a realistic appraisal. If you're concerned about losing a job, for example, you and a therapist will evaluate your work strengths, weaknesses and techniques for improvement. You learn to focus on problem solving by consulting with a therapist or by taking courses and reading books on time management, personal organization and problem solving.

Of course, some problems—like world peace—are usually totally out of your control. It's important for worriers to practice what George Burns preaches—to learn not to worry about the problems that are out of their control.

Set aside a worry period. Interestingly, setting aside a daily worry period can reduce overall worry levels over time. Leading worry researcher Michael Vasey, Ph.D., assistant professor of psychology at Ohio State University in Columbus, suggests set-

DISSIPATE WORRY WITH IMAGERY

While a certain amount of anxiety is normal, excessive worry can make you feel passive and helpless. Organized support groups led by trained professionals generally include a relaxation component to help control anxiety.

Breast cancer patients in the landmark study conducted by David Spiegel, M.D., professor of psychiatry and behavioral sciences at Stanford University School of Medicine and author of *Living Beyond Limits: New Hope and Help for Facing Life-Threatening Illness,* for example, learned and used a powerful imagery technique, called the screen technique. It specifically addresses worry in such a way that helps patients sort out possible solutions that can lead to positive change.

To practice the screen technique, go to a quiet place and get comfortable. Close your eyes and feel your body floating—in a bath, a lake, a hot tub or just in space. Learn to enjoy that pleasant sense of floating relaxation. As you continue to float, picture in your mind's eye an imaginary screen, like a movie screen or clear blue sky. Picture on it a pleasant scene—a place you enjoy being. Take a good look at it, and then notice how your memories and fantasies of this place help you and your body feel more comfortable.

Now, if you're worried about something, don't fight it—admit it—but picture some aspect of what you're worried about on that imaginary screen. Do so with the rule that no matter what you see on the screen, you will allow your body to continue floating. If you notice yourself starting to fidget, stop the image on the screen and

ting aside 30 minutes a day, always at the same place and time, to worry. "Focus on your worry for the entire period and try to think of solutions to the problem." For example, if your worry is that you will be fired, imagine the whole scenario—the firing and the consequences—and don't let the image drift away.

It's likely that your first reaction will be an increase in anxiety.

re-establish the sensation of floating. Keep practicing this until you are able to maintain the physical sense of floating while you picture the image of what worries you on your screen.

Then divide the screen in half, and put the image of what worries you on the left side of the screen. Use the right side to brainstorm solutions to the problem. At first, don't try to judge or perfect the ideas; just be open to your own thoughts. After reviewing some possible solutions, you can begin to select strategies for dealing with what worries you. Keep the floating sense in your body, but use this technique to face your feelings.

The women in Dr. Spiegel's support group used the screen technique to reflect on predominant emotional themes at the conclusion of group sessions. At one meeting, for example, they used the screen to voice frustrations over not receiving what they wanted from their families, concentrating on the idea that the best way to get what you want from people might be to give it to them. On the left side of the screen, they pictured "something I want from someone I love." On the right side, they pictured giving that very same thing (words of concern, a statement of affection, an offer of help) to that very same person.

"These exercises served to place whatever the problem was in a new perspective," says Dr. Spiegel. "The participants neither avoided the problem nor allowed it to become overwhelming. The problem was changed, not in itself, but rather by placing it in a new and broader context."

But resist the urge to distract yourself, says Dr. Vasey. "If you practice focusing on worries and thinking of solutions for 30 minutes each day for several weeks, your anxiety starts to taper off. You'll get better at generating solutions or realize it's not worth worrying about." Psychologists call this process desensitization.

Another benefit of worry periods is, "During the rest of the day, when you notice that you're worrying, you can say, 'I'm busy now; I'll worry during my worry period.' It frees you from worry for the rest of the day and teaches you how to let go of worries," says Dr. Vasey.

Visualize mastery. If you like, you can spend the last several minutes of your worry period imagining the best—not the worst. At the Albany clinic, therapists steer their clients through a visualization of their worst fear occurring. Half an hour is spent fixing on that image, and the other half-hour is focused on the client's ability to cope with the anxiety. Worriers learn to reduce their anxiety by rationalizing and dismissing their worst fears rather than by worrying about them.

Improve your thoughts. People who worry a lot tend to share the same ordinary concerns as nonworriers. The difference, says Dr. Vasey, is that worriers think that disasters are much more likely to occur. For example, if you ask nonworriers the likelihood that the elevator they are boarding will fall, they will accurately respond that it's extremely remote. But a worrier might rate the possibility at 20 percent or more.

Another difference between worriers and nonworriers is that worriers assume they won't be able to deal with their imagined disasters. "They typically have a perception of not being able to cope," says Dr. Abel. They assume that if they lose their jobs, they'll wind up on the street, get sick and die. Nonworriers, on the other hand, assume that after a transition they'll find other jobs.

That's why a technique called cognitive therapy is ideal for worriers. It's a way of correcting negative, inaccurate thoughts and replacing them with more realistic, positive thoughts. Worriers are taught to detect the early cues that they're starting to worry. At the first hint of muscle tension or anxiety, for example, they ask themselves, "What am I telling myself that's threatening?"

The next step in this technique is to seek a more reasonable perspective, says Dr. Vasey. "Here the patient must question her assumptions. If she does just a little research, she'll find out that it's virtually impossible that the elevator will fall."

Dr. Abel notes that cognitive therapy is different from "positive thinking." "It doesn't mean seeing the world through rose-colored glasses. With worry, you tend to look at the world through cracked glasses—everything looks bad. Our goal is to give people clear glasses, so they see things more accurately."

You can try cognitive therapy yourself by carrying a notebook around for a week. Write down every negative prediction. Then do some research to come up with more realistic thoughts.

Breathe through the worry. Relaxing the body can relax the mind. Therapists teach worried clients techniques like meditation and progressive relaxation, which involves relaxing the major muscle groups, from the legs on up, one by one.

Once they've mastered these techniques, says Dr. Abel, they can apply them as soon as they catch their anxiety starting to mount. When worry strikes, even taking a few long, deep breaths from the diaphragm can really help. (This relaxation technique is called diaphragmatic breathing.)

Focus on the moment. "Worry is almost always future oriented," says Dr. Abel. "So if we can focus on what we're doing right now—the sentence we're reading, the tone of voice of the person speaking—rather than thinking about what someone might say next or our worries, we're better off."

Take a chance. Worriers usually have behaviors that reinforce the worry habit, says Dr. Brown. "A wife might call her husband at work several times a day to make sure he's okay. A parent might watch the kids at the bus stop every second, despite the fact that there's a chaperone there. In the short term, those behaviors reduce anxiety. But over the long run, they reinforce the worry—you start to think that your call or your watching the kids actually decreases the likelihood of something bad happening. Part of our treatment for worry might be to give worry-behavior-prevention assignments, along with the cognitive technique of prediction testing, like 'Don't call your husband every day at work,' and 'Don't watch the kids every second,' " Dr. Brown explains. Then set a prediction on what could happen if you don't call your husband or you do leave the kids with a chaperone, and compare the prediction to the actual outcome. "Eventually, people learn that the dreaded consequences still aren't occurring, and that reduces worry levels."

GETTING HELP

Can people cure themselves of worry without undergoing some kind of therapy? Some people do, experts say. But if it's a lifelong habit, says Dr. Abel, "you may not be able to control it on your own. Treatment provides relief for most worriers." Look for a therapist or program that specializes in cognitive therapy and applied relaxation, she adds.

And by the way, most experts agree that medication is usually not an effective treatment for chronic worry. "They may help some people for a while, but when a person goes off the drugs, there's a high chance of relapse," says Dr. Brown. "With behavioral and cognitive programs, clients may actually learn techniques that last a lifetime."

—*Cathy Perlmutter*

DO WORRY, BE HAPPY

FEEL AS IF YOU'RE CARRYING THE WEIGHT OF THE WORLD ON YOUR SHOULDERS? RELAX— WORRYING HAS A WEALTH OF BENEFITS.

You name it, I worry about it," says Ellen Warren, 42. "I worry that my children aren't getting enough vitamins. That they're not drinking enough milk—or maybe they're drinking too much! I worry about my weight, my new job and about my car breaking down. I worry about crime and the ozone layer and. . . ."

Like this Chicago mother of two, many of us have a catalog of concerns, both real and imagined, serious and minor. "How can you live in the '90s and not be worried?" asks Gary Emery, Ph.D., a Los Angeles psychologist. "Every day we are bombarded with what can go wrong."

Worrying is certainly nothing new—people have been rubbing worry stones, massaging their temples and pacing floors for centuries. Yet it seems we are worrying more than ever. Of 500 women polled nationwide by EDK Associates, a New York City research firm, 58 percent said they are more worried about their family today than they were five years ago.

Of course, nobody likes to worry; it's distracting and, in extreme cases, can lead to health problems, such as weight gain or loss, headaches, muscle tension, insomnia, even depression. But now a growing number of experts are saying that, in small doses, worrying can be good for you.

"It helps us anticipate danger and stay out of trouble," says Elwood Robinson, Ph.D., associate professor of psychology at North Carolina Central University in Durham. Worry nudges us to turn off the iron before we leave the house. It sends us to the doctor when we're not feeling well. Concern about a problem can also motivate us to find a solution, and nag us until we take action. As one psychologist puts it, worry is that red signal on a car dashboard that lets the driver know something is wrong.

WORRIERS: BORN OR MADE?

"Certain people are naturally more anxious than others," says Michael Vasey, Ph.D., assistant professor of psychology at Ohio State University in Columbus. But many times, experts agree, we learn to worry from our parents. "It's like a family tradition that gets passed down," says Dr. Emery.

Ellen Warren says that her mother has always worried out loud. "She shares her concerns—just about all of them," says Warren. "When I was growing up, she would do things like have us say the rosary as we crossed over a bridge. I got the message that there are at least a million and one things to worry about."

Although Warren's mother's behavior may seem extreme, her tendency to voice her concerns is the norm for women. That could explain why women consistently report worrying two to three times as much as men. "A lot of men just don't tell anyone they worry because they think it threatens their image," says Dr. Robinson. "They don't like to admit that there may be something that's out of their control. There's definitely a macho element involved."

Women's worries are often exacerbated by their sense of responsibility, adds Dr. Emery. "Society expects women to worry about people's feelings." And once children enter the picture, our capacity for worrying reaches new heights. "Until I became a mother, I lived a reckless life. I drove too fast, ate and drank what I pleased, stayed out late," says Jette Davis, 40, of suburban Los Angeles. "Now you wouldn't recognize me." Davis says she worries about everything, from whether her two boys' bunk beds will collapse to the quality of the air they breathe. "It seems with kids there's always something to worry about," she sighs.

"Moms are usually the family worriers," says Boris Rifkin, M.D., associate clinical professor of psychiatry at Yale University School of Medicine. "Since women are still considered the ones in charge at home, that often means they take on the majority of day-to-day concerns."

But motherhood won't automatically turn a woman into a worrywart; her personality also plays a role. "Go-getters or confident people may worry, but they'll identify troubles and try to remedy them immediately," says Dr. Robinson. "People who are less sure of themselves can be 'worrywimps'—they recognize a problem, but instead of fixing it, they sweat about it."

WHAT'S ON WOMEN'S MINDS

Studies show that women's worries run the gamut: work, finances, intimate relationships, social skills, health and the world at large. These worries vary not only by situation but also by age. "As children and adolescents, we worry most about self-image. As we get older, family and financial concerns take over," says William R. Carter, Ph.D., a psychologist in private practice in Charlottesville, Virginia, who specializes in worry.

Parents have to juggle a whole other set of worries. According to a survey of 803 moms and dads by the National Safe Kids Campaign in Washington, D.C., parents most often worry that their kids will be victims of violence, take drugs or alcohol, get into car crashes, fall sick or be negatively influenced by peer pressure.

Surprisingly, death is not a major concern; a Gallup Poll found that 83 percent of Americans rarely think about dying.

"We get too caught up in day-to-day particulars to worry about the real biggies," says Thomas Borkovec, Ph.D., professor of psychology at Pennsylvania State University and a pioneer in worry research.

Some of our worries are topical; worries of the hour, day or month that shift constantly. "Our worry index rises with every shooting spree, child kidnapping or death from AIDS that hits the front pages," says Dr. Vasey. In general, though, those worries fade quickly and get replaced by other front-page traumas.

Most everyone has a pet worry. Sometimes it's related to an insecurity, one woman might fear losing her job; another, her husband; a third, her looks. Holly Whitmore Denton, 33, of Verona, New Jersey, worries about money. "Every time I do the bills, I can't help but think about how my husband and I haven't done much saving for the future," she says. Other pet worries can stem from bad experiences. Cindy Warnell, 39, a Haslett, Michigan, mom of two, almost drowned as a child. "Now I worry whenever my kids are in water," she says.

A HEALTHY EMOTION

Once we understand what we worry about and why, we can use it in a positive way. "Worry can be a motivating and energizing force," says Dr. Vasey.

In recent years health worries have given people an edge in preventing illness. Women worried about getting cervical cancer, for example, are more apt to get Pap smears. In a sense, publicity about the disease and the worry it engenders have reduced cervical cancer deaths by as much as 41 percent among all age groups.

Besides motivating us to take care of ourselves for the long term, worrying can also help us avoid dangerous situations. If you're worried about going for a drive because you heard it's going to rain heavily, you might postpone it.

And worry can safeguard our loved ones, too. Before motherhood, Kathleen O. Ryan, 34, of San Antonio rarely used a seat belt. Now she wears one without fail and makes certain her sons Tyler, 5, and Sam, 2, are buckled up for every trip. "Worrying has made me take more control of my life," she says.

Worrying is also an emotion that lets your family know how much you care. "This is the job of parents, to be concerned, to protect their young and, yes, to worry," says Dr. Rifkin. "How are you feeling? I'm worried about you," a parent tells a sick child. The words alone are medicinal. Studies of juvenile offenders reveal that the most troubled youths complain no one worries about them; children may assume they're not loved if no one voices concern about their welfare and safety. Adds Dr. Carter, "Plenty of people get upset that their spouses don't worry *enough* about them."

Sometimes worry is a form of intuition. When Hanke Gratteau, 38, couldn't shake the thought that there was something not quite right about the woman babysitting her nine-month-old twins, she tried to push it to the back of her mind. "I told myself don't worry about it, they're fine," she says.

Later one of the boys suffered a serious cut inside his mouth—an injury the pediatrician said may have been caused by force-feeding. Gratteau immediately fired the babysitter. "Now, I really pay attention to my worries," she says. "And I try to do something about them."

WORRIED SICK

Although worrying can be helpful, too much is dangerous. An estimated 3 percent of Americans are chronic worriers. They get mired in concerns and find it impossible to break out of the cycle by taking action, says Dr. Vasey. Even worse, they imagine the worst possible outcomes for their worries.

In one study Dr. Vasey conducted, he asked 24 students who were chronic worriers and 24 nonworriers to imagine the outcome of getting bad grades. At first, both groups came up with feasible scenarios. They could end up in a bad job and make less money. But the worriers didn't stop at mere financial loss. They went on to envision mental illness, terrible pain and even death—all from getting a D.

Nonstop worrying obviously takes its toll on job performance and personal relationships. It can even impair other brain functions. Dr. Robinson tested the memories of 35 men and women, and asked them to worry for 15 minutes. Then he monitored them again and found they had weaker recall ability. "The effects of worry linger on," he says.

Chronic worriers also affect those close to them. One woman recalls the influence her worrisome grandmother had on her. "Other kids were riding bikes and going swimming, but I just kept thinking about cracking my head open on the sidewalk or getting bit by turtles in the lake. I couldn't find anything pleasant about doing the things most kids do."

But over the years, she says, she's learned to take more risks because her past fears were never realized. And experts confirm that most of our worries are usually pessimistic projections rather than true prediction. As Mark Twain reportedly once said, "I have known a great many troubles, but most of them never happened."

—Pamela Warrick

THE GOOD FIGHT

TEN WAYS TO TURN SPATS, SCRAPES AND SNARLS INTO (BELIEVE IT OR NOT) ARENAS FOR POSITIVE AND MEANINGFUL GROWTH.

Tonya could feel herself getting more upset with each passing minute—10:36 on a Tuesday night and not so much as a phone call. Why was he doing this again? Didn't he realize how much it upset her? Work had consumed her husband lately; he'd been leaving her and the kids with nothing but his paycheck.

At 11:14 P.M., she finally heard footsteps on the back porch. Tonya was tired after a long day at work, but she vowed not to lose her cool.

"This was the day from hell," Donald said as he parked his briefcase by the door and began rummaging through the refrigerator. "Anything exciting for dinner?"

"You could have called," Tonya snapped, her control already slipping away. "You even had the kids worried this time."

"Sorry. Guess I lost track of time," Donald answered, his

mouth full of cold chicken. Tonya felt her temperature rising.

"You really don't care about us, do you?" she challenged. "This is your home, you know, not a motel! You're seeing someone else, aren't you?"

"What are you—nuts?" Donald spat. "I work these long hours because I care about this family. How much more do I have to care before I end up killing myself?"

"Sure, wake the kids and really show you care!" Tonya fumed. "You're nothing but a coldhearted, success-starved egomaniac. Why don't you just go live in that damned office of yours and do us all a big favor?"

"You said it, not me!" Donald yelled as he left, slamming the door hard enough to rock the house—and the very foundation of his marriage.

GET IT ON THE TABLE

Ah, the hazards of confronting someone you love. It can be risky business—like a game of hopscotch in a mine field. But it's business that must be done, the experts say. Trying to build a strong and meaningful relationship without tackling sticky issues is an exercise in futility.

"The relationship simply won't last," says psychotherapist Ronald Podell, M.D., co-founder of the Center for Mood Disorders in Los Angeles and author of Contagious Emotions. Filomena Warihay, Ph.D., agrees. "The strongest and most worthwhile relationships are those that deal with the difficulties of the present for the sake of the future," says the "head coach" (as she prefers to be called) of Take Charge Consultants, a management consulting firm located in Downingtown, Pennsylvania. "Time doesn't make these difficulties go away. If anything, it just allows them to become more rancid."

In other words, you can't keep a clean house by sweeping day-to-day dirt under the rug. You must lay potentially divisive issues on the table to avoid the need for a massive cleanup later. And this holds true for relationships of all types, not just those between lovers or spouses.

"Whether you're dealing with your children, your parents, a friend, a co-worker or even your boss, more can be gained by expressing rather than repressing issues of concern," says Fran Gaal, a marriage counselor and family therapist in Bethlehem, Pennsylvania, and author of *Marriage: The Ulti-Mate Affair*. "And the sooner these issues are confronted, the better. That way, you can prevent the kind of resentment and miscommunication that can break apart even very healthy relationships."

NO LOSERS ALLOWED

Confrontation is usually a good thing. But not always. For instance, confrontation merely for the sake of altercation can do more harm than good. Unless a confrontation benefits both parties, it probably shouldn't be attempted. Success is a "win-win" situation, if either participant loses, there is no winner and two losers. Keep this in mind if you're tempted to come out with guns blazing when an olive branch might do. In a good confrontation, it's as important to keep the peace as it is to preserve your dignity.

That said, let's look at ten confrontational techniques that can best achieve a dignified peace. These "commandments" may appear to be specific to marital problems, but they're applicable to discord in almost any type of relationship. The communication techniques that make for a good marriage can also foster good parenting, good friendships and even a better working relationship with your boss. Sex isn't the only benefit of seeing eye to eye.

Commandment no. 1: Communicate, don't denigrate. "It's probably the most common mistake people make in the confrontational process," says Dr. Podell. "Wanting to make sure their case is well-argued, they resort to ridicule and insult. And this always backfires because the person being attacked puts up defenses that keep any sort of real communication from getting through."

Consider Tonya and Donald. They lost all hope of confronting each other positively when Tonya accused Donald of not caring to the point of being unfaithful. Donald may well have been unresponsive to Tonya's needs, but to assume this stemmed from a lack of affection great enough to drive him to other women was a leap she was neither justified nor wise to make.

It only takes a spark to ignite a confrontational bonfire, Dr. Podell says, so don't be the one to throw it.

Commandment no. 2: Be nonflammable. By the same token, don't catch fire too easily from whatever sparks your partner may throw. "The ability to think and communicate rationally drops off sharply as emotions rise," Dr. Podell says. "So it's best to stay as calm as possible in the face of provocation, even if the effort is bordering on the unbearable."

Just give it a minute—have the sense to put your pride aside in the face of a potential holocaust, Dr. Podell says. This doesn't mean surrendering, just changing the rules of battle. Instead of screaming at Donald, for instance, Tonya would have done better to say, "We're both getting upset. Why don't we take time to cool off before we say or do something we may regret?"

This sort of response accomplishes two things: It defuses the argument, and it shows that you have the best interests of your relationship in mind. Granted, such self-control can be extremely difficult to muster, Dr. Podell concedes, but it's well worth the effort, given the "bloodshed" it can spare.

Commandment no. 3: Talk about feelings, not actions. Had Tonya confronted Donald with how she actually felt about his late arrival, instead of pointing out the character flaws it seemed to represent, their ballyhoo might not have occurred. Why? Because Tonya could have stated her position in such a way that Donald couldn't really contest it. Had she simply said, "Donald, it upsets me that you've been working so late because I miss your company," how could he, in good conscience, have gotten angry? Tonya's mistake was to attack Donald for his actions, when the feelings his actions had aroused were the issue.

"I see this so often in couples who communicate poorly," says Dr. Podell. "They fight about each other's behavior, when what really needs to be discussed are the feelings those behaviors represent."

Commandment no. 4: Switch the focus. To help make the shift from actions to feelings and avoid the accusatory tone that can sour even the best confrontational intentions, Dr. Podell suggests using the pronoun "I" instead of "you," whenever possible. You'll be amazed at the pacifying effect, he says. This technique forces you to address your degree of responsibility and involvement in a particular issue, not just your partner's.

Had Tonya not opened the conversation with "You could have called" but rather "I was hoping you'd call," she would have sounded less judgmental and expressed exactly how she felt. And later in their argument, when the heat was on, Tonya might have avoided the eventual boilover by saying "I feel like you no longer care about us" instead of challenging him with "You really don't care about us, do you?"

Commandment no. 5: Don't try to read minds. Dr. Podell calls it the mind-reading syndrome—assuming you know the intentions behind someone's actions and then reproaching them accordingly. It's a guaranteed fire starter, not just because it's an act of mental trespass, but because you come off sounding like a know-it-all. Tonya made this mistake with Donald when she accused him of working late for purely selfish reasons. She implied that she knew more about his psychological motivations than he did—and she didn't.

"Whatever thoughts you may have about why someone has done what he has done should be kept to yourself," Dr. Podell says. This doesn't mean you can't have opinions. But to treat them as fact is to pass a sentence far short of a fair trial.

Commandment no. 6: Plan for positive outcomes. People often enter the confrontational arena emotionally and, hence, inadequately prepared, says Dr. Warihay. They wait until they're at wit's end before initiating a confrontation. And as a result, they're less persuasive and less effective at defending themselves against a counterattack. Not only was Tonya poorly prepared for her confrontation with Donald, she was tired and upset when she started it. So she resorted to counterproductive diatribe when Donald attempted to defend himself.

"Plan what you're going to say, how you're going to say it and how you're going to respond to all possible replies," says Dr. Warihay. "Then wait for a time when you're feeling calm and the person you'll be confronting is in a relatively peaceful mood."

Frank Dattilio, Ph.D., associate professor of psychiatry at the University of Pennsylvania School of Medicine in Philadelphia, even suggests composing a letter detailing your argument, then practicing its presentation with a friend or alone in front of a mirror. "You want to appear as objective as possible, so the more rehearsed you can be, the better," he says.

Commandment no. 7: Consider "fault" a four-letter word. There's a big difference between being assertive and being self-righteous. "Nothing can turn a potentially productive confrontation sour like a holier-than-thou attitude," says Gaal. "You want to be firm, but not demeaningly so, and the way to do this is to be willing to share responsibility for the misunderstanding."

Tonya might have made more headway with Donald if she'd owned up to feeling threatened by his late nights at the office. By admitting, "I fear you don't love me when you work so late," Tonya would have done far more to achieve a peaceful understanding than she did by calling her husband "a coldhearted, success-starved egomaniac."

Accepting partial blame also means that you must share in the responsibility for arriving at a solution, Gaal points out. The more "team effort" that goes into solving the problem, the easier and less contestable the solution will seem.

Commandment no. 8: Use the Installment Approach. This strategy simply involves withdrawing when the argument begins showing signs of rotting irreparably. "People sometimes think they have to stick it out in order to save face, no matter how badly it may be going," Dr. Podell says. "With the installment approach, you give yourself the option of disengaging from the confrontation so that it may be resumed less emotionally and more constructively at a future date."

How do you do this in the midst of battle, when any retreat looks like surrender? By announcing, simply, that the discussion is becoming too heated to be productive and that you'd like to call a time-out to let the air clear. This strategy prevents the kind of major bloodletting that can snuff out the chance for a productive discussion of the topic later on.

Commandment no. 9: Enlist the help of humor. The grist for confrontational mills is no laughing matter. But comic relief can occasionally make a valuable contribution to the peacemaking process. Tension itself is often the culprit when confrontations go poorly, Dr. Podell says, so injecting a little humor—and, yes, dosage is important—may help you achieve a more relaxed and potentially more constructive atmosphere.

Had Tonya greeted Donald with a remark like "Gee, I was beginning to wonder if the next place I'd see your face would be on a milk carton," their confrontation may have started better.

Commandment no. 10: Get outside help. So, what if all your patience, understanding, objectivity, sensitivity, assertiveness, compassion and humor still fail to bring about peace with a significant other?

Then it may be time to explore your options—namely, professional help. Relationships often need compromise, but they should never involve punishment. If your situation proves intractable, you may benefit from professional assistance.

—*Porter Shimer*

MAKE PEACE WITH THE NEIGHBORS

ARE THE FOLKS NEXT DOOR OR DOWN THE BLOCK DRIVING YOU UP A WALL?

Good fences make good neighbors," wrote poet Robert Frost, but some fences make bad neighbors.

When the fence between Angela's house in State College, Pennsylvania, and that of the couple next door began falling down, the neighbor offered to split the cost of a new one. "I paid him in advance," says Angela. "He hired the builder, and now his side is beautiful and mine is trash—old boards painted black with nails sticking out half an inch. He said he'll take care of it, but it has been a year and a half and he still hasn't kept his end of the bargain. The experience taught me that you never really know your neighbors."

HARD TO LOVE THAT NEIGHBOR

What should you do when a neighbor is less than neighborly? In a Woman's Day survey of 500 women across the

"As you go from mediation to arbitration to litigation, procedures become more formal and the parties have less and less participation in and control over how the dispute is resolved," says Vivian G. Walker, Ph.D., adjunct faculty at Northwestern University's Kellogg Graduate School of Management in Evanston, Illinois, and an authority on dispute resolution.

The options include:

Negotiation. Parties simply talk face-to-face. According to guidelines developed by Community Boards of San Francisco, negotiation is most effective if both people allow plenty of time for the discussion, approach it in a calm frame of mind, think about what to say ahead of time, avoid blaming or name-calling, listen to the other person's point of view and describe possible solutions in specific terms.

Conciliation. A third party, such as another neighbor, a member of the clergy or a representative of the court, acts as a go-between, often by telephone. The conciliator might discuss the issues with each party separately and summarize her story to the other person, going back and forth until a resolution is reached.

Mediation. Both people meet in the presence of a neutral party, who assists them in reaching a solution but doesn't make a decision for them.

Arbitration. Both sides agree to abide by the decision of a neutral person, often a lawyer or retired judge. The decision may be legally binding, depending on state law. Arbitration offers the advantage of a quick and final decision but is more adversarial than mediation. If the decision is binding, only in rare circumstances may it be appealed.

Small claims court. Monetary damages of less than $1,000 and, depending on the jurisdiction, up to $3,000. Representation by an attorney is not always required.

Municipal county court. Both criminal cases and instances in which you are trying to collect damages. Busy courts, however, may require routine disputes between neighbors to be mediated or arbitrated.

country, a fourth reported having had at least one dispute with a neighbor. Noise led the list of most common complaints, followed by problems with children's behavior, pets and garbage. Many such conflicts are resolved quickly and amicably, but some remain chronically annoying for years, and still others end up making headlines.

Madonna was sued by a neighbor in Hollywood Hills who claimed the star's trees and hedges were blocking his view; a judge ordered Madonna to trim the shrubbery and pay her neighbor's attorneys' fees. Mr. T's neighbors, on the other hand, were horrified when the star of *The A-Team* cut down more than a hundred century-old trees that were growing on his suburban Chicago estate.

Other, less-publicized disputes are equally disruptive. Too often, a simple disagreement escalates until it approaches all-out war. To keep raccoons out of the garbage cans near their summer house in Columbia County, New York, 30-year-old Sharon Blake and her family had a latticed wooden box built around the cans. One neighbor protested that the new structure had been built on his property (it turned out to be a community road), another raised fears about liability, tempers flared at a community meeting and, says Blake, "two years later half of the community isn't speaking to the other half. The shelter is still sitting there, and it's nice not to have to deal with the raccoons. But lifelong friendships were ended over garbage!"

LITTLE EFFORT, BIG RESULTS

According to Madeleine Crohn, president of the nonprofit National Institute for Dispute Resolution (NIDR) in Washington, D.C., people tend to react to conflict in one of two ways: Either they give up and walk away in frustration, or they become outraged and take drastic action—such as calling the police or filing a lawsuit—without seeking more moderate measures. Taking an issue to court is no guarantee of satisfaction; litigation is expensive, decisions are often appealed, resolution can take years and community goodwill can be irreparably damaged. "People don't know that there are other options," says Crohn.

One of those options is mediation, in which a neutral third

party sits down with the disputants and helps them find their own solution to the problem. Over the past ten years, several hundred neighborhood mediation centers have been established around the country, part of a growing trend toward finding alternatives to legal action in resolving conflicts. Mediation is usually inexpensive and highly effective. Many neighborhood centers use volunteer mediators who have been trained in negotiation skills and are either free or charge a nominal fee for their services. (Private professional mediators charge an hourly rate.)

When a problem is jointly solved by the parties themselves, the solution is much more likely to stick, explains Rita Adrian, director of a 15-year-old neighborhood mediation program for Community Boards of San Francisco that was one of the nation's first. People often realize that their neighbor is driving them crazy, but he's not the devil incarnate, says Adrian. "They usually find out new information about each other that reduces the hostility—for example, one of them might have an elderly parent living with them who's sensitive to noise."

AVOID ALL-OUT WAR

A related but more formal alternative is arbitration, in which a final decision is made by a neutral party, not the people having the dispute. In considering their course of action Crohn encourages neighbors to think about what they want out of the process.

"If your goal is just to get it over with, you might turn to arbitration because somebody else will make a decision for you quickly. If you want to maintain a decent relationship with the person with whom you have had the dispute, mediation might be preferred. If you want to be vindicated, litigation might be appropriate. But remember that you may not win."

Even without outside intervention, patience, persistence and creativity can go a long way toward resolving disagreements. In the Seattle suburb of Clyde Hill, an area with spectacular views of Mount Rainier and the surrounding lakes, many residents' sight lines were blocked by a "living fence" of towering pines and hemlocks whose owner had refused to trim them for 15 years.

Instead of mounting a lengthy and potentially divisive court battle, the owner's neighbors, Cathey and Margaret, waited until he put the property up for sale. The two mustered community support and approached the buyer with a proposition: The neighbors whose trees blocked his view would allow him to trim their trees if he would allow them to trim those that blocked their view. To ensure neighborhood cooperation and to work out a fair division of the cost, the two organized a coffee hour followed by a walk around the neighborhood to observe which trees affected each resident's view. The pruning fees were pro-rated accordingly, and all but one family agreed to chip in.

"It was a very civilized experience," says Carolyn Greer, a ballet teacher who lives behind the newly trimmed property. "We had the chance to become acquainted with neighbors below us we'd never met. If we'd taken the matter to court, there would have been legal fees and more animosity—tempers were already running high. I don't think we'd have the wonderful feeling we have now. We just wanted our view back, and its magnificent!"

—*Janet Bailey*

SIX PHYSICAL REASONS YOUR MIND MAY BE MUSHY

WHAT'S CLOGGING YOUR THOUGHTS MAY NOT BE WHAT YOU THINK.

Thinking's easy. You do it all the time, and you've gotten pretty good at it. In fact—you could do it with both frontal lobes tied behind your back. Lately, however, the noggin's been nodding off. You're losing car keys more often—and when you find them, you spend 20 minutes in the mall parking lot searching for your car.

Amid the missed appointments and the mistakes in your checkbook, things seem a little foggy, and life is getting a little confusing. Call it cognitive cobwebs. Relax—you may be losing keys, but you probably aren't losing your mind. There may be physical reasons—unexpected or overlooked—for your fuzziness. In fact, you may be unwittingly mushing your mind in ways that could easily be prevented or treated.

MEDICINE-CABINET MUSHINESS

Behind that mirrored door is a collection of potential mind muddlers. "Impaired mental performance caused by drug side effects is an underestimated problem among the general population," says Rodney Richmond, a registered pharmacist with the Drug Information and Pharmacoepidemiology Center at the University of Pittsburgh. "Sedation, dizziness, drowsiness and fatigue are common but reversible—although they can become bad enough to cause a dramatic reduction in your overall performance."

Some of these problems can be egged on by Father Time. "As you age, your body finds it harder to process medication," says Arthur I. Jacknowitz, Pharm.D., professor and chair of the Department of Clinical Pharmacy at West Virginia University School of Pharmacy. Antihistamines, for example, can cause sedation and grogginess. They impair the function of cholinergic neurons—brain chemicals used in thought processes. "Since cholinergic neurons become less functional as you age, the drugs offer a double whammy," says Dr. Jacknowitz.

"Kidney function also declines with age in many people, and that, combined with drugs, can affect cognition," says Dr. Jacknowitz. "Certain drugs taken for peptic ulcer disease— cimetidine (Tagamet), for example—may not be metabolized as efficiently due to poor kidney function and may accumulate to higher-than-desired levels." These increased levels may lead to cognitive impairment that can, in rare cases, reach dementialike proportions. "Many of the nonsteroidal anti-inflammatory drugs (NSAIDs) can impair blood flow to the kidneys in some people, thus increasing the risk of memory loss, inability to concentrate, confusion and personality changes in older people taking these agents," according to Dr. Jacknowitz.

Because they enter the central nervous system, some blood pressure medications can also have mind-fuzzying effects. "Beta-blockers and calcium-channel blockers may also cause fatigue by slowing your heart rate," says Richmond.

"Of course, if you're experiencing some mental impairment, and you think it may be due in part to any medication you're using—see your doctor or pharmacist immediately," says Richmond. You may not need to stop taking your medications—just change dosage or switch to another drug, but only at your doctor's advice.

Take note, too, that mind-mushing side effects can sprout even from milder over-the-counter (OTC) medications. "If you're taking any over-the-counter drugs, read the labels carefully and ask your doctor or pharmacist what certain ingredients can do," says Richmond. "Mental impairment from OTC drugs isn't extremely common, but it's possible that they could be at the root of your cognitive trouble." Some possible mind-numbing OTC drugs:

Antidiarrheal agents. "Some of the ingredients found in these OTC products contain opiates and anticholinergic agents and can have sedative properties," says Richmond. "Some products contain an opiate called paregoric, while another (loperamide) is chemically related to a certain psychotropic drug—which can have potential for drowsiness and fatigue."

Analgesics. NSAIDs (like ibuprofen) can cause some drowsiness or dizziness in 3 to 15 percent of users. "Some analgesics and other sinus-allergy-headache products contain antihistamines that may compound the effect," says Richmond.

Antitussive agents. The cough suppressant in some popular OTC cough syrups may be codeine, while others may contain dextromethorphan, a mirror image of codeine. "Both can have sedative effects in some people," says Richmond. "Other products may contain diphenhydramine, which may have sedative effects in up to 50 percent of adult users."

And others can double as bar fare. "Any OTC using the title elixir contains alcohol—as much as 5 to 10 percent," says Richmond. "Some elixirs, however, can run as high as 25 percent alcohol—more than a hearty wine." Of course, the amount of alcohol in a typical dose is small and may not affect a 175-pound man. However, it may have an entirely different effect on a 50-pound tyke. "If it's for your child, that's even more reason to check the alcohol content," says Richmond. Further, alcohol can compound the sedating effects of any sedative drug. Look for new alcohol-free products out on the market now.

Antiemetic agents. "Some antinausea drugs can cause sedation in roughly half the people using them," says Richmond. Some of these OTC products contain meclizine or dimenhydrinate, which can have sedative-like effects.

Sleeping agents. "Most OTC sleeping medications contain antihistamines, which can stay in your body much longer than you'd like them to," says James Walsh, Ph.D., director of the Sleep Disorders and Research Center at Deaconess Health System in St. Louis, Missouri. "They can remain active for 12 to 15 hours, so four hours after you've gotten up, they're still trying to put you to sleep." Some sleeping aids also carry the above-mentioned diphenhydramine, which may affect your daily performance of repetitive tasks.

UNFITNESS FOG

Evidence suggests body fitness may enhance brain fitness. If that's indeed the case, then the opposite may also be true—that being out of shape may lead to a foggy state of mind.

Mental metabolism. "While you're improving your body's metabolism through exercise, you may also be boosting your cerebral metabolism," says Charles Emery, Ph.D., assistant professor of psychiatry at Duke University Medical Center in Durham, North Carolina, and exercise and cognition researcher. Although research in this area is in its infancy, exercise may help increase blood flow to the brain, which carries more oxygen to help boost function. Exercise may lead to changes in neurotransmitters in the brain as well. This mindful metabolism may also help accentuate glucose transport to the brain, packing the lobes with much-needed fuel for thought.

Cognitive confusion. The speed at which you might process material—and what Dr. Emery calls sequencing, or your ability to follow instructions—could be hampered by a lifestyle of inactivity.

"Sequencing is the way you would think if you were following directions," he says. Taking a wrong turn may, in part, result from a lot of time being sofa-bound—instead of walking or jogging.

Life's demands. If exercise prepares you for the rigors of reality by making you stronger, then it makes sense that lack of exercise may leave you overmatched by your daily activities. "Life demands a proportion of effort on your part," says Bryant Stamford, Ph.D., exercise physiologist and director of the health promotion center at the University of Louisville Division of Allied Health. "If your energy capacity is only equal in proportion to what's demanded from your daily activities, then you'll be tapped out. If your energy capacity outweighs the demand, then you'll have a reserve of energy, so you won't feel tired."

To enlarge your fuel tank for living, you need to exercise regularly. As exercise eases the demands of living, alertness and mental vigor won't be undermined by physical fatigue.

A quick mind-fix. Just one bout of exercise may work as an on-call cobweb cutter. If your mind is mush—or oatmeal—a brisk walk may stir it up. "I take a 20-minute walk in the afternoon to help reinvigorate myself," says Dr. Stamford. It may be the change of scenery that works. Exercise may also trigger an endorphin release—chemicals in the brain that may boost your mood. And because cognitive function may be hindered by depression or anxiety, improved cognitive function may come about from enhanced psychological well-being.

BRAIN BURNOUT

If you're stressed out from being overworked—and you're reading this sentence—chances are your mind has already strolled off this page. "Your ability to concentrate and make decisions, along with short-term memory, may be one of the first areas of mental functioning hit by stress," says Paul J. Rosch, M.D., president of the American Institute of Stress. "Some of this stems from information overload. The constant flood of information we now have to process and sort out for personal relevance may become too much to handle."

Loss of control. In a review of 82 studies and articles conducted by the Naval Training Systems Human Factors Division in Orlando, Florida, "perceived control" was the major factor implicated in good or bad performance caused by stress. "When there's a sense of loss of control, it can lead to high levels of job stress, cardiovascular disease and burnout," says Dr. Rosch.

In a recent study, 24 women were put through four hours of continuous mental activity, during which cortisol, a stress hormone, was tested. A test of their cognitive performance then followed. Women with elevated cortisol reactions—indicative of stress—scored much lower in attention during the cognitive testing. Stress is an unavoidable part of life—and up to a point, increasing stress or demand increases productivity at work.

"But there's a limit—once you exceed it, productivity plunges downward and mental and physical fatigue results," says Dr. Rosch. Stress is much like the tension on a violin string. If you don't have enough, it's going to produce a dull, flat sound. If it's excessive, the tone will be harsh or shrill; or worse, the string may break. "But with the right amount of stress, or tension, you can make beautiful music," he says.

Changing your perceptions. "Many stressful events aren't necessarily stressful, but it is rather our perceptions that cause problems," says Dr. Rosch. "Often we can change or correct faulty perceptions and regain control." Sit down and list all of the things at work or home you consider stressful and divide the list into those items over which you have no control and others where you can exert some influence. "Use your time and talent to change those things where you can make a difference, and learn to accept or avoid those things you can't do anything about," says Dr. Rosch.

BLOOD SUGAR

"For people with diabetes, low blood sugar clearly affects awareness, attention and other aspects of cognitive function," says Alan Jacobson, M.D., staff psychiatrist at the Joslin Diabetes Center in Boston. "Short-term memory and attention—the ability to stay focused—get hit first."

Because glucose functions as fuel for your brain, when it dips low, what your brain does best—thinking—may suffer. Staying alert or following complicated instructions can become a Herculean task. "This problem can go on for some time and you won't even be aware of it," says Dr. Jacobson. That's because these very symptoms keep you from recognizing it.

Friends as cognitive watchers. "Because fuzzy thinking may keep you from realizing you have a problem, it's key for your friends and family to be aware," says Dr. Jacobson. "These warning signs need to be heeded before blood sugars dive to a more dangerous zone." The unclear responses and slowness may be a tipoff that blood sugar is low. Treatment may be as simple as a glass of orange juice to get your sugar raised. (And obviously, blood sugar monitoring is key for all people with diabetes.)

The sweet slump. For people who do not have diabetes, eating habits may mush you up by lowering your blood sugar. "The human body wasn't designed for consuming a whole bunch of rapidly absorbed processed sugar," says registered dietitian Jay Kenney, Ph.D., nutrition research specialist at the Pritikin Longevity Center in Santa Monica, California, and Diplomate of the American Board of Nutrition. "It's doubtful a sweet snack will knock you out at your desk; though in a few people a snack of colas and candy bars may raise blood sugar levels quickly, causing their bodies to produce so much insulin that their blood sugar temporarily plummets—leading to a short period of grogginess or feeling weak. If this occurs infrequently, munching on a piece of bread or fruit will bring you back to normal within 10 to 15 minutes. If this reaction occurs frequently, and particularly if it's accompanied by anxiety or sweating, it may be reactive hypoglycemia. If it occurs consistently after eating a meal or snack high in refined carbohydrates, you need to have your blood sugar checked when you have the symptoms. If your blood sugar is very low, your physician may need to do other tests."

Graze past the daze. The "Thanksgiving dinner effect"—eating a large meal—may also cause a drop in energy level. "This is a normal physiological response to a very large meal and probably occurs because blood is shunted to the digestive tract to get all those extra calories transported and stored," says Dr. Kenney. "Eating two or three large meals a day may work for our schedules, but may not be best for our bodies," he adds. "To keep your function steady, eat in smaller amounts and choose from high-carbohydrate unprocessed foods," says Dr. Stamford. By eating smaller meals more often, or grazing, you may keep your blood sugar level and not hit the postmeal need-to-nap switch.

CAFFEINE ROLLER COASTER

What we use to stay alert can turn us into "grog monsters."

"Some—though not all—people often experience the symptoms of caffeine withdrawal, which include faintness, irritability and shakiness when the caffeine level in their blood drops," says Dr. Kenney. Considering that 75 percent of the U.S. population uses caffeine, there may be a whole lot of shakin'—and yawnin'—going on.

Getting mugged. Because caffeine's half-life in the body is roughly 3½ to 4 hours, by late afternoon, the morning buzz has finally made it out of your system. So, six to eight hours after those jolts of French roast, you're sliding into your chair. Because that cognitive dip comes after you've eaten lunch, you may blame it on what you ate. In truth, the main cause may be caffeine withdrawal.

One study of 62 regular coffee slurpers underlines caffeine's seesaw effect. They abandoned their mugs and instead got their caffeine in capsule form for two days (an amount equal to about 2½ cups of java). During a second two-day period, they received a dummy pill containing no caffeine. No one knew which pill they were taking during the study. During the caffeine-free period, half of the group experienced extreme fatigue, lack of concentration and impairment of motor performance.

To measure work performance, the group performed simple tasks. No surprise—they performed poorly when going through withdrawal.

Other caffeine fiends. Tea, chocolate, cola and some other soft drinks have caffeine, too—only in lesser quantities than coffee. Even some OTC analgesic and antihistamine medications contain 75 to 200 milligrams of caffeine per dose—roughly equivalent to a six-ounce cup of "Joe." Have a cup of coffee, followed by a candy bar and a cola for a snack (plus a combination analgesic for your headache), and you're setting yourself up for a big fall. Severe symptoms of withdrawal—like those seen in the study mentioned above—can begin 12 to 24 hours after the last use, peak at 20 to 48 hours and last roughly one week.

How much is too much?

This study suggests that anyone who gulps just two or more servings of caffeine-containing beverages can be at risk. If you think your fuzziness is caused by caffeine withdrawal, you might consider trying to wean yourself off the bean—slowly. Reduce the intake incrementally—halving portions and mixing them with decaf. Follow that strategy and you'll be off the buzz completely.

BEDROOM BEDLAM

If your sleep is screwed up, chances are you won't know it. The only sign that something is awry at night, then, is what's going on the next day. "Sleep disorders can cause lapses in attention and fatigue in the daytime, especially when you're faced with repetitive tasks requiring complete attention," says Peter Hauri, Ph.D., administrative director of the Mayo Clinic Sleep Disorders Clinic in Rochester, Minnesota, and author of *No More Sleepless Nights*. "The more attention demanded by the job, the greater effect lack of sleep can have on your performance." Here are some common sleep problems that may mush you up in the daytime.

Insomnia. "Insomnia isn't a disorder, but a symptom of other problems, from stress to depression or chronic arthritis," says Dr. Walsh. "How much sleep is disrupted will dictate how severe the grogginess is during the day." And that grogginess can turn dangerous. "Insomniacs have roughly 2½ times more accidents than normal sleepers," says Dr. Hauri.

"Because insomnia can be caused by any number of things, your first step is to pinpoint the underlying problem," says Dr. Walsh. "If you can narrow it down to one to three contributing factors, most insomniacs can be helped within a few weeks. Sleep medications can provide temporary help—but they won't address the root cause. If arthritis is the real cause, then sleeping pills won't help—the illness must be treated first," says Dr. Walsh.

Plus, you can do a lot to promote good sleep without drugs. "Exercise—but do it at least three hours before bedtime," says

Dr. Walsh. That's because exercise stimulates you initially, leaving you wide awake instead of sleepy. "The same thing goes for mental stimulation," he adds. Have a cool-down period—a very calming presleep routine for 30 minutes—before bed.

"Go to bed at the same time and get up at the same time every day," says Dr. Walsh. On weekends, limit the extra sleep that might cause Sunday night insomnia and the following Monday mushiness. "Sleep is partially controlled by your biological clock," says Dr. Walsh. "A regular sleep schedule can reinforce that rhythm to improve sleep."

Sound sleep means avoiding caffeine products at night. But aim for an earlier cutoff point. "Even at 4 P.M. caffeine can still be disruptive," says Dr. Walsh. And while alcohol may help you fall asleep, the net effect is a negative one. It's metabolized fast and your brain ends up rebounding in the second half of the night, leaving you stimulated.

Sleep apnea. Because breathing obstruction is the calling card of sleep apnea, causing sufferers to wake up to catch their breath 40 to 60 times an hour, they'll often demonstrate impaired daytime performance from sleep loss. "Most people won't remember waking up—so their only signal is their daytime grogginess," says Dr. Hauri.

Your most important step: If your spouse reports that you regularly stop breathing during loud snoring, see a physician for a professional evaluation. Sleep apnea can be life threatening.

"Once apnea is diagnosed, however, the treatment is successful in a vast majority of cases," says Dr. Walsh. For people who only experience sleep apnea when they sleep on their backs—while breathing fine on their sides or bellies—a custom-made nightshirt might help. It has a pocket that allows you to fit tennis balls along the spine—keeping you from rolling onto your back. Weight loss is also encouraged if the sufferer is obese.

More serious cases may require a continuous positive airway pressure machine. It's a bedside compressor connected to a face mask that delivers a steady stream of pressurized air into the nose throughout the night. Surgery is another option for more serious cases.

Unrefreshing sleep. These insomniacs think they sleep okay at night, but don't. Their sleep is very shallow, or unrefreshing.

"Those folks don't know that their daytime fatigue is due to light sleep," says Dr. Walsh. "They may wake up 10 to 15 times an hour and remember only a few," says Dr. Walsh. "This sleep fragmentation results in a lot of time in the light stages of sleep—without real slumber." Stress, pain or discomfort from arthritis or other chronic conditions might cause this. "Circadian rhythm disorders—mismatches between the time you sleep and the time your brain wants to sleep—can cause it, too," says Dr. Walsh.

Periodic limb movements. Many people experience a constant twitching of their legs throughout the night. "The typical patient will have a leg jerk once every 30 seconds for hours and hours during the night," says Dr. Walsh. And, like sleep apnea patients, they tend not to remember many of these awakenings—and feel tired the next day. "Although many people experience normal limb activity during the night, once it gets over 100 to 200 times a night, you've got a problem," says Dr. Walsh. The cause of this ailment isn't known, but it could be from some shenanigans in the spinal cord or brain.

"And it may be triggered by anemia or kidney failure," says Dr. Walsh. A drug containing levadopa and carbidopa, normally used in combination for Parkinson's disease, seems to work in most patients, he says.

Sleep cheats. You may also just be cheating yourself knowingly of slumber, causing your mental mushiness. "We're a nation of sleep skippers, and that courts disaster," says Dr. Walsh. "Thousands of accidents can be attributed to lack of sleep. You have to realize you need sleep to lead a productive life."

"Experiment with your sleep schedule," says Dr. Hauri. Try seven hours each night for one week. If toward the end of the week you're tired during the day, add an hour. "Just seeing how well one night of sleep works isn't enough—your body needs to adapt," says Dr. Hauri. If you feel you may have a sleep problem beyond your control, talk to your doctor about seeing a sleep specialist.

—*Greg Gutfeld*

SOURCES AND CREDITS

PART ONE

"The Process of the 'Pause' " was adapted from *The Pause* by Lonnie Barbach, Ph.D. Copyright © 1993 by Lonnie Barbach, Ph.D. Used by permission of Dutton Signet, a division of Penguin Books USA, Inc.

"How to Get More from Your Ob-Gyn Visit" was adapted from "How to Get More from Your OB-GYN Visit" by Stephanie Young, originally published in *Glamour*, October 1993. Courtesy *Glamour*. Copyright © 1993 by The Conde Nast Publications Inc.

"Don't Have a Stroke!" was adapted from "Don't Have A Stroke!" by Leslie Laurence, originally published in *Ladies' Home Journal*, November 1993. Copyright © 1993 by Meredith Corporation. All rights reserved. Reprinted from *Ladies' Home Journal* magazine.

"Female Hearts at Risk" was adapted from *The Woman's Heart Book* by Fredric J. Pashkow, M.D., and Charlotte Libov. Copyright © 1993 by Fredric J. Pashkow, M.D., and Charlotte Libov. Used by permission of Dutton Signet, a division of Penguin Books USA, Inc.

PART TWO

"Dating Your Husband" was adapted from "Dating Your Husband" by Sherry Suib Cohen, originally published in *New Woman*, February 1994. Copyright © 1994 by *New Woman*. Reprinted by permission.

"The Sex Offenders" adapted from "The Sex Offenders" by Michael Castleman, originally published in *New Woman*, September 1993. Copyright © 1993 by Michael Castleman. Reprinted by permission.

"Five Things You Should Never Do in Bed" was adapted from "Five Things You Should Never Do in Bed" by Judy Kuriansky,

Ph.D., originally published in *Ladies' Home Journal*, October 1993. Copyright © 1993 by Meredith Corporation. All rights reserved. Reprinted from *Ladies' Home Journal* magazine.

PART THREE

"How to Foil Purse Snatchers" was adapted from "How to Foil Purse Snatchers" by Debra Wishik Englander, originally published in *New Woman*, September 1993. Copyright © 1993 by Debra Wishik Englander. Reprinted by permission.

"The Striking Realities of Self-Defense" was adapted from "The Striking Realities of Self-Defense" by Susan J. Grill, originally published in *First for Women*, March 7, 1994. Copyright © 1994 by Micaela R. Grill. Reprinted by permission.

PART FOUR

"Dermatologist, Peel Thyself" was adapted from "Dermatologist, Peel Thyself" by Jean Godfrey-June, originally published in *ELLE*, January 1994. Copyright © 1994 by ELLE Publishing. Reprinted by permission.

PART FIVE

"The Myth and Promise of Herbal Weight Loss" was adapted from "The Myth and Promise of Herbal Weight Loss" by Michael Castleman, originally published in *Herb Quarterly*, Winter 1993. Copyright © 1993 by Michael Castleman. Reprinted with permission.

PART SIX

"A Nutritional Survival Guide for Women" was adapted from "A Nutritional Survival Guide for Women" by Liz Applegate, Ph.D. Copyright © 1994 by Liz Applegate, Ph.D. Reprinted by permission.

"Foods That Kill Pain" was adapted from "Foods That Kill Pain" by Robert Barnett, originally published in *First For Women*, November

22, 1993. Copyright © 1993 by Robert Barnett. Reprinted by permission.

"How Common Drugs Can Rob You of Vitamins" was adapted from *Nutrition for Women* by Elizabeth Somer, R.D. Copyright © 1993 by Elizabeth Somer, R.D. Reprinted by permission of Henry Holt and Co., Inc.

PART SEVEN

"Yoga: The Right Moves" was adapted from "Fitness" by Clint Willis, originally published in *Lear's*, November 1993. Copyright © 1993 by Clint Willis. Reprinted by permission.

PART EIGHT

"Do Worry, Be Happy" was adapted from "Do Worry, Be Happy" by Pamela Warrick, originally published in *Redbook*, March 1994. Copyright © 1994 by the Hearst Publications. Reprinted by permission of *Redbook* magazine. All rights reserved.

"Make Peace with the Neighbors" was adapted from "Make Peace with the Neighbors" by Janet Bailey, originally published in *Woman's Day*, August 10, 1993. Copyright © 1993 by Janet Bailey. Reprinted by permission.

INDEX

Note: Prescription drugs are denoted with the symbol Rx.

B

Babies, nutrition tips for, 228–29
Bacterial vaginosis
  diagnosis, 85
  drug treatment, 84–85
Banks, safety guidelines, 156. *See also* Automated teller machines
Basal metabolic rate (BMR), 207–8
Beauty, 167–90
  accentuating the positive, 169
  resolutions for, 168–70
Behavior management, for worry relief, 293–94
Benadryl, sexual side effects, 135–36
Beta-carotene
  to lower cancer risk, 63
  to smooth wrinkles, 189–90
Biking, stationary, 264–68
  boredom breakers for, 267–68
  getting comfortable during, 266–67
  keeping cool during, 266
  programming for, 265–66
  pulse monitoring during, 264–65
Bingeing, 7
Birth control pills
  dental care while taking, 89–90
  for menstrual cramps, 74–75
  nutrition effects, 245
  protective effects, 68–69
  sexual side effects, 133
  and stroke, 94
Bladder infections, home remedies for, 34–35
Blood cholesterol level
  lowering
    avocados and, 231–34
    nuts and, 233–34
    before menopause, 59
  tests for, 7
    guidelines, 25–26
Blood pressure checks, 7
  guidelines, 25–26

Blood pressure drugs
  mental side effects, 310–11
  nutrition effects, 244
  sexual side effects, 134
Blood sugar
  and cognitive function, 314–16
  and grazing, 315–16
Blood tests
  CA-125, 67
  cholesterol levels, 7, 25–26
  fecal occult, 30
Blush, suggestions for use, 182–83
BMR, 207–8
Bodybuilding, 252–63
  compound exercises, 252
  for extra tone, 262–63
  major muscle exercises, 259–63
  order of exercises, 252–53
  pushing yourself during, 256
  resistance-training exercises, 198–99
  resting between exercises, 255
  in sets, 255–57
  strength-training workouts, 257–63
Body/mind connection, 269–70
Body shaping, 247–75
Bone scans, guidelines, 31–32
Breakfast, 209
  as fat burner, 196
Breast cancer screening, 7–8
Breast-feeding
  and cancer risk, 63
  effect on sexual desire, 123
Breasts
  examination
    guidelines, 26, 27
    mammography, 22, 27–28
    test rates, 22
  painful or fibrocystic, home remedies for, 40
Breast self-examination (BSE)
  guidelines, 26
  test rates, 22
BSE. *See* Breast self-examination
Burning mouth, 90
Bus safety, guidelines, 155–56

C

Caffeine
  nutrition effects, 246
  during pregnancy, 229
  seesaw effect, 316–17
  withdrawal symptoms, 316
Calcium, 3
  for menstrual cramps, 39
  nutrition tips, 231
  for pain relief, 238–40
  supplements, 16–18
    Healthy Women Survey
      results, 4–5
    before menopause, 58
Cancer
  breast, screening for, 7–8
  colon, screening for, 30–31
  ovarian, 61–71
  risk factors, 62–63
Cancer drugs, sexual side effects,
    135
CA-125 blood tests, 67
Carbohydrates, 197
Cardio-nutrients, 234–37
Car safety, 149–50
  guidelines, 156–57
Cash machines, 156, 159
Cervicitis, drug treatment, 84
Child safety, 150
Chili peppers, for pain relief,
    242–43
Chinese ephedra, for weight loss,
    207–8
Chlamydia
  diagnosis, 85
  drug treatment, 84
Cholesterol level. *See* Blood
    cholesterol level
Cigarettes
  and menopause, 58
  nutrition effects, 245–46
  and stroke, 94
Cimetidine (Rx), for ulcers, 135,
    310
Cleocin (Rx), for yeast infections,
    85

Climacteric, 56
Clindamycin phosphate vaginal
    cream (Rx), for yeast
    infections, 85
Cognitive deficits
  and lifestyle, 312
  physical reasons for, 309–19
Colon cancer prevention tests,
    30–31
Communication techniques,
    301–5
  mediation, 306, 307–8
  negotiation, 306
Community support, as stress
    buster, 20–21
Competition, fitness benefits,
    250–51
Concealers, suggestions for use,
    183–84
Conciliation, 306
Confrontations
  communication techniques for,
    301–5
  conciliation, 306
  disputes, 305–7
  humor in, 304–5
  Installment Approach, 304
  mediation, 306, 307–8
  negotiation, 306
  suggestions for resolving, 119,
    299–305
  win-win, 301–5
Congenital heart defects, risk
    factors, 103
Contraceptives. *See* Birth control
    pills
Control, over stress
  immune system factor, 284–85
  loss of, 313–14
Copper, for pain relief, 240–41
Coronary heart disease, 100
Cortisol, side effects, 203
Cough syrups, mental side effects,
    311–12
Couples, 118–24, 130
  approach to sexually trans-
    mitted diseases, 83–84

E

Eating. *See also* Food; Nutrition
  bingeing, 7
  breakfast, 196
  exercise after, 198
  grazing, 197–98, 209, 228,
    315–16
  habits during your twenties,
    226–28
  healthy, 15–16
  to lose weight, 202–3
  for menopause, 57
  nutrition tips, 230
  substitutes for, 218
Emotional health, 277–319
Emotions. *See also* Stress
  anatomy of, 281–82
  immune connection, 282
  power of expression, 285–86
  talking about, 302
Endometrial tissue samples,
    guidelines, 29–30
Endometriosis, signs and
    symptoms, 74
Endorphins, 242
Environmental engineering, for
    weight loss, 221–22
Ephedrine, for weight loss, 207–8
Ergot drugs, for migraines, 134
Exercise, 4, 192–95, 248–52
  aerobics, 4
  age and, 3
  bodybuilding, 252–63
  body/mind connection,
    269–70
  and cancer risk, 63
  deficiency, 192–95
  for depression, 37
  after eating, 198
  with family, 251–52
  for fat loss, 196–97
  for fun, 113–14, 250–51
  for hot flashes or night sweats,
    38
  housework as, 251
  indoor, 266

  interval training, 199–200
  on the job, 249–50
  for menopause, 38, 57
  for menstrual cramps, 39, 76
  mind effects, 312–13
  mindful, 269–70
  motive for, 195, 270–71
  muscle, 259–63
  national deficit, 248–49
  for older women, 3, 231
  pleasure principle of, 12–14
  for posture, 170
  for premenstrual syndrome, 42
  resistance training, 198–99
  for romance, 112–14
  stationary bikes, 264–68
  strength training, 257–63
  for stress relief, 205
  time pressures on, 4
  walking, 4
  for weight loss, 7, 209–10,
    214–15
Exercises, 259–63
  bench press, 259
  biceps curl, 262
  compound, 252
  Kegel, 43
  lat machine pull-down, 261
  leg extension, 259
  leg press, 260–61
  military press, 261
  seated pulley row, 260
  sit-back, 263
  triceps push-down, 262–63
Exercise stress tests, 264–65
  guidelines, 26
Exfoliants, 175–76
Exfoliation, 175–78
  anti-aging, 182
  basics of, 177–78
  body, 178
  mechanical, 176–77
  nonmechanical, 177
Expression, power of, 285–86
Eye care
  anti-aging advice, 181–82
  beauty resolutions, 168–69

F

Family exercise, 251–52
Fantasies, sexual, 121–22, 142
Fast food, nutrition tips, 228
Fat
 body
  effects of stress on, 203–6
  top ten burners, 196–200
 dietary
  monounsaturated, 232–33
  saturated, 234
Fat budget, 212–13
Fatigue, home remedies for, 39–40
Fecal occult blood tests,
  guidelines, 30
Feelings
 anatomy of emotions, 281–82
 power of expression, 285–86
 talking about, 302
Fiber, for fitness, 199
Fibrocystic breasts, home
  remedies for, 40
Fibroid tumors, signs and
  symptoms, 74
Fights. *See* Confrontations
Fitness
 boosters, 12–14, 199, 250–51,
  252
 lifestyle and, 312
Fluid retention drugs, sexual side
  effects, 135
Folic acid, during pregnancy,
  228–29
Follicle-stimulating hormone
  (FSH) testing, 49
Food. *See also* Diet; Eating; Nutrition
 ethnic cuisines, 196
 fast, nutrition tips, 228
 high-energy, 200–203
 nutrition tips, 231
 for pain relief, 237–43
 during pregnancy, 229
 spicy, 196
 substitutes, 214
Forgetfulness, physical reasons for,
  309–19

Framingham Heart Study, 105
Friends, as cognitive watchers, 315
Fruit, nutrition tips, 230
FSH testing, 49
Fun, exercises for, 113–14
Fungal infection medications,
  sexual side effects, 135

G

Glutamate receptor antagonists,
  for stroke, 97
Glycolic acid peels
 anti-aging, 182
 used by dermatologists, 189
Golden years
 exercise in, 3, 231
 nutrition tips, 230–31
Gonorrhea, drug treatment, 84
Grazing, 228
 blood sugar effects, 315–16
 for weight loss, 197–98, 209
Gum health, during menstruation,
  88
Gynecological care, medical
  screening tests, 28–30
Gynecologic oncologists, how to
  find, 64

H

Hair care, beauty resolutions, 169
Haldol (Rx), for psychoses, 135
HDL, 26
Headache medications, 134
 sexual side effects, 133–34
Health
 effect of stress on, 280–87
 emotional and mental, 277–319
 nutrition connection, 225–46
Healthy Women Survey, 2–12, 22
 AIDS prevention results, 9–10
 calcium supplementation
  results, 4–5
 medical screening results, 7–9
 skin care results, 9
 stress relief results, 10–11
 weight concerns results, 5–7

Heart attack, risk factors, 102–3
Heart disease, 105–7
  coronary, 100
  diet and, 235–36
  exercise stress tests, 26
  gender bias in, 103–5
  medical screening tests, 25–26
  risk factors, 98–107
  and stroke, 95
  vitamins and minerals for
    preventing, 234–37
Hemorrhage, subarachnoid, 93
Hemorrhagic stroke, 92
Herbs, 209
  diuretic, 206–7
  stimulant, 207–8
  for weight loss, 206–10
High blood pressure, and stroke, 94
High blood pressure medications.
    See Blood pressure drugs
High-density lipoproteins (HDL),
    26
High-fiber diet, 4, 99
HIV test, guidelines, 32–33
Home remedies, 33–43
  for anxiety, 40–41
  for bladder infections, 34–35
  for depression, 36–37
  for fatigue and lethargy, 39–40
  for hot flashes or night sweats,
    37–38
  for menstrual cramps, 38–39,
    75–77
  for painful or fibrocystic
    breasts, 40
  for premenstrual syndrome,
    41–42
  for urinary incontinence, 43
  for vaginal dryness, 42–43
  for vaginal infections, 35–36
Home safety tips, 150–51
Hormone-replacement therapy
    (HRT), 59
Hot chili peppers, for pain relief,
    242–43
Hot flashes, 60
  home remedies for, 37–38

Hot spots, sexual, 142
Housework, fitness benefits, 251
HRT, 59
Human immunodeficiency virus
    (HIV) test, guidelines,
    32–33
Humor, for confrontations, 304–5
Husbands
  dating, 124–31
  listening to, 129–30
Hygiene, importance of, 185–86
Hypertension, and stroke, 94

I

Ibuprofen, for menstrual cramps,
    38–39, 73–74
Imagery, to dissipate worry, 290–91
Immune system
  control factor, 284–85
  emotional connection, 282
  stress factor, 282–84
Inderal (Rx), for migraine
    headaches, 133–34
Infections
  AIDS prevention, 9–10, 32–33
  bladder, 34–35
  drug treatments, 84–85
  HIV test guidelines, 32–33
  home remedies for, 34–35,
    35–36
  sexually transmitted diseases,
    83–84
  urinary-tract, 84, 85
  vaginal, 35–36
Injuries, benefits of yoga for,
    274–75
Insomnia, 317–18
Installment Approach, to
    confrontations, 304
Intercourse, painful, 122
Interval training, 199–200
Intimacy
  dating your husband, 124–31
  suggestions for, 142–43
Iron supplements, 236
"I" statements, 302–3

O

Obesity. *See* Overweight
Obstetrician-gynecologists, 78–87
  extra-curricular health services
    from, 78–79
  as primary care doctors, 78–79
Older women
  exercise for, 3, 231
  nutrition tips, 230–31
Oncologists, gynecologic, 64
Oophorectomy, effect on
    menopause, 52
Oral contraceptives. *See* Birth con-
    trol pills
OTC medications. *See* Over-the-
    counter medications
Ovarian cancer, 61–71
  familial, 65–70
  medical screening tests, 61–64,
    66–67
  prevention, 64–65
  risk factors, 62–63, 65–70, 70–71
Ovarian failure, premature, 52
Over-the-counter (OTC) medica-
    tions
  mental side effects, 311–12
  sexual side effects, 135–36
Overweight
  effect of exercise deficiency on,
    192–95
  effect of stress on, 203–6
Overwork, 313–14

P

Pacing, benefits of, 250
Pain, during intercourse, 122
Pain relief
  foods for, 237–43
  home remedies for, 40
Pap-smear tests, 8–9
  annual rates, 22
  guidelines, 28–29
Passion, rekindling, 114–24
Peanuts, for fighting cholesterol,
    233–34

Pelvic examinations, 66
  annual, 81–83
  guidelines, 28
  health data from, 83
Pelvic inflammatory disease, signs
    and symptoms, 74
Peppers, for pain relief, 242–43
Peptic ulcer drugs, mental side
    effects, 310
Perimenopause, 56
Personal safety, 145–64
  precautions, 158–60
  guidelines, 152–58
  self-defense, 161–65
  worst-case scenarios, 157–58
Physical fitness
  boosters, 12–14, 199, 250–51,
    252
  and mental fitness, 312
Physicians. *See* Doctors
Pickpockets, how to foil, 158–61
Play, fitness benefits, 252
Pleasure
  principle, of exercise, 13–14
  touching, 143
PMS. *See* Premenstrual syndrome
Posture
  exercises, 170
  importance of, 170
Potbelly, taming, 203–6
Potbelly syndrome, 204–5
Power snacks, 228
Prednisone (Rx), for allergic and
    inflammatory disorders,
    135
Pregnancy
  and cancer risk, 62–63
  dental care during, 88–89
    gingivitis, 88
  nutritional survival guide for,
    228–29
  oral health effects, 88–89
  and stroke, 94–95
Premenstrual syndrome (PMS)
  home remedies for, 41–42
  menopause connection, 46–47,
    57–58

Prescription medications
for migraine headaches, 134
sexual side effects, 131–36
Prevention/AMWA Healthy
Women Survey, 2–12, 22
Primary care physicians, 11–12
selecting, 23–25
Priorities, re-ordering, 121
Problem solving, learning, 289–90
Professional help, when to seek,
305
Propranolol (Rx), for migraine
headaches, 133–34
Prostaglandins, menstrual cramps
connection, 72–74
Protein, nutrition tips, 231
Psychoses, prescription medica-
tions for, 135
Pulse monitoring
guidelines, 26
during stationary biking,
264–65
Purse snatchers, how to foil,
158–61

R

Race, and stroke, 94
Rape
defense against, 161–65
safety tips, 151–52
Recommended Dietary Allowance
(RDA), 227
for stress-reduction, 278–80
Rehabilitation therapy, for stroke,
97–98
Relationships. *See also* Couples
suggestions for resolving fights,
299–305
unresolved anger in, 116–17
Relaxation techniques
for anxiety, 41
to control stress, 205–6
for menstrual cramps, 75–76
Resistance-training exercises,
198–99
Retin-A, beauty benefits, 173

Romance
exercises for, 112–14
second chance, 110–14
Ruth Stricker/MindBody Study,
269–70

S

Safecard Services, 159
Safety, 147–49
crime prevention, 146–52,
152–58
guidelines, 152–58
at home, 150–51
personal, 145–64
precautions, 158–60
on roads, 149–50
self-defense, 161–65
worst-case scenarios, 157–58
SAH, 93
Salad, nutrition tips, 231
Salt sitz baths, for vaginal
infections, 36
Saturated fats, guidelines, 234
Sedatives, sexual side effects,
132–33
Selenium, to smooth wrinkles,
189–90
Self-blame, sexual, 139
Self-care remedies. *See* Home
remedies
Self-control, and overweight,
203–6
Self-defense, 161–65
assertiveness training, 162
ground fighting, 163–64
Self-tanners, 178
Sex, 109–43
appreciation, 142–43
effect of drugs on, 131–36
effect of stress on, 117–18
fantasies, 121–22, 142
fitness benefits, 251
fluctuations in, 138–39
homework, 141–42, 142–43
hot spots, 142
during menopause, 60

Subarachnoid hemorrhage
(SAH), 93
Sugar, for pain relief, 241–42
Sun damage
anti-aging advice, 184
shielding from, 169–70
Sunglasses, suggestions for, 184
Sunscreen
guidelines, 174
suggestions for, 184
used by dermatologists, 186–87
Surprises
exercises for, 113
planning, 128–29
Sweets
as diet busters, 6–7
effect of, on blood sugar, 315
for pain relief, 241–42

T

Tagamet (Rx), for ulcers, 135, 310
Talcum powder, and cancer risk, 62
Talking
communication techniques,
301–5, 306, 307–8
to rekindle sexual desire, 119
Taxi safety, guidelines, 155–56
TCA peels. See Trichloroacetic
acid peels
Theft, 160–61
how to prevent, 158–61
Thorazine (Rx), for psychoses, 135
Thoughts, improving, 292–93
TIA, 95
Toning, muscle
benefits, 252–63
exercises, 259–63
Total-body stretch, ten-second, 279
Training
assertiveness, 162
crime prevention, 149
interval, 199–200
self-defense, 161–65
Train safety, guidelines, 155–56
Tranquilizers, sexual side effects,
132–33

Transcendental meditation, to
control stress, 205–6
Transient ischemic attacks (TIA),
95
Transvaginal ultrasound, 66–67
guidelines, 29
Travel
eating smart during, 228
safety precautions, 160
Trichloroacetic acid (TCA) peels
anti-aging, 182
used by dermatologists, 189
Tumors. See also Cancer
fibroid, 74

U

Ulcer drugs
mental side effects, 310
sexual side effects, 134–35
Ultrasound, transvaginal, 29,
66–67
Urethritis, drug treatment, 84
Urinary incontinence
home remedies for, 43
vaginal prolapse and, 123
Urinary-tract infections
diagnosis, 85
drug treatment, 84
Uri-Three test, 85
Urokinase, for stroke, 97

V

Vaginal creams, for vaginal
infections, 36
Vaginal dryness
home remedies for, 42–43
postmenopausal, 60
Vaginal infections
creams for, 36
diagnosis, 85
drug treatment, 84–85
home remedies for, 35–36
Vaginal lubricants
home remedies, 42–43
for menopause, 60